THE WAR FOR
IRELAND

1913–1923

OSPREY
PUBLISHING

THE WAR FOR
IRELAND

1913–1923

Peter Cottrell

CONTRIBUTING AUTHORS

Brendan O'Shea & Gerry White

First published in Great Britain in 2009 by Osprey Publishing,
Midland House, West Way, Botley, Oxford, OX2 0PH, UK
443 Park Avenue South, New York, NY 10016, USA

E-mail: info@ospreypublishing.com

A CIP catalogue record for this book is available from the British Library

ISBN: 978 1 84603 9966

Material in this book has been previously published as Campaign 180: *The Easter Rising*;
Essential Histories 65: *The Anglo-Irish War*; Essential Histories 70: *The Irish Civil War*; and
Warrior 80: *Irish Volunteer Soldier 1913–23*. All colour maps, 3D maps and artwork credited to
Peter Dennis is © Osprey Publishing

Peter Cottrell, Michael McNally, Brendan O'Shea and Gerry White have asserted their right
under the Copyright, Designs and Patents Act, 1988, to be identified as the Authors of this Work

Page layout by Myriam Bell Design, France
Index by Alison Worthington
Typeset in Adobe Caslon Pro and Myriad Pro
Maps by The Map Studio
3D maps by The Black Spot
Originated by PPS Grasmere, Leeds, UK
Printed in China through Worldprint Ltd

09 10 11 12 13   10 9 8 7 6 5 4 3 2 1

ACKNOWLEDGEMENTS:
I would like to thank Donal Buckley, Jim Herlihy, Richard Abbot, Sean Connolly, Sean Dunne,
Cormac Doyle, Peter McGoldrick, Kevin Myers, Keith Strange, Adrian Goldsworthy, and my
wife Heather for all their help, support and encouragement.

DEDICATION:
To my wife, Heather.

IMPERIAL WAR MUSEUM COLLECTIONS
Many of the photos in this book come from the Imperial War Museum's huge collections
which cover all aspects of conflict involving Britain and the Commonwealth since the start
of the twentieth century. These rich resources are available online to search, browse and buy at.
In addition to Collections Online, you can visit the Visitor Rooms where you can explore over
8 million photographs, thousands of hours of moving images, the largest sound archive of its kind
in the world, thousands of diaries and letters written by people in wartime, and a huge reference
library. To make an appointment, call (020) 7416 5320, or e-mail.

FRONT COVER:
This remarkable photograph, taken on 14 October 1920 by 15-year-old John J Hogan, an
apprentice photographer, is of British intelligence officer Lt Gilbert Arthur Price RTR, only
seconds before he was killed in a gun battle with the IRA during a raid on the Republican
Outfitters in Talbot Street, Dublin. IRA leader Seán Treacy was also killed during this incident.
© National Library of Ireland.

BACK COVER:
The Four Courts ablaze during the fighting in Dublin between Irish Free State troops and IRA
Irregulars between 28 June and 5 July 1922. © Corbis.

For a catalogue of all books published by Osprey
please contact:

NORTH AMERICA
Osprey Direct, c/o Random House Distribution
Center, 400 Hahn Road, Westminster,
MD 21157, USA
E-mail: uscustomerservice@ospreypublishing.com

ALL OTHER REGIONS
Osprey Direct, The Book Service Ltd.,
Distribution Centre, Colchester Road,
Frating Green, Colchester, Essex, CO7 7DW
E-mail: customerservice@ospreypublishing.com

Osprey Publishing is supporting the Woodland
Trust, the UK's leading woodland conservation
charity, by funding the dedication of trees.

www.ospreypublishing.com

CONTENTS

LIST OF ABBREVIATIONS

3 RI Rifles	3rd Royal Irish Rifles
3 RI Regt	3rd Royal Irish Regiment
10 RDF	10th Royal Dublin Fusiliers
AARIR	American Association for the Recognition of the Irish Republic
AC	Assistant Commissioner
ACA	Army Comrades Association
ADC	Aide-de-Camp
ADRIC	Auxiliary Division RIC
ASU	Active Service Unit
C.-in-C.	Commander-in-Chief
CID	Criminal Investigation Department
Comdt	Commandant
COS	Chief of Staff
DC	Detective Constable
DCI	Detective Chief Inspector
DI	District Inspector
DMP	Dublin Metropolitan Police
DORA	Defence of the Realm Act
DS	Detective Sergeant
FGCM	Field General Court Martial
GAA	Gaelic Athletic Association
GFA	Good Friday Agreement
GHQ	General Headquarters
GOC	General Officer Commanding
GOCinC	General Officer Commanding in Chief
GOI	Government of Ireland
GPO	General Post Office
HE	High Explosives

ICA	Irish Citizen Army
IG	Inspector General
IPP	Irish Parliamentary Party
IRA	Irish Republican Army
IRAID	IRA Intelligence Department
IRB	Irish Republican Brotherhood
ITGWU	Irish Transport and General Workers Union
IUP	Irish Unionist Party
IVF	Irish Volunteer Force
KSLI	King's Shropshire Light Infantry
NA	National Army
NCO	non-commissioned officer
OC	Officer Commanding
OTC	Officer Training Corps
PDF	Permanent Defence Force
PG	Provisional Government
PSA	Public Safety Act
RAF	Royal Air Force
RDF	Royal Dublin Fusiliers
RIC	Royal Irish Constabulary
RN	Royal Navy
ROIA	Restoration of Order in Ireland Act
RUC	Royal Ulster Constabulary
TD	Teachta Dálas
UK	United Kingdom of Great Britain and Ireland
USC	Ulster Special Constabulary
UUC	Ulster Unionist Council
UVF	Ulster Volunteer Force

INTRODUCTION

In 1798 a rebellion in Ireland, French-backed and Protestant-led, failed to create the non-sectarian republic that was intended. Instead it resulted in the British Government cajoling the Irish Parliament in Dublin to vote to merge the Kingdom of Ireland with Great Britain, to form the United Kingdom of Great Britain and Ireland (UK) in 1801. Despite the fact that Irish MPs were all Protestants the Act of Union did not enjoy universal support among those of that faith and it was passed by 158 votes to 115, indicating deep divisions in the Protestant community. Ireland's Catholic majority, disenfranchised and unrepresented in their Parliament, were even less enthusiastic about becoming subjects of an enlarged Protestant state and from the start there were attempts to break the Union. While there were several failed rebellions in the nineteenth century it was constitutional opposition to the Union that had the upper hand, and tragically it achieved its moment of triumph – and ultimate failure – in 1914, on the eve of World War I.

When the UK Parliament passed a Home Rule Act giving Ireland what would now be called devolution from Westminster, Ulster Unionists formed their own private army, the Ulster Volunteer Force (UVF), to oppose its implementation. Pro-Home Rule Nationalists responded by creating their own militia, the Irish Volunteer Force (IVF), presenting the UK Government with the prospect of civil war in Ireland. To make matters worse, elements of the British Army in Ireland were unwilling to oppose the UVF. The crisis was diffused only by the outbreak of World War I, and while the majority of Nationalists believed that Home Rule would be enacted after the war, a minority of them came to the conclusion that Irish freedom could be achieved only through bloodshed.

The first spark of rebellion came in Easter week 1916 when a thousand or so Irish Volunteers seized the centre of Dublin. Although the British Army crushed the rebellion, its treatment of the rebel leaders brought militant Republicanism from the fringes to the centre of Nationalist politics. By 1917 constitutional politicians had lost control of Irish Nationalism to Republican revolutionaries, who created the conditions

Prior to the Easter Rising, the 1798 United Irishmen rebellion was the last great uprising against Crown rule in Ireland. While the rebellion's leaders were mostly Protestant Irish Freemasons, the insurgents were drawn mostly from the Catholic majority. Although the United Irishmen received some military assistance from France, the majority were poorly equipped to face the muskets of the government troops. Many were equipped with old-fashioned pikes as this bronze sculpture at Barntown, Co. Wexford clearly shows. (© The Irish Image Collection/Corbis)

On 8 April 1886 the British Prime Minister, William Gladstone, attempted to solve the 'Irish Question' by introducing the first Irish Home Rule Bill. Although the Bill was supported by Charles Stewart Parnell and the IPP they were far from satisfied with its provisions. Gladstone urged MPs to vote for Home Rule in honour rather than being compelled to do so later in humiliation, but Unionists condemned it as a mandate for 'Rome Rule', and on 8 June 1886 it was narrowly defeated in the Commons by 341 votes to 311. (© Bettmann/Corbis.)

for a guerrilla war, known variously as the Anglo-Irish War, War of Independence or simply 'the Troubles', which would last from January 1919 to July 1921 and ultimately carve out an independent Irish state from 26 of Ireland's 32 counties.

While most of Ireland gained a form of independence in 1922, six Protestant-dominated counties in the north-east of Ulster refused to break with Britain and became what is known as Northern Ireland. This partition of Ireland into Northern and Southern states was enshrined in the treaty that ended the Anglo-Irish War. It divided the Nationalist community, and ultimately plunged Southern Ireland into a bitter civil war where former comrades-in-arms turned on each other. This book tells the story of the years from 1913 to 1923 that saw the breaking of the Union and the emergence of an independent Irish state. It is a story of sectarian bigotry, political violence and mutual misunderstanding that had major consequences on both sides of the Irish Sea and opened wounds that have only just begun to heal.

Military historian and retired Irish Army officer Capt Donal Buckley said in a speech on 7 October 2004 that '… history is what happened. We may not like some of it as it does not suit our notions of how we would have wanted it to be … We have to recognise how history was manipulated and how successive generations were manipulated with it.'

Capt Buckley's words strike at the heart of the problem when studying much of this period of Irish history. The story of Ireland's uneasy relationship with Britain – the events of Easter week 1916, the Anglo-Irish War and the ensuing Civil War – has survived in Ireland as an emotional experience rather than a piece of history, while in Britain these events have, almost deliberately, been forgotten.

In Ireland stories about the Irish Volunteers, the Easter Rising and the violence of 1913–23 persist and have been shaped into a narrative that mythologizes men like Michael Collins, Patrick Pearse and the 'boys' of the Irish Republican Army (IRA), while vilifying those who supported the British Crown as colonial oppressors, to such an extent that this version of history has largely been allowed to go unchallenged. Indeed, even when the Troubles stray into popular culture in films like *Michael Collins* (1996) and *The Wind That Shakes the Barley* (2006) they tend to reinforce stereotypes rather than objectively examine the facts. Consequently, it is extremely difficult to get to the truth about the events that took place in Ireland and Britain between 1913 and 1923, yet these events largely shaped Anglo-Irish relations throughout the last century while the Civil War essentially shaped the domestic Irish political landscape.

Irish Nationalist interpretations of this period internationalize the conflict, portraying it as a war of liberation against a foreign colonial occupier while ignoring the fact that Ireland's participation in the UK would have been impossible without the support of thousands of Irishmen in the Army, the police and the civil service; or, indeed, without the acquiescence of the vast majority of the population.

It also fails to come to terms with the fact that many of the Irish soldiers who helped put down the Easter Rising had themselves been members of the National Volunteers before they joined; although many may have supported Home Rule, and some did gravitate into the ranks of the IRA, thousands of others remained loyal to the Crown.

What is interesting is that these 'unionists' were by no means exclusively Protestant, no more than the Republicans were all Catholic, and in the words of Sean O'Faolain, who was both the son of a policeman and a member of the IRA during the conflict, 'Men like my father were dragged out … and shot down as traitors to their country … they were not traitors. They had their loyalties, and stuck to them.'

Like the Anglo-Irish War, the Civil War was essentially about Ireland's relationship with the UK, and rather than solving the problem the Anglo-Irish Treaty merely rearranged the pieces for another cycle of violence. In effect the Civil War was the endgame of the conflict. When the Treaty was put to the Irish electorate on 16 June 1922 they overwhelmingly supported it, and thus the anti-Treaty Republicans who took up arms against the first independent Irish state to exist since 1801 had no electoral mandate and consequently lacked the popular support enjoyed by the IRA during the Anglo-Irish War.

Patrick Pearse, the Volunteers'
Director of Operations and
leader of the IRB Military
Council addresses a meeting
in 1915 advocating his own
brand of Irish Nationalism.
(Irish Military Archive)

The anti-Treaty IRA viewed both the Irish state and Northern Ireland as equally illegitimate, and a cursory glance through Eunan O'Halpin's 1999 book *Defending Ireland – The Irish State and its Enemies since 1922* – highlights how much effort Ireland's security forces have expended containing them. In the *Cork Examiner* on 23 February 2000, Ryle Dwyer stated that 'as a people we have been largely ignorant of our history and have thus allowed ourselves to become virtual prisoners of these emotions'. He could not remember it ever being mentioned during his schooldays. This is perhaps why the emotional divisions of the Civil War persist without being fully understood.

More importantly, the lack of a clear-cut victory for the *Saorstát Éireann* (Irish Free State) and the failure to fully come to terms with the consequences of the political violence that began in Dublin in 1916 and ended in internecine bloodletting in 1922–23 has played a major role in determining how the people of the 26 counties view their own state as well as their immediate neighbours, and arguably it is only now, more than eighty years on, that the scars are perhaps beginning to heal.

CHRONOLOGY

1169	Anglo-Norman invasion of Ireland.
1172	The Pope recognizes Henry II of England as 'Overlord' of Ireland.
1690	
1 July:	William of Orange defeats the Irish army of James II at the battle of the Boyne.
1795	Orange Order founded.
1798	United Irishmen revolt. The rebellion degenerates into a series of sectarian massacres by both rebel and Government forces and is ruthlessly suppressed by British and Protestant-led Catholic Irish troops.
1801	Act of Union. The Irish and British Parliaments vote for a formal Act of Union creating the United Kingdom of Great Britain and Ireland.
1849	End of the Great Famine in Ireland.
1858	Foundation of the Irish Republican Brotherhood (IRB).
1859	Foundation of the Fenian Brotherhood in the United States of America.
1867	The Fenian revolt fails. The Irish Constabulary becomes the Royal Irish Constabulary (RIC).
1880	Charles Stewart Parnell becomes leader of Irish Parliamentary Party (IPP).
1885	Gaelic Athletic Association (GAA) founded.
1886	First Home Rule Bill fails to be passed by Parliament.
1890	Parnell deposed as leader of IPP.
1893	Second Home Rule Bill passed in the House of Commons, but defeated in the House of Lords. The Gaelic League is established.
1899	Arthur Griffith founds the newspaper *United Irishman*.

1905

28 November: The Sinn Féin League founded by Griffith.

1906 Liberal Party wins landslide election victory in Great Britain.

1908 Foundation of Irish Transport and General Workers Union (ITGWU).

1910 Two general elections held in Britain – IPP effectively holds balance of power.

Sir Edward Carson is elected leader of Ulster Unionists.

1911 Parliament Act removes power of veto from the House of Lords.

1912 Third Home Rule Bill passed by the House of Commons. The House of Lords imposes two-year delay on its implementation as law.

Unionists sign Solemn League and Covenant.

1913

13 January: Carson founds the Ulster Volunteer Force (UVF) by unifying several existing Loyalist militias.

31 August: On 26 August the ITGWU began a series of strikes known as the Dublin Lockout. On Sunday 31 August the Dublin Metropolitan Police (DMP) kills one demonstrator and injures 400 others dispersing a demonstration in Sackville (now O'Connell) Street. To this day the Irish Labour movement remembers this event as 'Bloody Sunday'.

25 November: The Irish Volunteer Force (IVF) is established in Dublin as a response to the creation of the UVF.

1914

March: The Curragh Mutiny – British Army officers in Ireland threaten to resign if they are ordered to suppress Unionist opposition to Irish Home Rule.

25 April: UVF lands 24,600 German rifles at Larne and Bangor, Co. Down.

26 July: The police and the Army attempt to prevent the IVF from landing 900 rifles and 26,000 rounds of ammunition at Howth, Co. Dublin.

August: IVF lands arms and ammunition at Kilcoole.

4 August: Britain declares war on Germany.

8 August: The Defence of the Realm Act (DORA) was passed.

18 September: Third Home Rule Bill enacted as law but suspended for the duration of hostilities.

20 September: IPP leader John Redmond urges IVF members to enlist in the British Army.

24 September: IVF splits to form the Irish Volunteers under Éoin MacNeill. The majority, named 'National Volunteers', follow Redmond.

1916

January: IRB Military Council agrees on insurrection for Easter weekend.

21 April: The *Aud* scuttled after being intercepted by the Royal Navy.

22 April: Éoin MacNeill issues countermand order to stop the Rising.

24–29 April: The Easter Rising.

3–12 May: The leaders of the Rising are executed.

3 August: Sir Roger Casement is executed.

December: Prisoner releases begin.

1917

July: Éamon de Valera elected MP for East Clare by-election.

25 September: Thomas Ashe dies while on hunger strike.

1918

14 December: Sinn Féin wins a landslide victory in the General Election.

1919

21 January: Dáil Éireann convenes. The IRA kills two RIC constables at Soloheadbeg, Co. Tipperary. The Anglo-Irish War begins.

31 January: The IRA is ordered to target the RIC.

8 September: The 'Sack of Fermoy'.

20 August: The IRA required to swear allegiance to Dáil Éireann.

1920

2 January: RIC recruitment in Britain begins.

25 March: RIC recruits from Britain begin to arrive in Ireland. They become known as Black and Tans.

4 June: The IRA orders a boycott of the RIC and their families.

27 July: First recruits join the Auxiliary Division RIC (ADRIC).

Several events in Irish history have been christened 'Bloody Sunday', the first being during the 1913 Dublin Lockout. This contemporary cartoon is less than complimentary about the DMP's conduct. (Jim Herlihy)

9 August:	Restoration of Order in Ireland Act (ROIA) passed.
26 August:	Ulster Special Constabulary (USC) formed.
20 September:	The 'Sack of Balbriggan'.
25 October:	The Lord Mayor of Cork, Terence MacSwiney, dies in Brixton Prison on the 74th day of a hunger strike.
21 November:	Bloody Sunday. The IRA kills 12 men believed to be British intelligence officers. Fourteen civilians are killed in Croke Park, Dublin by Auxiliaries.
28 November:	Kilmichael ambush, Co. Cork.
10 December:	Martial law declared in counties Cork, Kerry, Limerick and Tipperary.
23 December:	The Government of Ireland (GOI) Act passed.

1921

28 February:	Six IRA prisoners are executed in Victoria Barracks, Cork. The IRA shoots six British soldiers in Cork City in retaliation.
19 March:	Crossbarry Ambush, Co. Cork.
25 May:	The IRA attacks and burns the Customs House in Dublin.
11 July:	The Truce comes into effect, bringing an end to the Anglo-Irish War.
14 September:	Dáil selects five delegates to negotiate and conclude a settlement with the British Government.
6 December:	The Anglo-Irish Treaty signed. The IRB calls for unity and the Dáil votes in favour of the Treaty. The IRA's General Headquarters (GHQ) splits.

1922

January:	de Valera resigns as President of the Dáil. Arthur Griffith becomes President.
7 January:	Dáil approves the Anglo-Irish Treaty.
10 January:	de Valera and his followers leave the Dáil chamber.
14 January:	Pro-Treaty Dáil creates a Provisional Government (PG). Michael Collins becomes chairman of the Executive Committee; Richard Mulcahy becomes Minister for Defence, and Éoin O'Duffy becomes National Army (NA) Chief of Staff (COS).
16 January:	Dublin Castle is handed over to the PG, who assume control of the *Saorstát Éireann* (Irish Free State).
31 January:	British hand over Beggars Bush Barracks, Dublin. It becomes the NA HQ.
February:	Co. Limerick IRA reject the PG.
21 February:	Civic Guards formed.

The headquarters staff of the Cork Brigade photographed outside the Volunteer Hall, Cork City in 1915. These halls were the centre of Volunteer activity in the years 1914–16 and the diversity of dress is quite evident. (Gerry White and Brendan O'Shea)

March:	A standoff develops between the NA and the anti-Treaty IRA in Limerick. The Dáil prohibits the IRA Convention planned for 26 March. Mulcahy orders the suspension of IRA officers who attended the Army Convention. The Army Convention rejects the authority of both the PG and GHQ.
9 April:	Anti-Treaty delegates attend an Army Convention in Dublin, electing their own 'Army Executive' with Liam Lynch becoming the alternative IRA COS.
13 April:	Anti-Treaty IRA occupy the Four Courts, Dublin.
May:	Fighting breaks out in Kilkenny. The planned IRA offensive in Northern Ireland fails. Collins and de Valera make their electoral pact. The British suspend troop withdrawals from Southern Ireland leaving 5,000 men in Dublin. The Northern Ireland Government bans all Republican organizations.
1 May:	Senior NA officers meet with anti-Treaty officers and sign a document aimed at unification of the Army.
31 May:	RIC disbanded.
1 June:	Royal Ulster Constabulary (RUC) formed.
3 June:	British troops parade through Phoenix Park, Dublin, to celebrate the King's birthday.

16 June:	Pro-Treaty candidates win 78 per cent of the seats in the General Election.
22 June:	Sir Henry Wilson is assassinated by the IRA in London.
28 June–5 July:	The Civil War begins. During the fighting in Dublin 65 people are killed, 281 wounded and £3–4m of property is damaged. Cathal Brugha is among the dead. Lynch establishes his GHQ in Limerick.
5 July:	The Provisional Government issues a national call to arms.
July:	The PG War Council chaired by William Cosgrave is established. Collins becomes NA Commander-in-Chief (C.-in-C.). IRA prisoners are offered parole if they undertake not to fight against the *Saorstát*. NA troops capture Blessington, Co. Dublin and the towns of Kilkenny, Waterford, Limerick and Tipperary. Kilmallock, Co. Limerick is captured by anti-Treaty forces. Co. Mayo is also overrun after an NA amphibious landing.
August:	NA amphibious landings in south-west Munster secure key towns in Co. Kerry, Co. Limerick and Co. Cork. The IRA abandons conventional operations and commences a guerrilla campaign. Griffith dies and is replaced by Cosgrave.
22 August:	Collins is killed in an ambush at Béal na mBláth in West Cork.
September:	The Southern Irish Parliament, created by the 1920 Government of Ireland Act, sits and merges with the Dáil. Anti-Treaty *Teachta Dálas* (TDs), or members of Dáil Éireann, create an alternative 'Republican' government. The Dáil passes the Public Safety Act (PSA).
October:	The PG offers an amnesty to the IRA, who surrender by 15 October. The Army Emergency Powers Act and the *Saorstát* Constitution come into force.
November:	On 17 November the first PSA executions take place. Lynch establishes an HQ in Dublin and orders the assassination of all TDs and high-profile supporters of the PSA. Erskine Childers is arrested by NA troops, court-martialled and executed on 24 November. Further executions of IRA follow, and Emmet Dalton resigns from the NA.
December:	The British Acts creating the *Saorstát* and its constitution are given royal assent and ratified by the Dáil. Tim Healy becomes Governor-General, Cosgrave becomes President of the Executive, Lord Glenarvy becomes Chairman of the Senate and all TDs take the oath of allegiance to the Crown. Northern Ireland votes itself out of the *Saorstát*. The 'Neutral' IRA is formed.
7 December:	Pro-Treaty TD Seán Hales is assassinated.
8 December:	IRA prisoners Rory O'Connor, Liam Mellows, Joe McKelvey and Dick Barrett are executed. Attacks on TDs cease. A further nine IRA are executed under the PSA.

1923

January: Thirty IRA executed and Liam Deasy, a prominent anti-Treaty leader, is captured. Paddy Daly takes command of the NA in Co. Kerry. The houses of 37 senators are burned out in the first two months of 1923. The 'Old' IRA is formed.

February: Lynch orders reprisals if executions continue. The PG offer a second amnesty to the IRA. Deasy and IRA prisoners in Limerick, Cork and Clonmel gaols appeal for an end to the war. Both sides reject the Neutral IRA's call for a truce.

March: IRA prisoners are killed in Ballyseedy, Killarney and Caherciveen, Co. Kerry, and 26 others are shot. The anti-Treaty Executive votes to continue the struggle. The PG place the NA under civilian control and establishes a Supreme Army Council.

April: NA success in Co. Mayo. Austin Stack and Dan Breen are captured and 13 IRA executed.

10 April: IRA COS Lynch is killed. He is succeeded by Frank Aiken.

27 April: The anti-Treaty leadership decide to suspend offensive operations (though orders to cease fighting are not issued until 14 May). More than 12,000 IRA are in captivity.

30 April: Aiken orders all anti-Treaty forces to suspend offensive operations.

May: The PG rejects de Valera's peace terms. Two IRA prisoners are executed in Ennis, Co. Clare.

24 May: Aiken orders the IRA to dump arms. The Civil War is over. Michael Murphy and Joseph O'Rourke are the last IRA members to be executed, on 30 May.

8 August: Civic Guards renamed the *Garda Síochána*.

3 August: The Defence Forces (Temporary Provisions) Act 1923 comes into force, placing the NA on a statutory footing.

22 August: NA victory parade is held in Phoenix Park, Dublin.

BACKGROUND TO THE WAR

Irish Republican tradition has it that Ireland's struggle for freedom from England began in 1169, when Anglo-Norman mercenaries began a process that ended in the kings of England becoming the titular rulers of Ireland. While there is some merit in this argument, it is too sweeping a generalization. In reality the conflict of 1913–23 had its roots in the failures of the 1798 United Irishmen rebellion, in constitutional Nationalism, the agrarian disasters of the 1840s and the rise of militant Hiberno-American Republicanism.

Before 1798 Irish rebellions may well have been about ending English domination over Ireland but they were never about removing the authority of the Crown. Even Arthur Griffith, the founder of Sinn Féin, originally favoured an Austro-Hungarian style 'dual monarchy' as the solution to Anglo-Irish relations. The failure of the French-aided 1798 rebellion, at a time when Britain was locked in a prolonged struggle with revolutionary France, resulted in an Act of Union being passed by both the Irish and British Parliaments to create a United Kingdom of Great Britain and Ireland (UK) in 1801.

The Act of Union is still controversial and its undoing lay at the heart of Nationalist political agitation. Although the Act was perfectly legal – in that it was passed by Ireland's Parliament – its opponents questioned its legitimacy because the country's Catholic majority was unrepresented. This, however, was not a democratic age and neither the Irish nor the British Parliaments were democratic institutions in the modern sense.

Even doctrinaire Republicans like Éamon de Valera, who played a prominent role in the Easter Rising and who was the political leader of the Republican movement during both the Anglo-Irish War and the Irish Civil War, recognized that Britain had a legitimate right to protect its vulnerable Atlantic flank. What they objected to was Ireland becoming a province of the UK. While the UK could countenance

David Lloyd George, 'The Welsh Wizard', was the British Prime Minister throughout the Anglo-Irish War and once commented that dealing with de Valera was like trying to pick up mercury with a fork. A consummate intriguer himself, Lloyd George and his political ally Winston Churchill eventually manoeuvred Michael Collins into accepting Dominion status during the treaty negotiations of December 1921.
(© Bettmann/Corbis)

Sir Edward Carson inspects
UVF Volunteers in 1913.
(National Library of Ireland)

Irish devolution through Home Rule it could not tolerate opposition to the Crown. To many Nationalists it was apparent that an independent Irish Republic was utterly unacceptable to the British.

For hundreds of years the main centre of power in Dublin was a large complex of buildings just off Dame Street, known as 'The Castle'. After the Union the Castle was home to the Chief Secretary, who in theory answered to the Lord Lieutenant or Viceroy, who lived in the Viceregal Lodge (now *Áras an Uachtaráin*, the official residence of the President of Ireland) in Phoenix Park. In reality the Chief Secretary was *de facto* head of the Irish government and a member of the British Cabinet.

Despite sectarian discrimination, economic decline, abysmal land management and famine, the lot of Ireland's Catholics steadily improved during the nineteenth century. Catholic emancipation in 1829 and hard-won land reform ensured that Irish Catholics began to share in the country's prosperity, and by 1921 over 400,000 of the country's 470,000 smallholdings were owned and occupied by Catholics.

Thus, throughout the nineteenth century the majority of Irish Nationalists supported constitutional rather than revolutionary change. The Irish Parliamentary Party (IPP) publicized Irish affairs by disrupting Parliamentary business and under the leadership of Charles Parnell sought Home Rule for Ireland *within* the UK.

By 1914 the IPP had managed to force a weak Liberal government to pass a Home Rule Bill granting limited devolution to Ireland. Although Home Rule fell far short of independence it was bitterly opposed by Irish and especially Ulster Protestants, who resolved to resist it. To Ulster's Protestants, Home Rule was nothing less than Rome Rule.

To make matters worse the British Army, with its disproportionately large number of Anglo-Irish Protestant officers – making up what Robin Neillands called the nearest thing to a Junker class that the British have ever known – could not be counted upon to enforce Parliament's will in Ireland. The ensuing crisis, remembered as the 'Curragh Mutiny', when a number of British Army officers serving in Ireland made it known that they would not force the Unionists to accept Home Rule, was only really diffused by the outbreak of World War I.

Although constitutional politics dominated Irish Nationalism, revolutionary groups did not die out in 1798 and, succoured by Irish émigrés in the USA and Australia, groups like the Fenian Brotherhood and the Irish Republican Brotherhood (IRB) kept the idea of armed insurrection alive. Until 1921 none of their attempts were successful and the British made a conscious effort to portray Irish rebels as common criminals rather than soldiers. Thus, the Royal Irish Constabulary (RIC) became the front line in the battle against Republicanism and paid a heavy price during the Anglo-Irish War.

By 1913 Ireland may have appeared a relatively stable and prosperous part of the UK but beneath the surface it was riddled with sectarian and political divisions. To make matters worse, increasingly militant Socialists in the Irish Transport and General Workers Union (ITGWU) and its Irish Citizen Army (ICA) stoked fears of a Marxist revolution in both the Castle and Westminster. It seemed that as long as every Irish political party had its own paramilitary organization, any form of political change faced the threat of violence. The political status quo, however, would also soon provoke a bloody uprising.

THE EASTER RISING

Undoubtedly, getting the Third Home Rule Bill through Parliament was the high-water mark of John Redmond's (MP for New Ross, Co. Wexford and leader of the IPP) political career. Liberal Prime Minister H. H. Asquith had grave reservations about Home Rule but his party was dependent upon the IPP to form a government and had little alternative.

In modern terms Home Rule meant devolution and, ironically, was unpopular with both Unionists and Republicans. For the former it went too far and for the latter not far enough. For the bulk of Irishmen, however, it was sufficient.

'The Solemn League and Covenant', with its biblical overtones that was signed by 447,197 Ulster Unionists on 28 September 1912, committed them to use 'all means which may be found necessary to defeat the present conspiracy to set up a Home Rule Parliament in Ireland'.

In January 1913, the Unionists' leader Sir Edward Carson suggested the creation of a 100,000-man Protestant militia to defend the Union, and so the UVF was born. Field Marshal Lord Roberts persuaded retired Gen Sir George Richardson to lead it. Richardson established an HQ in Belfast and Col Hacket Pain became his Chief of Staff. They set about training and equipping a force capable of destroying Home Rule.

In March 1914, Gen Sir Arthur Paget, General Officer Commanding in Chief (GOCinC) (Irish Command) began formulating plans to contain the potential civil unrest in Ulster. The subsequent orders were vague and badly worded, implying that officers from the Province would be temporarily excused duty for the duration of operations, while the only alternative for officers not covered by this exemption would be to resign their commissions and leave the Army.

At the Army camp at the Curragh, in Co. Kildare, Brig Gen Hubert de la Poer Gough, an Irishman from Gurteen, Co. Wexford, and 57 officers of the 3rd Cavalry Brigade were among the minority of officers who chose to tender their resignations, and a meeting was subsequently set up between Gough and Col John Seeley, the Secretary of State for War, in an attempt to heal the rift in the Army's ranks.

O'Connell Street in 1900. Known as Sackville Street before independence, it was and still is at the heart of Dublin. The colonnades of the GPO can be seen on the left hand side of the picture, as can Nelson's Pillar – Dublin's version of Nelson's Column – in the background. O'Connell Street was the scene of savage fighting in 1916 and 1922, and Nelson's Pillar was blown up by the IRA in 1966. (© Corbis)

The first military operation undertaken by the Volunteers was the landing of 900 Mauser rifles and 26,000 rounds of ammunition at Howth Pier on 26 July 1914. Although discovered by the security forces, the Volunteers still managed to carry the weapons to storage points by strapping them to the crossbars of their bicycles. These weapons became the main armament of the Volunteer movement.
(National Museum of Ireland)

The outbreak of war in August 1914 saved Ireland from its troubles and many Irishmen believed that as Britain had joined the conflict to defend the rights of a small nation – Belgium – Ireland's rights would similarly be respected after the war. Although the war split the IVF, thousands of Irish Nationalists volunteered to fight for 'King and Country'; 200,000 Irishmen – Orange, Green and indifferent – signed up voluntarily.

Although the Government allowed the UVF-dominated 36th Division to use 'Ulster' in its name, it objected to both the 10th and 16th Divisions using 'Irish' in theirs. All three divisions served with distinction, with the 10th suffering appalling casualties at Gallipoli, and the 16th and 36th supporting each other on the Western Front.

By 1916 the IRB had gained control of the Irish Volunteers and planned to use them in an uprising against the British. Among these hardliners was an Anglo-Irish diplomat, Sir Roger Casement. However, the failure of his efforts to garner support in the USA and Germany during 1915–16 convinced him that any rising would fail. Thus he decided to return to Ireland and try to prevent the rising from taking place.

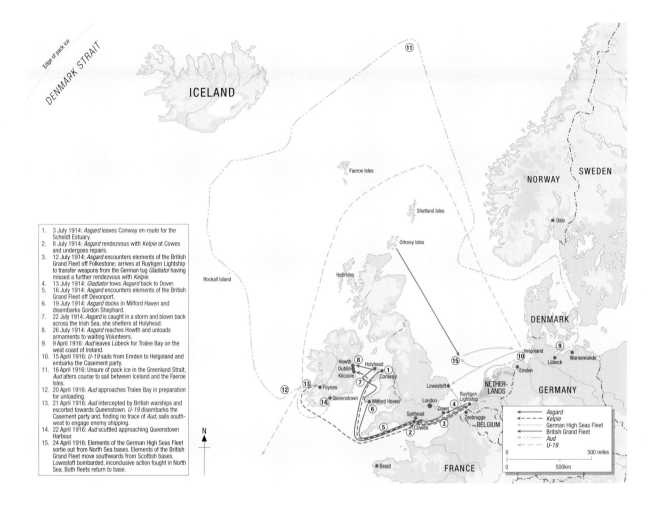

1. 3 July 1914: *Asgard* leaves Conway en-route for the Scheldt Estuary.
2. 8 July 1914: *Asgard* rendezvous with *Kelpie* at Cowes and undergoes repairs.
3. 12 July 1914: *Asgard* encounters elements of the British Grand Fleet off Folkestone; arrives at Ruytigen Lightship to transfer weapons from the German tug *Gladiator* having missed a further rendezvous with *Kelpie*.
4. 13 July 1914: *Gladiator* tows *Asgard* back to Dover.
5. 16 July 1914: *Asgard* encounters elements of the British Grand Fleet off Devonport.
6. 19 July 1914: *Asgard* docks in Milford Haven and disembarks Gordon Shephard.
7. 22 July 1914: *Asgard* is caught in a storm and blown back across the Irish Sea, she shelters at Holyhead.
8. 26 July 1914: *Asgard* reaches Howth and unloads armaments to waiting Volunteers.
9. 9 April 1916: *Aud* leaves Lübeck for Tralee Bay on the west coast of Ireland.
10. 15 April 1916: *U-19* sails from Emden to Helgoland and embarks the Casement party.
11. 16 April 1916: Unsure of pack ice in the Greenland Strait, *Aud* alters course to sail between Iceland and the Faeroe Isles.
12. 20 April 1916: *Aud* approaches Tralee Bay in preparation for unloading.
13. 21 April 1916: *Aud* intercepted by British warships and escorted towards Queenstown. *U-19* disembarks the Casement party and, finding no trace of *Aud*, sails south-west to engage enemy shipping.
14. 22 April 1916: *Aud* scuttled approaching Queenstown Harbour.
15. 24 April 1916: Elements of the German High Seas Fleet sortie out from North Sea bases. Elements of the British Grand Fleet move southwards from Scottish bases. Lowestoft bombarded, inconclusive action fought in North Sea. Both fleets return to base.

Arguably, Patrick Pearse, the Volunteers' director of organisation and a member of the IRB's Military Council, did not care whether a rising succeeded or not, and there is considerable evidence to suggest that he was more enthusiastic about heroic failure than success. Perhaps he realized that in 1916 his brand of Republicanism, with all its martial imagery and rhetoric, was not that popular among ordinary people and that his aims could be achieved only by provoking the British to overreact. It is equally possible that, as revolutionaries often are, he was so divorced from reality that he believed that all they had to do was rise up and declare a republic and every man in Ireland would rally round the green flag.

Despite being a 'minority within a minority within a minority', as Collins called it, the Military Council went ahead with its plans, ignoring the objections of Volunteers Chief of Staff (COS), Éoin MacNeill. Thus, on Easter Monday 1916, parties of Irish Volunteers and ICA seized strategic locations around Dublin and Pearse declared, 'in

Arms shipments to Ireland, 1914–16. Unlike the UVF, the IVF did not enjoy the tacit support of the British establishment and had to rely on weapons smuggled into Ireland to equip its Volunteers.

the name of dead generations', an Irish Republic from the main entrance of the General Post Office (GPO) on Sackville (now O'Connell) Street. The Easter Rising had begun.

COMMANDERS OF THE EASTER RISING

The rebels

DMP Assistant Commissioner William Harrell was forced to resign over his handling of the Volunteers' landing of weapons at Howth in 1914. (Jim Herlihy)

Publicly the rebel command structure revolved around the Irish Volunteers Executive, but in reality focused on the IRB's Military Council headed by Tom Clarke. Clarke was 59 years old in 1916 and had already spent 15 years in prison for his part in a bombing campaign in Britain in 1883. He had been the main liaison between the *Clan na Gael* (the family of Gaels) – an American-based group of Republican émigrés that had grown out of the divisions in the Fenian Brotherhood after its failed rebellion against the British in 1867 – and the IRB. By 1912 Clarke was a member of the IRB Supreme Council along with Seán MacDermott and John Bulmer Hobson. Hobson was later ejected from the Council after he sided with Redmond when the IVF split in 1913.

Clarke set about infiltrating the Irish Volunteers and in early 1915 he recruited Pearse, Joseph Plunkett and Eamonn Céannt, respectively the Volunteers' directors of organization, operations and communications, to become the Military Council of the IRB. In one fell swoop the IRB had driven a wedge between the Volunteer Executive and the rank and file, for no orders would be dispatched by its COS, MacNeill, without first passing through the hands of the Military Council.

The membership of the Council remained unchanged until April 1916, when James Connolly, who had deserted from the British Army in 1889 and was both the leader of the Irish Transport and General Workers Union (ITGWU) and commander of the ICA, was co-opted into it along with Thomas MacDonagh, commander of the 2nd (Dublin City) Battalion of the Irish Volunteers. Together these seven men were to form the Provisional Government (PG) of the Irish Republic.

The British

The British forces opposing the rebels were commanded by three men with extensive experience of operations in India and South Africa – Lt Gen Sir John Grenfell Maxwell (late Black Watch) was GOCinC (Irish Command); Col William Henry Muir Lowe (late 7th Dragoon Guards) commanding 3rd Reserve Cavalry Brigade; and Col Ernest William Stuart King Maconchy (late Indian Army Staff Corps) commanding 178th Infantry Brigade, 59th Division. Maxwell was an associate of the British Secretary of State for War, Field Marshal Lord Kitchener, from his days as Sidar of the Egyptian Army, while Lowe had earned a reputation for aggressive tactics in South Africa. Maconchy was a retired Indian Army officer who had been recalled to the colours when war broke out in 1914.

Given their collective experience of suppressing rebellions in Sudan, South Africa, India and Burma, none of the three had much time for the Irish rebels who had taken up arms against their lawful sovereign.

ARMED FORCES IN IRELAND, 1916

The rebels

The Irish Volunteers were organized on lines very similar to those of the British Army, and their drill, tactics and procedures all emulated contemporary British practices. A Volunteer battalion had eight companies – A to H – each consisting of 79 officers and men. When additional personnel were added, a Volunteer battalion numbered 650 men. Each battalion was based on a single recruiting area and grouped to form regional regiments. Thus all the Dublin battalions made up the City of Dublin Regiment. By 1915 the term 'Regiment' had been substituted by 'Brigade' and its colonel became known as Commandant (Comdt).

Because of the split in the IVF the Irish Volunteers' City of Dublin Brigade was much smaller than its predecessor, and each battalion had six companies instead of eight. They wore grey-green uniforms cut along British lines, with a Boer-style slouch hat or a British-style service dress cap.

There was also a women's auxiliary called the *Cumann na mBan*; a youth movement, the *Fianna*; and the Volunteer Auxiliary, whose members were unable to commit the required amount of time to training, but were expected to learn marksmanship and basic military skills.

Alongside the Irish Volunteers was the smaller ICA, led by James Connolly. The ICA existed primarily to protect ITGWU members and wore a uniform of similar cut to the

Volunteers, albeit of a darker-colour cloth, while the brims on their slouch hats were pinned up with a badge in the shape of the red hand of Ulster. During the course of the Rising the combined ICA and Volunteer force was known colloquially as the IRA.

The major challenge facing the Volunteers was arming itself. It had to rely on a mixture of shotguns, sporting rifles, stolen military rifles and several hundred obsolete M1871 single-shot Mausers that had been landed by Erskine Childers at Howth in 1914. The Mausers' 11mm black powder cartridges led the British to accuse the rebels of using dumdum bullets in 1916.

The British

When the Easter Rising broke out, the bulk of British troops in Ireland were 'Reserve' or 'third-line' training formations whose chief purpose was to provide cadres of trained recruits for their first- and second-line parent formations. The 15th (Ulster) Reserve Infantry Brigade, responsible for the North of Ireland, was based in Belfast; with the 25th (Irish) Reserve Infantry Brigade based at the Curragh, and responsible for the middle of the country as well as the garrisoning of Dublin. A third reserve brigade was based in and around Cork.

By 1915 an infantry battalion, commanded by a lieutenant colonel, had five 200-man companies (HQ and A–D), giving an effective strength of 1,000 men. However if we compare this with, for example, the troop returns for the three infantry battalions in Dublin on 24 April 1916, we can see that they were chronically under-strength, not just in terms of common soldiers but, more importantly, in terms of both experienced officers and non-commissioned officers (NCOs).

During the fighting some units were brought up to strength with drafts from other regiments and soldiers on leave, but in combat these *ad hoc* groups did not function well and at least two officers were accidentally shot by soldiers who did not recognize them.

The other formations in Ireland at the time were the 5th Reserve Artillery Brigade at Athlone and the 3rd Reserve Cavalry Brigade based at the Curragh. The 3rd Reserve Cavalry Brigade was primarily a training formation, but differed in that instead of supplying trained recruits for a battalion within the same regiment, each of the reserve cavalry regiments incorporated the training squadrons of several individual units, which were then rotated through basic training before being returned to their parent formation. Thus regimental strength fluctuated greatly.

Once it became apparent that additional forces would be required to put down the rebellion, elements of the 59th Division – which was designated as the 'rapid reaction force' for the Home Army – took ship for Ireland. The 59th was a Territorial Force Division still undergoing training at all levels early in 1916.

ORDERS OF BATTLE

Rebel Forces in Dublin – April 1916

Composite Headquarters Battalion (150 men rising to 350)
Commandant General and Commander-in-Chief (C.-in-C.) of Irish Volunteers: Patrick Pearse
Commandant General and Commander Dublin Division Irish Volunteers: James Connolly
Commandant General: Joseph Mary Plunkett
Aides-de-Camp (ADCs) to Comdt Gen Plunkett: Capt Michael Collins,
    Capt W. J. Brennan-Whitmore

1st (Dublin City) Battalion Irish Volunteers (less D Company) (250 men)
Comdt: Edward Daly
Vice-Comdt: P. Beaslai

D Company, 1st (Dublin City) Battalion Irish Volunteers (12 men)
Comdt: Capt Seán Heuston, D Company, 1st (Dublin City) Battalion, Irish Volunteers

2nd (Dublin City) Battalion Irish Volunteers (200 men)
Comdt: Thomas MacDonagh, Commander Dublin Brigade Irish Volunteers
Vice-Comdt: Maj James MacBride

3rd (Dublin City) Battalion Irish Volunteers (130 men)
Comdt: Éamon de Valera, Adjutant Dublin Brigade Irish Volunteers.

Special Section, A Company, 4th (City of Dublin) Battalion, Irish Volunteers. Striking a martial pose, members of Céannt's 4th Battalion are shown here in full Volunteer uniform. (Courtesy National Museum of Ireland, Dublin)

Irish Citizen Army outside Liberty Hall, Dublin. The ICA's Marxist agenda made the British Government fear that Republican violence was the beginning of a Communist revolution. (National Library of Ireland)

OPPOSITE
Broadsheet published in Dublin showing 16 portraits of the rebel leaders. Of the subjects, the O'Rahilly was the only one to be killed in action, whilst Ashe, Markiewicz and de Valera all received prison sentences. The remainder, including Willie Pearse and Michael Mallin, were executed at Kilmainham Gaol between 3 and 12 May. (Imperial War Museum, Q70583)

4th (Dublin City) Battalion Irish Volunteers (100 men)
Comdt: Eamonn Céannt
Vice-Comdt: Cathal Brugha

5th (North Dublin) Battalion Irish Volunteers (60 men)
Comdt: Thomas Ashe

Irish Citizen Army (100 men)
Comdt: Michael Mallin

Irish Citizen Army (detachment) (30 men)
Capt: Seán Connolly

Kimmage Garrison (56 men)
Capt: George Plunkett

Total rebel forces
1,100–1,500, all ranks

British order of battle – Ireland 1916

Dublin Garrison: Col Kennard
Marlborough Barracks, Phoenix Park – 6th Reserve Cavalry Regiment (ex-3rd Reserve Cavalry Brigade) – 35 officers and 851 other ranks (5th/12th Lancers, City of London/1st County of London Yeomanry)
Portobello Barracks – 3rd (Reserve) Battalion, Royal Irish Rifles – 21 officers and 650 other ranks

IRISH REPUBLICAN ARMY
Leaders in the Insurrection, May, 1916

IRISH REBELLION, MAY 1916.

THOMAS MacDONAGH
(Commandant of Bishop Street Area).
Executed May 3rd, 1916.
One of the signatories of the "Irish Republic Proclamation."

J. J. HEUSTON.
One of the leaders of the Rebellion.
Executed May 8th, 1916.

CORNELIUS COLBERT
(Who took a prominent part in the Rebellion).
Executed May 8th, 1916.

SEAN MAC DIARMADA.
Executed May 9th, 1916.
One of the signatories of the "Irish Republic Proclamation."

THE O'RAHILLY.
One of the Leaders, who was Shot in Action, G.P.O. Area.

MAJOR JOHN McBRIDE.
(Born in Westport, May 7th, 1866).
Executed in Kilmainham Prison, May 5th, 1916.

P. H. PEARSE.
Commandant-General of the Army of the Irish Republic.
Executed May 3rd, 1916.
One of the signatories of the "Irish Republic Proclamation."

JAMES CONNOLLY.
(Commandant-General Dublin Division).
Executed May 9th, 1916.
One of the signatories of the "Irish Republic Proclamation."

THOMAS ASHE.
(Leader of the North County Dublin Volunteers in the Rising).
Sentenced to Death;
Sentence commuted to Penal Servitude for Life.

E. DALY.
(Commandant of the North-West Dublin Area).
Executed May 4th, 1916.

EAMONN CEANNT.
(Commandant of the South Dublin Area).
Executed May 8th, 1916.
One of the signatories of the "Irish Republic Proclamation."

COUNTESS MARKIEVICZ.
(Who took a prominent part in the Rebellion, Stephen's Green Area).
Sentenced to Death;
Sentence commuted to Penal Servitude for Life.

MICHAEL O'HANRAHAN.
(Author of "The Swordsman of the Brigade," etc.).
Executed in Kilmainham Prison, May 4th, 1916.

ED. de VALERA.
(Commandant of the Ringsend Area).
Sentenced to Death;
Sentence commuted to Penal Servitude for Life.

THOMAS J. CLARKE.
Executed May 3rd, 1916.
One of the signatories of the "Irish Republic Proclamation."

JOSEPH PLUNKETT (son of Count Plunkett),
Commandant-General Irish Republican Army.
Executed May 4th, 1916.
Who was married a few hours before his execution.

Printed and Published by the Powell Press, 22 Parliament Street, Dublin.

Richmond Barracks – 3rd (Reserve) Battalion, Royal Irish Regiment (Lt Col R. L. Owens) –
18 officers and 385 other ranks

Royal Barracks – 10th (Service) Battalion, Royal Dublin Fusiliers – 37 officers and
430 other ranks

The Curragh Camp: Col (temp Brig Gen) W. H. M. Lowe

Elements 25th Reserve Infantry Brigade

5th (Extra Reserve) Battalion, Royal Dublin Fusiliers

5th (Extra Reserve) Battalion, The Prince of Wales' Leinster Regiment

3rd Reserve Cavalry Brigade: Col Portal

8th Reserve Cavalry Regiment (16th/17th Lancers, King Edward's Horse,
Dorsetshire/Oxfordshire Yeomanry)

9th Reserve Cavalry Regiment (3rd/7th Hussars, 2nd/3rd County of London Yeomanry)

10th Reserve Cavalry Regiment (4th/8th Hussars, Lancashire Hussars, Duke of
Lancaster's/Westmoreland/Cumberland Yeomanry)

Athlone

5th Reserve Artillery Brigade – eight 18-pdr field guns (only four artillery pieces were found
to be serviceable)

Belfast

Composite Infantry Battalion (drawn from elements of 15th Reserve Infantry Brigade) –
1,000, all ranks

Templemore

4th (Extra Reserve) Battalion, Royal Dublin Fusiliers (ex-25th Reserve Infantry Brigade)

59th (2nd North Midland) Division: Maj Gen A. Sandbach

B Squadron, the North Irish Horse

59th (2/1st North Midland) Divisional Cyclist Company

C Squadron, 2/1st Northumberland Hussars

59th Divisional Signal Company

176th Infantry Brigade (2nd Lincoln & Leicester): Brig Gen C. G. Blackader

2/4th Battalion, the Lincolnshire Regiment

2/5th Battalion, the Lincolnshire Regiment

2/4th Battalion, the Leicestershire Regiment

2/5th Battalion, the Leicestershire Regiment

177th Infantry Brigade (2nd Staffordshire): Brig Gen L. R. Carleton

2/5th Battalion, the South Staffordshire Regiment

2/6th Battalion, the South Staffordshire Regiment

2/5th Battalion, the North Staffordshire Regiment

2/6th Battalion, the North Staffordshire Regiment

178th Infantry Brigade (2nd Nottingham & Derby): Col E. W. S. K. Maconchy

2/5th Battalion, the Sherwood Foresters

2/6th Battalion, the Sherwood Foresters

2/7th Battalion, the Sherwood Foresters – 'The Robin Hoods'

2/8th Battalion, the Sherwood Foresters

Divisional Elements
295th Brigade, Royal Field Artillery
296th Brigade, Royal Field Artillery
297th Brigade, Royal Field Artillery
298th Brigade, Royal Field Artillery (H)
59th Divisional Ammunition Column
467th Field Company, Royal Engineers
469th Field Company, Royal Engineers
470th Field Company, Royal Engineers
2/1st North Midland Field Ambulance
2/2nd North Midland Field Ambulance
2/3rd North Midland Field Ambulance
59th Divisional Train, Army Service Corps
59th Mobile Veterinary Section
59th (North Midland) Sanitary Section

Miscellaneous units
Trinity College, Officer Training Corps (OTC)
Detachment, Army School of Musketry – Dollymount (Maj H. F. Somerville)
Home Defence Force '*Georgius Rex*'

THE REBEL PLAN

The rebels' original plan was simple but heavily flawed. Casement and Joseph Plunkett put the proposal to the German government that they send a force of several thousand troops on ships around the north of Scotland to land on Ireland's west coast.

At the same time, the Volunteers in and around Dublin would rise against the British who, with their attention thus polarized, would be unable to prevent the invaders from moving inland and securing the 'line of the Shannon'. From there it would be a simple matter of picking off isolated British garrisons before a decisive encounter, which would be fought in terrain inhibitive to the cavalry who, they informed the Germans, formed the bulk of the British Army in Ireland. The Germans demurred when neither Plunkett nor Casement could explain how a convoy of German ships could slip past Scapa Flow, the home base of the British Grand Fleet, without endangering the Kaiser's High Seas Fleet.

Thus they came up with a more modest proposal that would involve the transfer of the 'Irish Brigade', in reality 55 Irish PoWs of questionable quality, with a number of German 'advisers' to Ireland, and an agreed cargo of arms and ammunition. The weapons would be ones captured from the Russians, but they were wary of committing themselves to using their military personnel in any such adventure.

The strain was proving too much for Casement, who went to a Munich sanatorium suffering from nervous exhaustion, and Plunkett returned to Ireland in order to make arrangements for the anticipated landing. Casement's place was taken by Robert Monteith, a former British soldier, whose job was now to assist in the final training of the 'Irish Brigade'.

Despondent at what he saw as German duplicity Casement began to retreat into himself and Monteith, who had by now got the measure of his rag-tag unit, began to think in terms of how to abort his mission and avoid an unnecessary waste of lives. Meanwhile, Plunkett's return to Ireland was hailed as a success by his colleagues within the IRB. Plunkett's return meant that plans for an insurrection could begin in earnest and in January 1916 a possible threat to their plans was neutralized when they secured the services of probably the most effective of the rebel leaders during the Rising – James Connolly.

The signal for rebellion would be the mobilization of the Volunteers' 3,500-strong Dublin Brigade, who would secure a series of strategic buildings in Dublin and invite attack, thus drawing British troops towards the east and away from Fenit, Co. Kerry, where the German convoy was supposed to land sometime between 20 and 23 April.

Of the estimated 13,000 Volunteers in the provinces, the Cork, Kerry, Limerick and Galway Brigades were to deploy in order to cover the initial landings and then move towards the Shannon, while the remainder of the Irish Volunteers would adopt a guerrilla role – the Ulster companies were ordered to march westwards to link up with

The Tralee Battalion being reviewed in the summer of 1914 by Col Maurice Moore, the Volunteers' Inspector General. By the time this picture was taken most units had been organised into companies and battalions. (Irish Military Archive)

the forces from Galway but were ordered not to provoke or interfere with either British Army units or the UVF while on the march.

The Military Council also believed that once a significant quantity of German arms had been landed, the majority of the National Volunteers would abandon Redmond and join the revolt. In the event such hopes proved naively optimistic. In addition, the rebels hoped that the colossal battle of Verdun that had raged since 21 February 1916 would prevent the British from diverting troops to Ireland for fear of not being able to contain a German breakthrough.

THE REBELLION

German

It is probably a testimony to the incompetence of the Castle and their perception of Pearse and the Volunteers' irrelevance that the rebellion came as a surprise to both the Government and the majority of Irishmen, despite the fact that the Royal Navy had cracked Germany's diplomatic codes early in 1915 and knew all about Casement's movements.

The DMP Chief Commissioner, Lt Col Sir Walter Edgeworth-Johnstone, warned the Government that Sinn Féin was getting better organized and on 12 April 1916, the same day that a U-boat left Germany carrying Casement, the RIC was asked to examine the feasibility of arresting its leaders. Disturbingly, the RIC never replied to the Castle's request.

On 18 April word of Casement's departure had reached the British, along with the news that the Germans were in the act of dispatching 20,000 rifles, ten machine guns and 5,000,000 rounds of ammunition to Ireland on board the 'Norwegian' steamer *Aud* – in reality the German ship SMS *Libau* commanded by *Kapitänleutnant* Karl Spindler.

The RN intercepted the *Aud* on 22 April and Casement was arrested within hours of landing. Both events were kept quiet by the Castle and on the evening of 23 April, the Lord Lieutenant – Lord Wimborne – and the Chief Secretary, Sir Matthew Nathan, decided that in the circumstances they should arrest all leading Sinn Féin and Irish Volunteers leaders still at liberty.

British diplomat turned Irish rebel, Sir Roger Casement, was executed for his part in the events of 1916. (National Library of Ireland)

Their decision came too late, as the rebels struck the next morning, on Easter Monday, 24 April 1916.

The Rising began in confusion for both the Castle and the Irish Volunteers. Monday was a bank holiday, and also Race Day at the Fairyhouse racetrack, so the streets were largely deserted when around 1,100 men of the Irish Volunteers and ICA, calling itself the IRA, seized some two dozen key points across the city. Pearse, calling himself the Commandant-General of the IRA, led the party that occupied the GPO in Sackville Street.

When Pearse – as President of the Provisional Government, dressed in a Volunteer uniform crowned with a Boer-style slouch hat – stood on the front step of the Post Office and declared that Ireland was an independent republic, free from the oppression of the British, his announcement was met by indifference from passing Dubliners. Sadly, Pearse's expectation that ordinary people would answer his call to arms was overoptimistic.

A rare, although clearly staged, picture of members of the socialist Irish Citizen Army standing guard on the roof of Liberty Hall, Dublin on the first day of the Easter Rising. (© Bettmann/Corbis)

In Co. Limerick more than 100 Volunteers did mobilize but disbanded on MacNeill's instructions. Contradictory orders flew back and forth across the country and MacNeill even took out an advert in the *Sunday Independent* telling Volunteers to stay at home. In Castlebellingham, Co. Louth, Volunteers under Seán MacEntee – who had failed to get a commission in the British Army only 12 months before – captured RIC Constable McGee and an officer from the Grenadier Guards, and summarily shot them. McGee died of his wounds but the officer, left for dead, later recovered.

In Belfast and Co. Tyrone there was no cohesive attempt to rise, and it soon petered out. Enniscorthy, Co. Wexford was occupied by Volunteers on 27 April while the local RIC barricaded themselves inside their station. Near Ashbourne, Co. Meath, Comdt Thomas Ashe and 60 men of the 5th Battalion ambushed 40 RIC led by a District Inspector (DI), and after a five-hour firefight killed eight, wounded 15 and captured the remainder, who surrendered when they ran out of ammunition. Ashe's ambush was arguably the high point of the rebellion outside Dublin, while its low point was probably the surrender of 600 Volunteers on the historically significant Vinegar Hill after barely firing a shot. In the end, fewer than 2,000 of the 13,000 or so known Volunteers attempted to do anything.

MONDAY 24 APRIL – A CITY TAKEN UNAWARES

On the morning of 24 April, the British garrison of Dublin numbered a little over 2,400 officers and men, deployed across four of the city's barracks. A short distance from Army HQ at Parkgate, the Marlborough Barracks held some 886 members of the 6th Reserve Cavalry Regiment while the nearby Royal Barracks was the depot for 467 officers and men of the 10th Royal Dublin Fusiliers (10 RDF).

The Richmond Barracks near the western suburb of Kilmainham was home to 403 men of the 3rd Royal Irish Regiment (3 RI Regt), and completing the garrison were the 671 troops of the 3rd Royal Irish Rifles (3 RI Rifles) at the Portobello Barracks, just south of the Grand Canal. Furthermore small pickets were distributed across Dublin, mounting guard on buildings such as the GPO in Sackville Street, the Magazine Fort in Phoenix Park and the military warehouses at the North Wall Docks.

In addition to the previously mentioned units, some quasi-military units were also available – the Officer Training Corps had cadres at Trinity College and the Royal College of Surgeons, and, in addition, a body of veteran former soldiers known as the 'Georgius Rex' or, as they were more colloquially referred to, the 'Gorgeous Wrecks' –

were also available. Thus, not only were the majority of British troops in Dublin Irishmen but they were also in the west of the city, well away from the areas in which the rebels were planning to assemble. However, the only military activity was a route march by the 'Georgius Rex', in the hills south of Dublin, and a troop of the 6th Reserve Cavalry Regiment, under the command of 2nd Lt G. J. Hunter, who had been sent to the North Wall Docks to escort an ammunition convoy through the city to the Magazine Fort in Phoenix Park.

Despite MacNeill's attempts to cancel the insurrection, the Military Council managed to muster about 1,100 all-ranks. Ned Daly's 1st Battalion mustered about 250 men around Blackhall Street and a dozen men from D Company, led by Capt Seán Heuston, in Mountjoy Square; it would later be acting under the direct orders of James Connolly. Daly's task would be to occupy and fortify an area of the city centred around the Four Courts complex on King's Inn Quay, extend his lines north towards Phibsboro, and

Initial movements of the Easter Rising, 24 April. The British Army was taken completely by surprise on the first day of the Rising and Irish Volunteers were able to occupy a series of key points around Central Dublin.

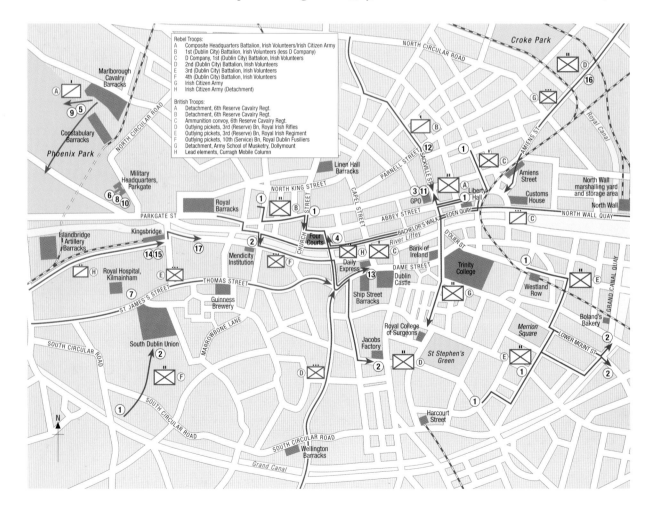

guard against attacks coming in from the west of Dublin, primarily from British troops moving from both the Marlborough and Royal Barracks. In north-east Dublin the men of MacDonagh's 2nd Battalion had been originally ordered to meet at Father Matthew Park in Fairview but were redirected to St Stephen's Green. This resulted in confusion among the men, and several stragglers ended up in the GPO instead.

American-born Éamon de Valera managed to muster a meagre 130 men of his 3rd Battalion in Brunswick Street, Earlsfort Terrace and Oakley Road. His battalion was originally intended to neutralize the British forces in Beggars Bush Barracks in Cranmer Street and block any reinforcements from the naval base at Kingstown, but his lack of numbers made either role implausible.

The 4th Battalion, commanded by Eamonn Céannt, had been given arguably the hardest task of all – to defend against the inevitable British counterattack that was expected to come from the base at the Curragh in Co. Kildare, some 30 miles south-west of Dublin. In the end he managed to muster only 100 men to occupy the largest battalion area, centred on South Dublin Union to the south of Kilmainham.

The Volunteers ranged from men in full uniform to those who wore ammunition bandoliers over civilian clothes and a yellow armband denoting their Volunteer membership. Their weapons varied from modern rifles to pikes that would have not been out of place in 1798.

One group of Volunteers was a group of Irish expatriates known as the 'Kimmage Garrison', who had mustered in the grounds of the Plunkett family estate. Commanded by Capt George Plunkett, they made their way into the south-west of the city. En route Plunkett stopped a tram at gunpoint and as his heavily armed men boarded the vehicle he holstered his pistol and, opening his wallet, turned to the driver with the immortal words, 'Fifty-two tuppenny tickets to the city centre, please.'

Meanwhile 400 rebels mustered at Liberty Hall. For the first time in over a century armed men stood in Dublin's streets with the intention of overthrowing the Castle. Connolly ordered his deputy, ex-British soldier Michael Mallin, to take a group of 100 or so and occupy St Stephen's Green to act as a link between the 2nd and 3rd Battalions and to control a position from which pressure could be applied to both Dublin Castle and Trinity College.

Mallin was assisted by one of the more colourful members of the Volunteer movement – the Countess Constance Markiewicz, an Anglo-Irish aristocrat who, having married a Polish count, had wholeheartedly embraced the Republican cause. Resplendent in her immaculately tailored uniform, she brandished an oversized pistol to encourage the men as they moved off.

At St Stephen's Green the rebels started to dig in within the lawns and bushes and construct roadblocks, often using the power of a loaded weapon to ensure compliance.

The Irish poet James Stephens recalled in his journal of *The Insurrection in Dublin* that he witnessed a workman being gunned down when he tried to extract his horse-drawn lorry from a barricade. His impression was that ordinary Dubliners far from approved. Strangely enough for an ex-soldier, Mallin failed to occupy either the Shelbourne Hotel or the Royal College of Surgeons, which dominated the area and overlooked his positions.

Connolly also sent a small detachment under the command of Capt Seán Connolly to seize the area around City Hall and interdict the movement of British forces attempting to use the main gateway to the Castle or the entrance to the Ship Street Barracks. Connolly joined Pearse and his men to occupy the GPO on Sackville Street at about 11.50 a.m. Although the GPO had been taken without a shot being fired, the killing had begun in the Upper Yard of Dublin Castle when Capt Connolly mortally wounded 48-year-old Dublin Metropolitan Police (DMP) Constable James O'Brien from Kilfergus, Co. Limerick, and occupied the yard.

Capturing the Castle could have been a decisive coup for the IRA because the Chief Secretary was within its walls at the time. However, they failed to appreciate that the six soldiers they had captured were the only garrison, and inexplicably withdrew to some buildings opposite its gate. By early afternoon the Castle was occupied by troops from 3 RI Rifles and 10 RDF as well as troops from 6th Reserve Cavalry Regiment and the moment was lost.

A party of IRA bluffed their way into the Magazine Fort on the pretence of recovering their football in order to destroy the ammunition stored there. The raid was frustrated because the Orderly Officer had taken the keys with him to the Fairyhouse races.

The premature detonation of their explosives merely alerted neighbouring British troops and ultimately this attack did little to damage the British major arms dump, and resulted in the killing of the unarmed 17-year-old son of a British officer, by Volunteer Gary Holohan as he attempted to raise the alarm.

Ironically, the first troops to react to the rebels were Irish, and within an hour of the shooting beginning most of the rebel enclaves were cordoned off by soldiers from two Irish regiments: 3 RI Rifles and 10 RDF. Interestingly 10 RDF was a 'Redmondite' battalion full of former members of the IVF while 3 RI Rifles, from Ulster, comprised former members of the UVF.

On entering the GPO the rebels herded its occupants – whether employees or customers – into the public hall and began the process of securing the building and preparing it for defence. One party headed to the telegraph room and came face to face with a group of British soldiers on guard duty; before the troops could react, one of the Volunteers fired his pistol and wounded the sergeant in command.

At this point the troops surrendered after lowering their unloaded rifles and their wounded sergeant was taken away for treatment. Another accidental captive was

2nd Lt A. D. Chalmers of the 14th Royal Fusiliers, who was captured in the act of sending a postcard to his wife. With no facilities as yet organized for the holding of prisoners, Chalmers was trussed up with telephone cable and left in one of the public phone booths. For the next hour or so, the entire building was a scene of organized chaos as the IRA fortified their position, under the watchful eyes of Connolly and Capt W. J. Brennan-Whitmore, one of Joseph Plunkett's aides.

As these events unfolded, Lt Hunter led his men at a slow trot from North Wall, heading along the quays parallel to the Liffey. Unknown to the cavalryman was the fact that his entire route was under observation by parties of Volunteers manning outlying positions to cover the GPO area. With strict orders to hold their fire, the Volunteers allowed the convoy to pass.

All changed, however, when the small column passed in front of the Four Courts. A group of IRA building a barricade on the corner of Church Street grabbed their weapons and fired off a loose volley. Several men were hit, including Hunter, who was mortally wounded, and the formation scattered with the majority finding

British cavalry on patrol in Sackville Street, May 1916. Although taken after the Rising, this photograph gives a perfect illustration of the composition of a unit of the cavalry reserve. All patrol members are armed and equipped as per their parent units – lancers, yeomanry, etc. The fact that these troopers are indeed mounted would suggest that they are members of the 6th Reserve Cavalry Regiment, the only such unit to retain their horses during the fighting. (Corbis)

Detail of the Upper Gate, Dublin Castle. As the Citizen Army seized the guardhouse – seen here through the gate, on the left – the gate itself was slammed shut and secured, thus robbing them of the opportunity of seizing the symbol of British rule even as the Republic was being proclaimed. (David Murphy)

themselves in Charles Street near Ormonde Market. Dismounting, they broke into the Collier Dispensary and the Medical Mission opposite, and began to barricade their position, bringing the bulk of the arms and ammunition into the buildings.

The explosion at the Magazine Fort and the small-arms fire outside Dublin Castle should have galvanized the Government forces into action but Col Kennard, the senior officer in Dublin, was missing and precious minutes were lost in trying to locate him.

Assuming command, the adjutant, Col Cowan, immediately telephoned the Portobello, Richmond and Royal Barracks to advise the battalion commanders there of events, and he instructed them to send their ready units – approximately 100 men per battalion – to Dublin Castle to assist in its defence pending the full mobilization of the city garrison. Another hurried call was made to Col Hammond in Marlborough Barracks asking for troops to be sent to Sackville Street to investigate the situation there. After Cowan hung up, Hammond decided to take personal command of the patrol and left at the head of at least two full troops of cavalry for the junction of Parnell and Sackville streets.

Next, Cowan placed a call to the headquarters of Central Command at the Curragh Camp and apprised Col W. H. M. Lowe, commander of the 3rd Reserve Cavalry Brigade, of the situation. Lowe immediately ordered the remaining three regiments of his brigade to entrain for Dublin without delay (the 6th was already in the city).

Several further telephone calls were made and soon reinforcements were being mustered in Athlone, Belfast and Templemore. It is also possible that at this time the Army Musketry School at Dollymount in north-west Dublin was also alerted about the situation, as a Maj H. F. Somerville was soon en route for the city at the head of a combined body of instructors and trainees. Finally, the only thing remaining was to alert the War Office in London, and an officer wearing mufti cycled to the Naval Base at Kingstown to transmit the message from the wireless station there, which he reached at 1.10 p.m.

By now, crowds had started to gather outside the GPO and Pearse's famous declaration was greeted by stony indifference. Shortly afterwards Hammond's troopers appeared at the top of Sackville Street, and many of the onlookers cheered, waiting to see what short work the Army would make of the insurgents.

A small knot of horsemen detached itself from the main body and began to walk down the centre of the road heading towards the Liffey. On both sides of the street, men either crouched behind their improvised breastworks or hung back in the shadows. Connolly, standing by one of the lower windows in the GPO, whispered to the men nearby, exhorting them to keep calm, hold their fire and wait for their targets to present themselves. When the horsemen drew level with the GPO, a shot rang out, quickly followed by another and another until finally a ragged volley broke the silence.

As the cavalrymen approached, a group of men were waiting in one of the side streets opposite the GPO. They were the men of the Rathfarnham Volunteer Company who – falling outside of the formal battalion organization – had come to join the Headquarters Battalion.

As the British troopers advanced they chose that moment to sprint across Sackville Street, gathering beneath the windows on the southern façade in an attempt to gain entrance to the building. The rifle fire that checked the British probe undoubtedly saved a number of lives and the company was a welcome addition to the GPO garrison.

Despite the obvious disadvantage of being caught in a crossfire, British casualties were absurdly light – only four troopers were hit, three of whom were killed outright and the last fatally wounded. A fifth British casualty was narrowly avoided when a spent bullet fired from opposite the GPO hit the telephone booth in which Lt Chalmers lay.

The scouting party hurriedly withdrew to the main body and Hammond pulled his troops back to barracks, both to report the incident and await further instructions, while amid the inevitable cheers Connolly returned to the business in hand and began to send out requisitioning parties to secure supplies from neighbouring shops and hotels, many of which were by now becoming the targets of civilian looters.

As an unarmed force, the DMP was withdrawn shortly after the firing started and thus, despite the Volunteers' best intentions, there was little that could be done to check this outbreak of lawlessness. The Dublin Fire Brigade, although able to contain initial spontaneous examples of arson, was also soon withdrawn for the same reasons, with calamitous consequences.

Although it was the farthest away from its objective, the picket from 3 RI Regt was the first into action. As the troops approached the Mount Brown area they could see outposts manned by members of Céannt's 4th Battalion, and so a detachment of 20 men under Lt George Malone was detailed to continue to Dublin Castle and spring any ambush while the remainder of the force took up defensive positions in support. The British advanced with rifles sloped and unloaded but soon came under point-blank fire from a group of IRA under John Joyce. A number of soldiers were killed immediately and the remainder attempted to force their way into some buildings opposite the rebel positions, with Malone being hit and his jaw shattered as he attempted to drag one of his dying men into cover.

It was clear that the picket was insufficient to force a passage past the 4th Battalion's positions and so 3 RI Regt's commander, Lt Col Owens, brought up the rest of his men from the Richmond Barracks. 'A' Company supported by a Lewis gun deployed in the nearby Kilmainham Hospital with orders to lay down covering fire, while the remainder of the battalion under the command of Maj Milner moved along O'Connell Road and entered the South Dublin Union from its southern side. Dividing his force into three sections, commanded by Capt Warmington, Lt Ramsay and himself, Milner prepared for action and the signal for the attack, which came at 12.55 p.m. when the company in Kilmainham Hospital opened fire.

The troops pushed their attack with vigour and Ramsay – a veteran of Gallipoli – was mortally wounded while leading an assault on the entrance to the Union. A short truce allowed the British to retrieve their dead and wounded and, as hostilities resumed, Capt Warmington led another attack on the gateway. He was killed almost immediately and his men broke under the intense fire coming from Céannt's positions. A second ceasefire was then permitted, to give the British the opportunity to retrieve the casualties suffered during this second, failed attack.

Attempts were made to move eastwards and thus outflank the rebels, but here the Volunteers' deployment initially paid dividends, with the infiltrators being enfiladed from the Jameson's Distillery in Marrowbone Lane. Numbers and superior firepower eventually told, and there was nothing that Céannt could do to prevent his outer defences from being breached by the grinding attacks that continued all that afternoon, finally securing lodgements in the Women's Infirmary and Wards 16/17 of the Union by 5.30 p.m.

The fate of 10 RDF was much the same as that of 3 RI Rifles, coming under intense but inaccurate fire from the Guinness Brewery and the Mendicity Institution as they prepared to cross the Liffey by the Queen Street Bridge. Suffering minimal losses, 130 men were able to make their way towards Dublin Castle at about 1.45 p.m., while a detachment of 50 men with a trolley-drawn Maxim gun from the Portobello Barracks had been able to make their way past MacDonagh's positions around the Jacob's biscuit factory and enter the Castle via the Ship Street entrance. As the sporadic fighting continued around the South Dublin Union, the first reinforcements began to reach Dublin. Although a column under Maj Somerville of the Musketry School at

Dollymount was able to press through into the city and secure the rail terminus and dockyard facilities at North Wall, an attempt by a second group of soldiers from the school to take the Amiens Street Station was beaten back by a detachment of MacDonagh's 2nd Battalion led by Capt Thomas Weafer, who then relocated to the GPO.

At 4 p.m., the 'Georgius Rex' were returning from their route march and heading towards the Beggars Bush Barracks in two columns. When the second group approached Northumberland Road, they came under heavy fire from outposts of de Valera's 3rd Battalion. Many were killed but the remainder of the formation was able to reach safety by scaling the barracks' walls. When word reached him of the killings, Pearse immediately tried to defuse the moral backlash by ordering the Volunteers not to fire on unarmed men, whether in uniform or not, but the damage had been done.

At the same time, the leading elements of the Curragh Mobile Column under Col Portal alighted at Kingsbridge Station near Kilmainham and over the next 90 minutes 1,500 dismounted troopers arrived at the rail terminus. After assembling some handcarts to transport ammunition and supplies, Portal's first act was to send 400 men from the 8th Reserve Cavalry Regiment by the loop-line railway to bolster the defences at North Wall. Covered by a large number of troops in open order, he then led the remainder of the column to Dublin Castle. Moving along the quays and past the Guinness Brewery the men filtered through the side streets without meeting serious opposition, eventually reaching the Castle at around 5.30 p.m.

The final British position south of the Liffey at Trinity College had at first seemed ripe for capture by the IRA, but as they had seemingly ignored the building complex the temporary commander of the OTC was able to increase the garrison to almost 50 men by 5 p.m. After he had armed a number of the students and co-opted some servicemen on leave – a force strengthened by the arrival of two regiments of dismounted cavalry within supporting distance at Dublin Castle – the chances of the rebels seizing the college simply evaporated.

The arrival of British Army reinforcements not only stabilized the situation, but also altered the balance of forces considerably; the British could now count on something in the region of 4,500 officers and men, while the IRA could probably only muster a quarter of the number. Now, the question for the British was how best to proceed.

The nearest IRA position to the Castle was City Hall, which had been occupied by Seán Connolly's men since their failed attempt to occupy the Castle and from where they had been continually sniping at the Castle garrison. Connolly was shot dead in a firefight at some time that afternoon. As evening approached, a composite storming party assembled in the Castle yard.

A hundred men rushed City Hall and took the Provost Marshal's building, but failed to penetrate further because of internal barricades that the insurgents had erected for just

Almost as soon as they had occupied the GPO, the rebels began to fortify the building using whatever materials came to hand – furniture, postal sacks, ledgers – anything that would serve to block a window or provide a modicum of cover. From this improvised post, the Volunteers opened fire upon a detatchment of the 5th and 12th Lancers and two regiments of London Yeomanry. (Peter Dennis © Osprey Publishing)

such an eventuality. Another attack was thrown at the building to add impetus to the first, but was halted by enemy fire and forced back when its commanding officer was killed.

With the streets now impassable, a third party – this time also armed with bombs – was sent through the Castle cellars and, emerging on the far side of City Hall while machine guns from the Castle suppressed the enemy riflemen on the roof, broke into the building from behind the defenders' positions.

As it became certain that their position had been turned, the IRA withdrew to the upper floors of the building and, in the confusion, each of the British forces continued to fire at the dust-obscured figures to their front, unaware that the enemy had slipped away to relative safety. With night falling, the ground floor of City Hall was occupied by British troops, while the remainder of the building was still in the hands of rebel forces who spent the night anxiously waiting for the inevitable dawn assault.

With events in Dublin unfolding, Capt Alpin RN, the Chief Naval Officer at Kingstown, having received a request from Col Cowan that an RN vessel be deployed on the Liffey, decided to investigate matters for himself and sailed for Dublin in an armed trawler escorted by the patrol vessel HMY *Helga II*.

Although he saw no cause for alarm and returned to Kingstown, Alpin ordered the *Helga* to remain 'on station' on the Liffey, supported by a second armed trawler, HMS *Sealark II*, which had been refitting in the Dublin docks.

TUESDAY 25 APRIL – THE NOOSE BEGINS TO TIGHTEN

At 3.45 a.m. more troop-trains arrived at Kingsbridge Station, carrying not only additional reinforcements – 5th Leinsters and 5 RDF – but also Col Lowe, who became the highest-ranking British officer in Dublin. Lowe was aware that his tenure of command would most likely be short, as the previous afternoon Lord French, C.-in-C. Home Forces, had authorized the transfer of the 59th (North Midland) Division to Ireland to assist in operations and thus he adopted a methodical, almost simplistic approach to the problem.

The rebel forces on either side of the Liffey would be separated by a wedge of British troops stretching from Kilmainham through to Trinity College and, as more troops became available, pockets of resistance would be surrounded and, depending on individual circumstances, either crushed or left 'to wither on the vine'.

The first stage of the operation had commenced shortly after midnight when a force of 100 men and four machine guns under Capt Carl Elliotson was ordered to occupy the Shelbourne Hotel on the north side of St Stephen's Green. Leaving the Castle at 2.15 a.m., the heavily laden soldiers filtered through the backstreets to Kildare Street and occupied the Shelbourne and the adjacent United Services Club shortly after 3.20 p.m.

They barricaded the lower windows against attack and deployed their machine guns on the fourth floor of the hotel. This gave them a perfect field of fire across the whole of St Stephen's Green and the troopers then grabbed whatever rest they could before daylight.

Dawn on Tuesday morning was punctuated by the staccato sound of machine guns. From Dublin Castle, the suppressing fire was the signal for the British troops

Statue of Cuchulain, GPO, Dublin. The death of the mythical Irish hero Cuchulain, killed while single-handedly defending Ulster against its enemies, has been used here as an allegory of the Irish struggle against the might of the British. (Michael McNally)

who had spent all night in occupation of the ground floor of City Hall to assault the stairwells. The building fell quickly, with all bar one of the rebel garrison being either killed or captured.

At St Stephen's Green, Mallin's command was given a rude awakening as British machine guns in the Shelbourne Hotel continually raked his position. For three hours his men endured the fusillade, returning a desultory fire as and when possible, but it was no use and it was now apparent that the failure to occupy the hotel had been a costly mistake. Mallin was faced with only one viable option – withdrawal.

Just after 6.30 a.m. word began to filter through the ranks to pull back to the West Gate and from there make a run for the Royal College of Surgeons on the corner with York Street. The first group made the short dash unscathed, but the second and subsequent groups had to run the gauntlet of British fire from the north side of the green. This was not the only danger, as three IRA from one of the outlying positions found when they were chased up to the college by a mob of irate civilians hurling abuse and rotten vegetables.

Mallin's men were undoubtedly in a better position inside the building than outside in the open, but it was cold, with an inoperative heating system. The only real food supply consisted of what the men and women under his command had remembered to gather up before the mad sprint from the green and, as if this were not enough, many of the garrison later complained of the permeating odour of formaldehyde and other medical preservatives.

Throughout the morning, the skirmishing continued around the South Dublin Union, but, unsure of the size of the rebel forces defending the facility and confounded by fire coming from supporting positions, the British contented themselves with simply maintaining contact with the enemy.

Had either Lowe or Lt Col Owens been aware that the force opposing them had mustered a paltry 100 men the previous day, then the arrival of the 4 RDF during the early afternoon would no doubt have spurred them into making a more aggressive showing; but this is with the benefit of hindsight, and so Céannt and his men continued to hold off a force almost 20 times their number, while the 5th Leinsters were pushed forwards to reinforce the garrison of Trinity College.

Although the IRA in the east of the city, with the exception of the GPO garrison, had been largely passive, the British position was further consolidated when a composite battalion of 1,000 men drawn from the units of the 15th Reserve Infantry Brigade arrived from Belfast. Their arrival facilitated the dispatch of an 'armoured train' from Amiens Street Station to repair damage to the railway lines, but as its crew were working on the tracks near Annesley Bridge they came under attack from a detachment of IRA and lost several men as prisoners.

British soldiers equipped with a machine gun and .303cal rifles man a barricade somewhere in central Dublin as part of the operation to cordon off the city centre and contain the insurgents. Although it is not clear which regiment they are from, the use of 1914-pattern leather equipment suggests that they are from one of Kitchener's New Army battalions. (© The Granger Collection/ TopFoto)

Buoyed by the success of the early morning, troops from the Castle continued to attempt to clear the surrounding buildings and a series of bayonet charges were launched at the *Mail & Express* offices a little after 2.15 p.m., with the troops taking only a few moments to gain entry to the ground-floor entrance. Connolly's pre-Rising lectures on urban warfare, however, had been well learned by the rebels and as subsequent waves of soldiers dashed out of the Upper Castle Yard they found their progress inhibited by their comrades who were making little or no progress against IRA firing from behind barricades. A fifth wave was thrown at the building and the increasing pressure finally broke the defenders, who left 22 of their comrades in the smoking ruins.

Farther to the east, the *Helga* began her participation in the suppression of the Rising during mid-afternoon, with a short and desultory bombardment of Boland's Mills at the behest of Army HQ. A detachment of four 18-pdr Mk. 1 QF guns from the Artillery Depot at Athlone also arrived in the city, giving the British a substantial boost in firepower.

The guns themselves were drawn from the 144th and 145th Field Batteries of the 5th Reserve Artillery Brigade and were in a pretty poor state. According to Lt Gerrard, an Athlone-based gunner caught up in the defence of Beggars Bush Barracks, the guns were in such bad repair that they had to be cannibalized for parts in order to send artillery pieces to Dublin. A total of four 18-pdrs could be salvaged to form a composite battery, presumably one section of two guns being drawn from each of the two reserve units. That the guns were Mk. 1 QF 18-pdrs is borne out by Gerrard when he states that the only shells available for the guns were 'fixed shrapnel'; thus their usefulness was limited by the lack of high-explosive (HE) or incendiary shells, despite the attestations of many Republican survivors to the contrary.

Upon arrival in Dublin, the battery split up into two sections. One deployed initially in the grounds of the Grangegorman Lunatic Asylum, while the other moved by a circuitous route, crossing the Liffey to the west of the city and then following the line of the British advance to Trinity College.

At 3 p.m. the Grangegorman guns opened fire on an IRA barricade on the North Circular Road near Phibsboro while machine guns that had previously deployed to cover Broadstone Street Station were brought up to join the barrage. A substantial detachment from the 6th Reserve Cavalry also left Marlborough Barracks on foot with instructions to flush out any rebel-held strongpoints and clear the North Circular.

At 3.45 p.m. they came within range of the barricade and less than an hour later were able to force the rebels to abandon the position. This effectively ended the rebel operations in the north of the city, with the various detachments attempting to disengage and retire towards the Headquarters Battalion at the GPO. While the machine guns certainly encouraged the rebels to keep their heads down, the artillery simply punched holes in the barricade, if anything meshing its constituent parts together rather than causing tangible damage to the structure.

It was as the day's fighting was beginning to lull that a British picket from the Portobello Barracks arrested Frank Sheehy-Skeffington – a journalist renowned in the city for his civil rights activities – on suspicion of being a rebel sympathizer or 'Shinner' as they were now known, an abbreviation of the Republican movement Sinn Féin.

Despite the fact that the British were unable to charge him legally with anything, Skeffington was held until midnight when Capt J. C. Bowen-Colthurst RI Rifles, a member of the Co. Cork landed gentry who was about to lead a raiding patrol into the streets, demanded that the prisoner be turned over to him both as a hostage and a guide. Once outside the barracks, he handed Skeffington over to his second in command with the admonition that if it became clear that the raid had gone wrong he was to shoot the prisoner. Bowen-Colthurst then ran amok, first killing a teenager named Coade,

The rapid build-up of British forces in Dublin, 24–25 April, allowed the British to isolate and contain the rebel Volunteers. Once in place it was only a matter of time before the rebel forces would be overwhelmed.

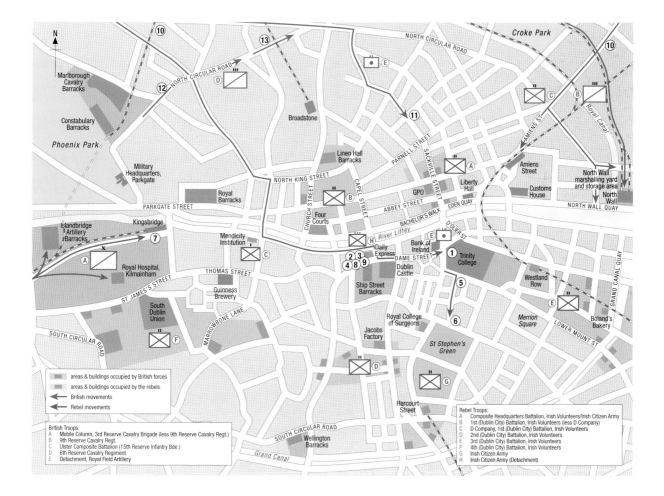

British Troops:
A   Mobile Column, 3rd Reserve Cavalry Brigade (less 9th Reserve Cavalry Regt.)
B   9th Reserve Cavalry Regt.
C   Ulster Composite Battalion (15th Reserve Infantry Bde.)
D   6th Reserve Cavalry Regiment
E   Detachment, Royal Field Artillery

Rebel Troops:
A   Composite Headquarters Battalion, Irish Volunteers/Irish Citizen Army
B   1st (Dublin City) Battalion, Irish Volunteers (less D Company)
C   D Company, 1st (Dublin City) Battalion, Irish Volunteers
D   2nd (Dublin City) Battalion, Irish Volunteers
E   3rd (Dublin City) Battalion, Irish Volunteers
F   4th (Dublin City) Battalion, Irish Volunteers
G   Irish Citizen Army
H   Irish Citizen Army (Detachment)

areas & buildings occupied by British forces
areas & buildings occupied by the rebels
British movements
Rebel movements

claiming that he was acting under the provisions of martial law that had been enacted that day, and then raiding the wrong address where he took two journalists as additional prisoners, bringing his three victims back to the barracks where they were held under arrest, but never charged.

At 10.05 the following morning, Bowen-Colthurst ordered the sergeant of the guard to assemble the three prisoners in the guardhouse yard and arrange a firing party. As soon as the squad had assembled, the prisoners were ordered to walk to the wall at the far end of the yard. As they did so, he rapidly barked out the command 'READY – AIM – FIRE!' and as the three men fell he simply turned to walk away.

As the bodies were inspected, it was believed that Skeffington was still alive and when the departing officer was asked for further instructions he ordered the firing party to shoot again. This time the bodies remained still.

The Sherwood Foresters

In April 1916 the Hertfordshire-based 59th (North Midland) Division (Territorial Force) was Britain's rapid reaction force. Its units were deployed across a series of rail hubs north of London to counter any German invasion. Late on Monday afternoon the divisional commander, Maj Gen Arthur Sandbach, received orders to dispatch 177th Brigade (Brig Gen Carleton) and 178th Brigade (Col Maconchy) to Dublin immediately, while 176th Brigade (Brig Gen C. G. Blackader) and the remainder of the division were to follow with the least possible delay.

Similar scenes were enacted at brigade headquarters as had been seen in Dublin earlier that day, but eventually some order was injected into the situation and at 4 a.m. the 2/5th and 2/6th Sherwood Foresters departed for Liverpool, followed by the 2/7th at 8.30 a.m. and the 2/8th at 10 a.m.

Awaiting the troops was the packet steamer *Ulster*, which would transport the initial lift of troops to the naval base at Kingstown (eventually several additional transports were made available to transfer the division); the brigade being formed there in the early hours of Wednesday 26 April.

As soon as he arrived in Liverpool, Maconchy was informed that his troops had moved with minimal ammunition – an estimated average of 50 rounds per man – and that, as they had trained to counter a German invasion, no one knew Dublin and its surrounding area. To resolve the former, he made a terse call to the War Office insisting that a total of 400 rounds per man and 10,000 hand grenades be made available at Kingstown before the brigade left the port; to resolve the latter, members of the headquarters staff were detailed to obtain as many maps of Dublin as possible, the majority of these being torn from hotel guidebooks.

The munitions were duly delivered to the Kingstown Docks where the small-arms rounds were found to be Mk. VI .303cal ball rather than the Mk. VII with which the troops had been issued while in camp. Although of an identical calibre, the difference in their capabilities would require the men's service rifles to be 'zeroed in' to suit the new rounds, if they were not to suffer from a loss of accuracy at long and medium ranges.

One oft-mentioned incident in the transfer of the 178th Brigade that needs clarification is that the battalion Lewis guns were left behind as a result of a clerical error or an overzealous embarkation officer. They were indeed left behind, but it was a *deliberate* action. A full-strength battalion would muster some 1,000 officers and men, which would mean that each of the two brigade columns would have had anything up to 2,000 men, whereas the *Ulster* was designed to carry just 1,400 passengers safely.

A Lewis-gun section was not simply a two-man crew, but a group of 26 soldiers and two horses and an ammunition wagon. Simply put, there was insufficient room on the vessel for the sections, and the intention undoubtedly was that they would follow on as soon as adequate transport had been arranged. Indeed, D Company, 2/8th Sherwood Foresters, would likewise remain behind in Liverpool and not rejoin the brigade until the additional transport capacity had been made available and its parent battalion committed to action.

At 8.30 a.m. on the Wednesday morning, Maconchy held a staff meeting in the Kingstown Yacht Club to issue his orders. During the night intelligence had been received from Irish Command that the British forces in Dublin had been taking severe losses and that the direct route into the city was known to be blocked by a number of strong IRA positions.

Maconchy sent a 300-man battle-group based around a rifle company from 2/5th Sherwood Foresters under Capt Rickman to march to Arklow, south of Dublin, in order to secure the arsenal and armaments factory. Meanwhile the remainder of the battalion, along with the 2/6th, would march to Kilmainham via the Stillorgan Road. The balance of the brigade was to take the direct – enemy-held – route to Dublin Castle. Both columns were due to start their march at 10 a.m. and, as they awaited their orders, the company officers went among their men, instructing them to move to the quays, face out to sea and load their weapons.

Maconchy is quite adamant in his account of the brigade's actions in Ireland that the munitions arranged by the War Office had not been distributed before the columns moved off, meaning that the Foresters loaded their weapons with the ready ammunition with which they had been issued before transiting to Kingstown.

The reason for the officers' insistence that their men load their weapons while facing out to sea is apparent when one considers that marksmanship was the one area in which the bulk of the troops had yet to complete their training. As Maconchy later wrote:

It will therefore be apparent that at the time when the Brigade was called upon to fight in Ireland in this month only a very small proportion of the men had ever fired a service bullet out of their rifles … With the exception of training in musketry, the Brigade was now in a very efficient condition, thanks to the untiring energy and loyal zeal displayed by the Battalion officers and the keenness and ready response of the rank and file. Discipline was excellent and crime practically non-existent.

WEDNESDAY 26 APRIL – PLANS AND BLUNDERS

This third day of combat would prove to be perhaps the most crucial, not merely as a result of the fighting that took place but also because Lowe had by now formulated the tactics which the British would employ. Two cordons would be established to isolate the rebel enclaves north of the river and surround them in a 'ring of steel', while south of the Liffey the bulk of the Government forces would then be directed in overwhelming force against the remaining rebel positions.

At 8 a.m. the *Helga II* and her escort, the *Sealark*, sailed back upriver and occupied berths opposite the Customs House at George's Quay. Supported by a section of 18-pdrs they began an hour-long bombardment of Liberty Hall, which was assumed to be both a concentration point for the insurgents and a major arsenal. After an hour's shelling, the guns ceased fire and the Ulster troops launched a bayonet charge from the Customs House, sweeping across Beresford Place, taking a deserted Liberty Hall and sealing off one end of Lower Abbey Street and Eden Quay, which brought the troops within a few hundred yards of Sackville Street and the GPO.

Across the city, similar preparations were taking place as men of the Dublin Fusiliers arranged for the evacuation of civilians in preparation for the launching of a major attack on the small garrison in the Mendicity Institution. Over the next three hours, the troops filed into position, harassed by rifle fire from within the building, but at 12.15 p.m. bombing parties advanced, hurling grenades at the windows while other infantry followed in their wake.

Initially Heuston's men were able to catch a number of grenades and hurl them back into the oncoming khaki ranks, but the British fire was too intense and casualties grew. At 12.30 p.m. Heuston became the first rebel commander to surrender his position to the British. His orders from Connolly had been to hold the position for three hours, yet he had managed against near-insurmountable odds to do so for almost three days.

At Trinity College, Col Portal was again showing his industriousness. At 2 p.m. machine-gun teams were sent to occupy various positions in and around D'Olier Street in order to be able to lay down suppressive fire on the rebel positions, and shortly afterwards he ordered his section of artillery into D'Olier Street from where he could engage an enemy strongpoint known as 'Kelly's Fort', situated on the corner of Bachelor's Walk and Sackville Street.

This was an extremely hazardous proposal for the artillerymen, for not only would they be at the mercy of IRA snipers but in addition the streets were paved with large stones known as 'square setts' and all attempts to prise up the stones and expose the sand beneath to give the guns some traction failed.

Thus, with their suppressors working inefficiently the gunners were expected to operate their pieces on a surface on which they would be unable to anchor the gun-trails in order to absorb some of the recoil – it was to be like deploying the guns on sheet ice.

The 'Irish Thermopylae'

As they left Kingstown, the Sherwood Foresters were mobbed by cheering crowds who, showering the troops with gifts, demonstrated where their sympathies lay. Most of the soldiers had little idea where they were; however, Capt F. C. Dietrichsen, adjutant of 2/7th Sherwood Foresters, knew the area well.

Dietrichsen had sent his Irish wife and children to stay with her parents in the Dublin suburb of Blackrock and he was delighted when they came to meet him as his men marched north, unaware of what awaited the column in the quiet suburban streets ahead.

Known as the 'Robin Hoods', the Nottinghamshire men marched towards Ballsbridge, their column led by Capt Frank Pragnell's C Company. They were followed in succession by Capt H. C. Wright's A Company, Capt H. Hanson's B Company with Capt L. L. Cooper's D Company bringing up the rear.

Pragnell's command was to be deployed in a 'box' formation of platoons, with one leading the advance in line abreast and one on each side of the road – in column – whose job would be to clear houses and cover all side streets. A fourth platoon acted as support. The battalion commander, Lt Col Cecil Fane, attached himself to the advance party, while the actions of the remainder of the regiment were coordinated by Maj F. Rayner.

After an interval of 400 yards came the 2/8th Sherwood Foresters, under the command of Lt Col Oates, marching in a similar formation though without a rearguard company as a result of the involuntary detachment of D Company – which was led by the battalion commander's son, Capt J. Oates.

By midday the column had reached Ballsbridge, where a joint headquarters was established for the 177th and 178th Brigades in the nearby Pembroke Town Hall. The troops were given 15 minutes' rest while Maconchy conferred with his two battalion commanders. The latest information from Irish Command was that heavy opposition was to be expected in the area around the Mount Street Canal Bridge, and that the rebels had fortified a schoolhouse on the right-hand side of the road.

Shortly after the troops resumed their march a number of shots rang out from nearby Carisbrooke House, forcing them to take evasive action, but under their company officers the men reacted calmly and efficiently. The ambushers soon melted away, however, and Lt Col Fane gave the order for the advance to continue, albeit more cautiously, and he led D Company into Northumberland Road while Maj Rayner and the bulk of the battalion followed at a reasonable distance.

Ahead of them lay a detachment from de Valera's 3rd Battalion, occupying a number of houses in Northumberland Road, covering the approaches to the Mount Street Canal Bridge and the direct route towards Dublin Castle and Trinity College. The projected killing zone was rectangular in shape and stretched from the canal bridge to the junction of Northumberland Road with Haddington Road and Cranmer Street, and comprised four separate firing positions.

As the troops moved towards the bridge, they would be met by fire from No. 25, on their left flank, which was occupied by two men who had been picked for their skill with a gun – Lt Michael Malone, who was one of de Valera's best officers, and James Grace, who had deserted from a militia unit in Canada to take part in the Rising. Malone's command had originally consisted of Grace and two others, but after assessing his party's chances of surviving contact with the enemy he decided to keep Grace with him and send the others back to battalion HQ.

Further along the left-hand side of the road, five men occupied No. 5. It was a red-brick building used as a hall for the Parochial School, which was opposite at No. 10. The school itself had been initially occupied by a small party, but was evacuated and the occupants divided between the Parochial Hall and the final position – Clanwilliam House, a building standing on the far side of the bridge at the corner of Lower Mount Street and the Grand Canal Quay.

The doors and ground-floor windows of these houses had been barricaded to impede access; the Volunteers occupied the upper floors so that they could fire down on any British troops and were able to fire at the rear of any column, thus increasing the possibility of causing confusion and panic.

In all a dozen or so men lay in wait for the approaching troops. The plan was simple and involved letting the leading British elements pass unmolested. When Malone and Grace opened fire it would act as a signal for the remaining positions to engage the

British troops man a barricade made of empty barrels taken from the St James's Gate Guinness Brewery, which suggests that the barricade was somewhere nearby. The soldiers have stripped off their webbing equipment and carry ammunition in cotton bandoliers. (© Top Foto)

▼ EVENTS

1. 0800hrs, 26 April: HMY *Helga II* and *Sealark II* (Q) sail upriver and anchor off George's Quay

2. 0830hrs, 26 April: Liberty Hall bombarded for one hour by HMY *Helga II* (Q) and 18-pdr guns (L) from Tara Street.

3. 0930hrs, 26 April: Composite Battalion of 15th Reserve Infantry Brigade (D) launches a bayonet attack across Beresford Place towards Eden Quay and Lower Abbey Street.

4. 1200hrs, 26 April: 10th Royal Dublin Fusiliers (H) launches final attack on Rebels (3) holding the Mendicity Institution.

5. 1215hrs, 26 April: D Company, 1st (City of Dublin) Battalion, Irish Volunteers (3) surrenders after holding the Mendicity Instutution for three days.

6. 1215hrs, 26 April: 2/7th (O) and 2/8th (P) Sherwood Foresters advance along Northumberland Road towards the Mount Street Bridge.

7. 1225hrs, 26 April: Sherwood Foresters ambushed in Northumberland Road, taking several casualties. The leading elements become pinned down under fire.

8. 1240hrs, 26 April: Beginning of the battle of Mount Street Bridge.

9. 1400hrs, 26 April: Troops from Trinity College (C) begin to occupy buildings in D'Olier and Westmoreland Streets and supported by artillery (L) open fire on rebel positions opposite.

10. 1415hrs, 26 April: British cordon is completed with aggressive patrols, forcing Rebel outposts to contract in on themselves.

11. 1900hrs, 26 April: After several hours' fighting and over 300 casualties, 2/7th (O) and 2/8th (P) Sherwood Foresters clear the Insurgent positions around the Mount Street Bridge, but during the night are withdrawn from the front line, their place being taken by the 2/6th South Staffordshires (S).

12. 0400hrs, 27 April: 2/5th (M) and 2/6th (N) Sherwood Foresters move from Kilmainham to Dublin Castle, and thence to the Four Courts area, coming under fire from Daly's 1st Battalion (2).

13. 0515hrs, 27 April: British begin using improvised armoured cars to transport men and materiel to reinforce the cordon around the Volunteers Headquarters (1) and 1st Battalion (2) positions.

14. 0900hrs, 27 April: 2/5th (R) and 2/6th (S) Sherwood Foresters begin street-clearing operations in the north of the western cordon.

15. 1000hrs, 27 April: Firing random shots, British artillery begins to shell Sackville Street area. 18-pdr shell hits the Irish Times' paper store, igniting several rolls of newsprint.

16. 1030hrs, 27 April: As the fire begins to spread, British troops move forward under the cover of smoke but are stopped by fire from Middle Abbey Street.

17. 1200hrs, 27 April: 2/5th (R) and 2/6th (S) South Staffordshires push forward along Lower Mount Street towards Trinity College, establishing sniper positions that engage de Valera's 3rd Battalion (5) until the early evening.

BRITISH FORCES

A	6th Reserve Cavalry Regiment
B	Dublin Castle Garrison
C	Trinity College Garrison
D	Composite Battalion, 15th Reserve Infantry Brigade
E	Detachment, Army School of Musketry
F	3rd Royal Irish Regiment
G	3rd Royal Irish Rifles
H	10th Royal Dublin Fusiliers
I	4th Royal Dublin Fusiliers
J	Elements, 25th (Irish) Reserve Infantry Brigade
K	Section, 5th Reserve Brigade, Royal Field Artillery
L	Section, 5th Reserve Brigade, Royal Field Artillery
M	2/5th Sherwood Foresters
N	2/6th Sherwood Foresters
O	2/7th Sherwood Foresters
P	2/8th Sherwood Foresters
Q	HMY *Helga II*, Trawler *Sealark II*
R	2/5th South Staffordshires
S	2/6th South Staffordshires
T	5th Leinsters
U	8th Reserve Cavalry Regiment
V	9th Reserve Cavalry Regiment
W	10th Reserve Cavalry Regiment

XXX
LOWE

GRANGEGORMAN LUNATIC ASYLUM
K

ROYAL HOSPITAL, KILMAINHAM
I J M N T
H

SOUTH DUBLIN UNION

JAMESON'S DISTILLERY
F

GUINNESS BREWERY

FOUR COURTS BUILDING

13
2
14
5
12
3
6
4

CITY HALL
DUBLIN CASTLE
1

JACOBS BISCUIT FACTORY
B U W

4

18

G

CONSOLIDATION
The containment of the Rebel positions, Wednesday 26–Thursday 27 April 1916.

This map is 4.4 x 3km

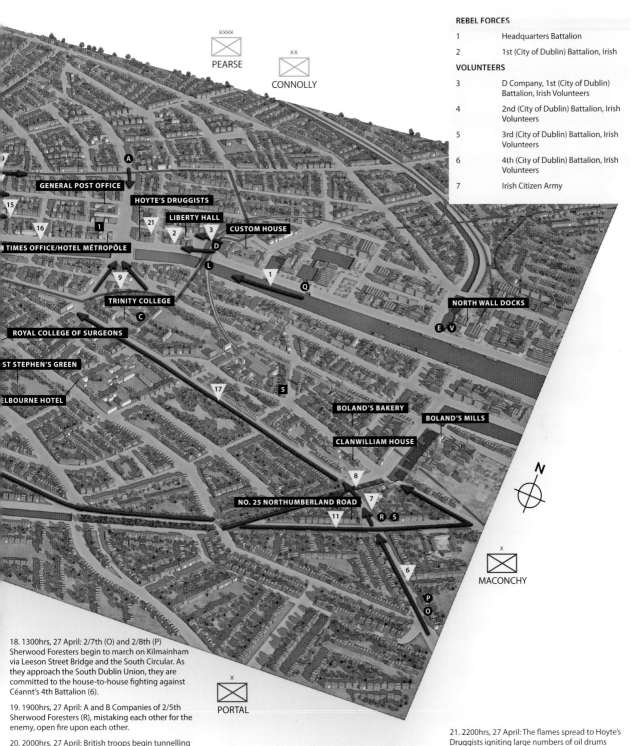

REBEL FORCES

1   Headquarters Battalion

2   1st (City of Dublin) Battalion, Irish

VOLUNTEERS

3   D Company, 1st (City of Dublin) Battalion, Irish Volunteers

4   2nd (City of Dublin) Battalion, Irish Volunteers

5   3rd (City of Dublin) Battalion, Irish Volunteers

6   4th (City of Dublin) Battalion, Irish Volunteers

7   Irish Citizen Army

18. 1300hrs, 27 April: 2/7th (O) and 2/8th (P) Sherwood Foresters begin to march on Kilmainham via Leeson Street Bridge and the South Circular. As they approach the South Dublin Union, they are committed to the house-to-house fighting against Céannt's 4th Battalion (6).

19. 1900hrs, 27 April: A and B Companies of 2/5th Sherwood Foresters (R), mistaking each other for the enemy, open fire upon each other.

20. 2000hrs, 27 April: British troops begin tunnelling through houses to reach objectives in order to avoid enemy fire.

21. 2200hrs, 27 April: The flames spread to Hoyte's Druggists igniting large numbers of oil drums and chemicals held in storage; the fire spreads out of control.

enemy, trapping them in a crossfire that would hopefully disorientate them and belie the Volunteers' lack of numbers.

Nervously the raw Nottinghamshire Territorials began to bunch together, advancing down the narrow street as one by one the British companies entered the killing zone. Malone and Grace watched the troops pass below their position until Malone nodded silently to his partner, aimed his Mauser C96 semi-automatic pistol out of the window and emptied the ten-shot magazine into the street below. As he ducked back inside, Grace engaged another section of the column and after a momentary delay the other positions began to open fire at the British infantrymen, who had instinctively dropped to the ground. Among the first to fall was Capt Dietrichsen, who tragically had been reunited with his family just hours before.

Waiting until there was a slackening in the enemy fire, Fane and Pragnell got to their feet and, with drawn swords, led the men immediately around them in a charge on the entrance to No. 25. As they reached the stairwell the two Irishmen poured a deadly volley into the milling troops. The other company officers began to form up for an assault on the bridge, but their onslaught was broken when the column was hit by fire from Clanwilliam House and almost immediately enfiladed by the men holding the Parochial Hall.

With the attack stalled, Fane detached Capt Hanson's B Company south-west toward the Baggot Street Bridge, with orders to outflank the ambushers by doubling back along the canal bank. As the young soldiers moved off, Malone moved into the bathroom and twice emptied his Mauser into the group of men, wreaking havoc in their tightly packed ranks.

Luckily, Hanson's men were soon out of Malone's line of fire and cautiously made their way to the bridge, convinced that a second ambush would be sprung at any moment. Leaving a platoon to guard the crossing, the remainder of the company began to move eastwards along Percy Place.

At the crossroads the situation was becoming desperate; fire was being directed at the four corner houses, although only No. 25 was actually occupied by the IRA. Then disaster struck as Fane was hit in the left arm and severely wounded. Waving away assistance he calmly handed over command to Maj Rayner and only then consented to withdraw to cover and accept treatment. Rayner seemed to lead a charmed life as he stood in the middle of the road giving orders, his uniform being shredded by rifle fire.

The fighting had been going on for a little over an hour but, despite the heavy casualties and their unpreparedness, the Foresters held on. A number of houses opposite Malone and Grace's position were now occupied and a steady if ineffectual fire began to be poured in their direction, although the sheer volume encouraged the raw troops.

Along the canal bank in Percy Place, Hanson's men were soon spotted and engaged from the side windows of Clanwilliam House. The soldiers went to ground almost immediately, but the coping stones lining the towpath gave them inadequate cover, and their opponents were able to track the khaki uniforms as they inched forward towards the Mount Street Bridge. Despite losing their company commander and two subordinates, the men continued to advance led by a senior NCO; however, as they reached the bridge they came under fire from another of de Valera's defensive positions and the flanking manoeuvre was stopped dead in its tracks.

A sketch of Dublin during the Rising. This contemporary drawing shows how the fighting was depicted in the British press. (*Illustrated London News*)

For several hours, a small number of Volunteers inflicted horrendous casualties on the Sherwood Foresters at Mount Street Canal Bridge, They suffered almost half of the total casualties received by the British forces during the whole of the Easter Rising, and their experience in undoubtedly gave rise to a more cautious British approach during the rest of the Rising. (Peter Dennis © Osprey Publishing)

Fane then decided to try to turn the enemy position from the east, and directed Capt Wright to move his men around via Beggars Bush Barracks. Almost immediately the manoeuvre ran into trouble as the barracks commander, Col Sir Frederick Shaw, commandeered one of the platoons to assist in defending his compound.

This attempt to turn the Volunteers' position came to naught as Wright's men came under fire from an enemy outpost in Boland's Mills on Grand Canal Quay. In retrospect the men were fortunate as, if they had managed to cross the canal at this point, they would have blundered into the sights of de Valera's main position at Boland's Bakery in Grand Canal Street.

At 2.45 p.m. Lt Col Fane reported to Brigade HQ that, although his men were pinned down by enemy fire and that all attempts so far to turn the position had been thwarted, if given machine-gun support and a number of grenades he still might be able to push through to the objective. Following a suggestion from Irish Command, the Bombing School at Elm Park was contacted and its commander, Capt Jeffares,

The officers of the North Midland Field Ambulance Section, 59th Division, pose for the camera. (Imperial War Museum, Q90436)

volunteered to lead a number of his men to assist the column, giving Maconchy some much-needed expertise in the use of grenades and explosives.

The Sherwood Foresters were rapidly running out of options, and Fane decided to make another attack. Capt Cooper's D Company, which had lain in reserve until now, was brought forward and the men deployed around the crossroads, while the survivors of Pragnell's men were withdrawn and ordered to move via Percy Lane – an alley parallel to Northumberland Road – to reinforce Hanson's company.

Again, Malone was waiting for the troops to move and, before they passed from view, accounted for another dozen or so soldiers. In Northumberland Road, meanwhile, the front of the house was the target for a whole company of British troops, mistakenly aiming for the unoccupied ground- and first-floor windows, even as their officers' whistles summoned their men for another assault on the bridge.

For Maconchy it was now clear that his remaining battalion would need to be committed if the situation were to be salvaged. Accordingly, Lt Col Oates of the 2/8th was ordered to advance along the road with two of his three companies and to detach A Company under Capt Quinnell in order to turn the Volunteers' left flank. Even as the troops were forming up another message was received from Brig Gen Lowe at Kilmainham, rescinding permission for the flanking manoeuvre. The bridge was to be taken at the point of the bayonet.

At the head of Percy Lane, Pragnell readied his company for a sprint towards the objective, but as they left cover they ran straight into the sights of the men who had earlier so effectively halted B Company's advance. Pragnell was badly wounded when he was forced to halt short of the objective, accompanied by a mere six men.

Fane's battalion was shattered, with two companies pinned down in Percy Place and a third being flayed by enemy volleys as it attempted to force its way across the narrow bridge; it was all that he could do to hold on until reinforcements arrived.

A short distance away at Boland's Bakery, the men of de Valera's 3rd Battalion could only listen to the sounds of gunfire as their comrades fought against the advancing troops. Despite the failure of the flanking attack, the fact that the attempts had been made had persuaded de Valera that he could not afford to send any men to reinforce those engaged at the Mount Street Bridge. This was a missed opportunity, as even a token gesture may well have broken Fane's raw troops.

By 5 p.m. Capt Jeffares and his bombers had arrived and the fighting began to move inexorably to its climax. Grenades were 'posted' through broken windows and then, under the cover of the explosions and sustained rifle fire from the houses opposite, the front door was blown in. With the entrance in ruins, there was inexplicably no attempt to immediately carry the building, and Grace and Malone kept up their harassment of the troops below until finally a section of D Company charged across the street. As soon as they saw the troops forming up, Grace went downstairs and waited for Malone to join him, but the soldiers swarming into the house prevented their junction. Diving for the cellar, Grace snapped off a few quick shots at the milling infantrymen but an answering volley felled Malone as he stood at the top of the stairs. The British then threw a number of grenades into the cellar to take care of Grace, but he took cover behind an old gas cooker, and remained hidden until the fighting had moved on and he was able to escape in the darkness.

With No. 25 neutralized, Oates held a hurried orders-group. B Company would spearhead the attack, closely supported by A Company, with C Company acting as a general reserve to exploit any potential success. Rushing up Northumberland Road, the 2/8th were soon taking casualties.

Shortly afterwards D Company 2/7th, led by Lt Foster, arrived without any orders. Oates used these unexpected reinforcements to force their way into the Old Schoolhouse at the top of the road, and take up positions from which they could engage Clanwilliam House. Foster was exasperated by his men's fire, crying, 'How is it that normally the platoon has plenty of excellent marksmen and first-class shots and yet now you can't hit a whole terrace at 50 yards' range?' Breaking cover, B Company stormed across the bridge but went to ground just short of the objective when both of its officers were killed shortly after reaching the northern bank.

The collapse of Malone's position had a grave effect on the viability of the Parochial Hall defence, and in the face of increasing numbers of British troops the men in the

Parochial Hall evacuated their position but were captured in Percy Lane. It was a minor success that would make Maconchy's task only marginally easier.

With the southern side of the bridge cleared, Oates began to deploy troops in buildings and behind walls to give the men a direct line of fire on Clanwilliam House, and he started massing the rest of his troops in the lee of a stone advertising hoarding at the top of Northumberland Road.

The strategy, such as it was, was that the column would storm across the bridge and overrun the IRA position. Although the plan was remarkably similar to earlier attempts, this latest assault would be preceded by bombers lobbing grenades into Clanwilliam House, and fire-support from platoons who were now in possession of several buildings from which they would be able to lay down a heavy, suppressive volume of fire into the enemy strongpoint. Accuracy no longer mattered as long as the suppressive fire was sufficient to keep the rebels' heads down.

In the end it was an unnecessary precaution as the bombs ignited the house's gas supply and the building was soon wreathed in flames, with the majority of its occupants able to make their escape in the confusion. With the area backlit by flame, the Sherwood Foresters began to consolidate their hard-won position and prepared to make the final push on Dublin Castle at daybreak. As night progressed, however, a message was received ordering the men back to Ballsbridge, and their positions were taken over by Brig Gen Carleton's 177th Brigade, which consisted of the four Staffordshire battalions.

THURSDAY 27 APRIL –
A CITY IN FLAMES

As dawn broke, the city fell back into what had become its normal state – British troops slowly pushing forward only to be met by rifle fire from the rebel positions, while from vantage points and rooftops snipers engaged each other in a deadly game of cat and mouse.

At 10 a.m., the calm was shattered as field guns began to fire shells into the Sackville Street area. Although the guns were undoubtedly firing at maximum elevation and without spotters, they were soon to have a crucial effect on the battle; shortly after they opened fire a number of shells plunged into a warehouse owned by the *Irish Times*.

Despite the fact that the munitions used by the 18-pdrs were intended as anti-personnel weapons, the building was filled with combustible materials and all it took was a single spark to ignite them. As the flames took hold they began to spread in all directions, not just into neighbouring buildings but also across some of the hastily erected rebel barricades that were constructed of furniture and paper bales taken from the warehouse. From the roof of the GPO, sentries reported that a number of fires had been started by British incendiary shells but, given the British ammunition limitations, a more reasonable explanation is that these fires were caused by burning debris falling from the Métropole Hotel on the opposite side of Princes Street.

Connolly was seemingly everywhere at once in the GPO. He issued orders, responded to reports from the various outposts and was hit while overseeing the construction of a barricade in Princes Street. Draping his jacket over the wound he then went up to Capt Mahony, a British prisoner who was assisting the medical staff, and, ducking behind a screen, asked him to dress the wound.

Later on during the afternoon, he was supervising the occupation of a new position in Middle Abbey Street when a bullet ricocheted off the pavement and smashed into his ankle. In agony, he crawled back into Princes Street where he was found and carried into the GPO. This time there was no possibility of concealing either the wound or its severity, and he was propped up on a mattress in the public hall.

From Kilmainham the 2/5th and 2/6th Sherwood Foresters were ordered to Capel Street to reinforce the cordon and commence street-clearing operations. Supporting the troops were two improvised personnel carriers, which had been built at the Inchicore Iron Works the previous afternoon. Two flatbed lorries had been fitted with boilers supplied by the Guinness Brewery and, drilled with loopholes and vision slits, they provided adequate protection for the transport of troops and supplies.

Interior of the GPO building, *c.*1430hrs, 27 April 1916

As neighbouring buildings in Princes Street begin to smoulder, we see here the situation within the eastern or A Block of the General Post Office. Following the excitement of the attack on the British cavalry on Easter Monday, the garrison has now reverted into a more reactive mode in anticipation of a British assault on the building. Despite being wounded earlier on in the day, here we see James Connolly (1) giving orders to Lt. Oscar Traynor for the establishment of a new outpost in Middle Abbey Street. It was whilst overseeing this operation that a ricocheting bullet shattered Connolly's ankle. Sheltered behind the main counter, a Volunteer mans an *ad hoc* arsenal (2), whilst a captured British officer Capt. George Mahoney, attends to the wounded in a makeshift hospital area (3).

To protect the main entrance to the public hall, the main doors are being barricaded (4) whilst a number of Volunteers and ICA men man the windows (5). Upstairs, Tom Clarke and Seán MacDermott have taken over one of the offices (6), where a signaller uses a tin can tied to a length of twine (7) to carry messages between the GPO and the Rebel positions on the opposite side of Sackville Street. From the balustrade several sentries (8) watch anxiously for signs of movement by the British forces, whilst two men guard the entrance to the van yard (9). Following Connolly's wounding the scene would change dramatically as flaming debris set light to the upper storeys of the building eventually blazing out of control and ultimately forcing the Headquarters Battalion to abandon its positions during the Friday evening. (Peter Dennis © Osprey Publishing)

As they reached their destination, they began an almost textbook street-clearing exercise, with each company allocated to a fixed area and each platoon or section within the company being likewise assigned to specific streets and houses. Once the men were established and operations begun, the armoured cars were used to bring back the artillery from the Grangegorman Asylum, which was then used in a direct support role against known enemy positions.

A few streets away from Clanwilliam House, the majority of de Valera's 3rd Volunteer Battalion had spent an uneasy night with several false alarms of British attacks, a number of which were simply the product of their commander's imagination.

At midday the 2/5th and 2/6th South Staffordshires recommenced the drive towards Trinity College and, tempered by the events of the preceding afternoon, they were content to isolate the Volunteers by dropping off sniper teams en route whose task was to engage de Valera's men and hold them in position until additional troops followed up. The irony of the situation is that had the Staffordshires made a more resolute showing they would have most likely swamped the rebel positions and destroyed the 3rd Battalion as a fighting force. The truth of the matter is that they were both untrained in street fighting and unaware of the meagre size of the opposing forces.

Still recovering from their ordeal of the previous day, and by now reunited with the errant D Company, 2/8th Battalion, the remainder of the 178th Brigade received orders to move around the south of the city to Kilmainham and, as news had been received that the remainder of the brigade had reached that same destination without incident, a fresh optimism began to permeate the ranks.

At 1 p.m. Lt Col Oates' battalion led the brigade westward through the southern suburbs. Their progress was uneventful until the leading elements began to cross the Rialto Bridge leading into the southern part of the South Dublin Union and Céannt's outposts forced them to go to ground. The situation was an ominous echo of the previous afternoon's attack in Northumberland Road, but here the terrain was more open and the British forces were able to clear a way through to the South Dublin Union.

Oates then sent his second-in-command, Capt 'Mickey' Martyn, to lead a fighting patrol into the buildings to engage the enemy while the rest of the column pushed ahead to Kilmainham. The men came under enemy fire almost as soon as they entered the grounds, with Martyn noting that 'I found that a bullet in Dublin was every bit as dangerous as one in No-Man's Land … In some ways the fighting in Dublin was worse – in France you had a fair idea of where the enemy was and where the bullets were going to come from. In Dublin you never knew when or from where you were going to be hit.'

The British troops edged their way into the complex, but the volume and accuracy of the Volunteers' fire was a testament of how well Céannt had deployed his few men.

Gathering any tools they could find, the Foresters tunnelled their way from room to room. As they broke into the Nurses' Home, Martyn and a Sgt Walker began bombing their way forward when they were joined by Capt Oates and successfully forced an IRA barricade inside the building. Céannt narrowly escaped being shot as the British broke into the Nurses' Home and soon afterwards his deputy, Cathal Brugha, was hit several times and critically wounded.

The rebels' situation was becoming critical. Céannt had already lost more than 20 men killed and wounded, while another dozen or so had been captured. The long-range sniping that had characterized the early stages of the fighting in the Union had given way to a series of close-quarter engagements. Céannt realized that he had no effective response to the enemy's superior numbers and firepower and decided that the best course of action would be to fight in the enclosed rooms and corridors in the hope that the confusion would cause the British to miscalculate the defenders' strength.

The morale of the men of the 4th Battalion had now reached an all-time low. The euphoria of the first day's fighting had given way to the relentless pressure of the succeeding days, and now it seemed as if all was lost, with many believing that they should wait for the British to take them prisoner. What saved the situation was the badly wounded Brugha, who had put himself into a position from which he could interdict the British advance and was now singing Republican songs at the top of his voice. The singing lifted the men from their lethargy and they rushed back to man the barricade.

For over an hour Oates and his men huddled on one side of the barricade nervously awaiting an IRA assault, while the rebels clung to their position fearing an imminent British attack. As darkness fell, a message came from battalion HQ that the column had broken through to the Royal Hospital and that Oates was to withdraw. For the second time that day the British forces had come within an ace of eliminating one of the Volunteer battalions, only to pull back at the moment of truth.

As night fell, a red haze lay over the centre of Dublin. The fire that had begun in the *Irish Times* warehouse had now spread into several neighbouring areas and the glow was echoed by that above the Linenhall Barracks, which had earlier been set alight by men of Daly's 1st Battalion. But at 10 p.m. this all – literally – paled into insignificance when Hoyte's Druggists and Oil Works, which lay on the opposite side of Sackville Street, exploded in a column of flame, scattering flaming debris over a wide area.

The situation within the GPO was becoming critical as the surrounding buildings were awash with flame and fire hoses were deployed to douse any surfaces that looked as if they might catch fire. In the public hall, Connolly was propped up on a mattress still masterminding the IRA defence, supported by the rest of the Provisional Government who had by now all congregated in this central area.

EVENTS

1. 0001hrs, 28 April: The blaze that originated in the Times Building and Hoyte's Druggists is now beginning to spread out of control as the Dublin Fire Brigade has been effectively stood down due to the danger from indiscriminate small-arms fire.

2. 0200hrs, 28 April: General Sir John Maxwell arrives at North Wall Docks to assume command of the British forces.

3. 1000hrs, 28 April: The newly arrived 2/4th Lincolns ordered to assist in throwing a cordon around de Valera's 3rd Battalion (6), taking over from the 2/6th South Staffordshires (S).

4. 1000hrs, 28 April: Maxwell orders the 2/5th (R) and 2/6th (S) South Staffordshires to move from Trinity College in on the Four Courts area.

5. 1020hrs, 28 April: 2/5th (M) and 2/6th (N) Sherwood Foresters and the 3rd Royal Irish Regiment (F) are ordered to close in on the GPO from the west and the 5th Leinsters join the eastern cordon.

BRITISH FORCES

A 6th Reserve Cavalry Regiment
B Dublin Castle Garrison
C Trinity College Garrison
D Composite Battalion, 15th Reserve Infantry Brigade
E Detachment, Army School of Musketry
F 3rd Royal Irish Regiment
G 3rd Royal Irish Rifles
H 10th Royal Dublin Fusiliers
I 4th Royal Dublin Fusiliers
J Elements, 25th (Irish) Reserve Infantry Brigade
K Section, 5th Reserve Brigade, Royal Field Artillery
L Section, 5th Reserve Brigade, Royal Field Artillery
M 2/5th Sherwood Foresters
N 2/6th Sherwood Foresters
O 2/7th Sherwood Foresters
P 2/8th Sherwood Foresters
Q HMY Helga II/Trawler Sealark II
R 2/5th South Staffordshires
S 2/6th South Staffordshires
T 2/5th North Staffordshires
U 2/6th North Staffordshires
V 2/4th Leicesters
W 2/5th Leicesters
X 2/4th Lincolns
Y 2/5th Lincolns
Z 5th Leinsters
AA 8th Reserve Cavalry Regiment
AB 9th Reserve Cavalry Regiment
AC 10th Reserve Cavalry Regiment

6. 1030hrs, 28 April: 3rd Royal Irish Regiment (F) occupies Great Britain Street.

7. 1155hrs, 28 April: An 18-pdr field gun (K) is brought up to the corner of Great Britain Street and Coles Lane. The shellfire starts a small blaze in Arnott's store in Henry Street, which is extinguished by the building's sprinkler system.

8. 1900hrs, 28 April: The Headquarters Battalion (1) is unable to extinguish the fire that has taken hold of the GPO. The Provisional Government agrees to evacuate the building in favour of a new headquarters at Williams & Woods in Great Britain Street.

9. 2000hrs, 28 April: The O'Rahilly leads a sortie from the GPO to clear a British barricade in Moore Street but his men are cut to pieces, and he himself is mortally wounded.

10. 2000hrs, 28 April: The Headquarters Battalion (1) pulls in its outlying positions preparatory to staging a breakout to the new Headquarters at Williams & Woods.

11. 2015hrs, 28 April: The Headquarters Battalion (1) is forced to take shelter in No. 15 Moore Street and attempts to tunnel through to Great Britain Street.

12. 1100hrs, 29 April: The 3rd Royal Irish Regiment (F) reinforced by 100 men of 2/6th Sherwood Foresters (N) prepares to assault the ruins of the GPO.

13. 1245hrs, 29 April: To avoid further civilian casualties, the Provisional Government aggress to establish contact with the British commander to discuss surrender terms.

14. 1430hrs, 29 April: Brigadier Lowe meets Pearse at the British barricade in Moore Street. The terms given are unconditional surrender. Countersigned by James Connolly, the order is to be brought to the battalion commanders by Nurse Elizabeth O'Farrell and Lowe's ADC, Captain de Courcey-Wheeler. Although it will take several hours before all insurgent forces comply with the surrender orders, the Rising is effectively at an end.

THE FINAL CURTAIN

The British cordon and the failed breakout attempt, Friday 28-Saturday 29 April 1916.

This map is 4.4 x 3km

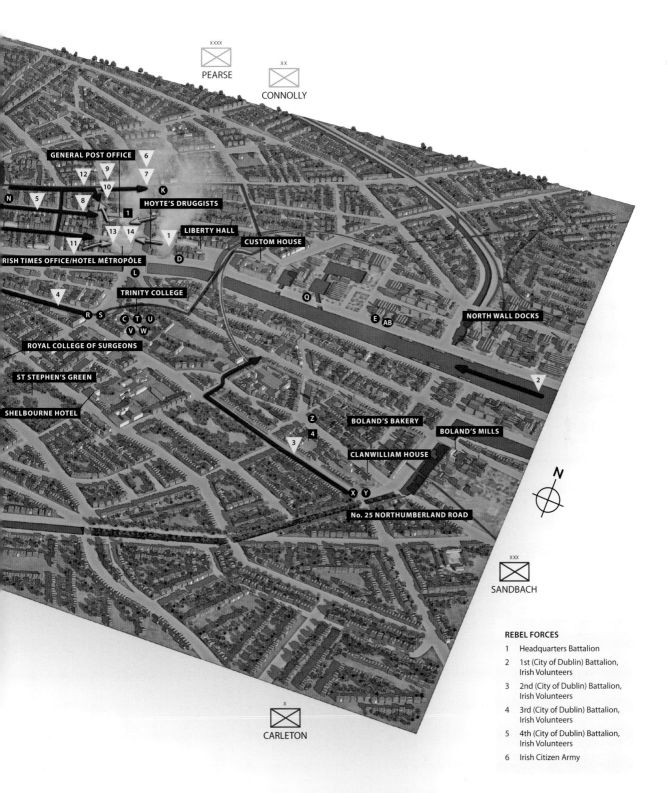

PEARSE

CONNOLLY

GENERAL POST OFFICE

HOYTE'S DRUGGISTS

LIBERTY HALL

CUSTOM HOUSE

IRISH TIMES OFFICE/HOTEL MÉTROPÔLE

TRINITY COLLEGE

NORTH WALL DOCKS

ROYAL COLLEGE OF SURGEONS

ST STEPHEN'S GREEN

SHELBOURNE HOTEL

BOLAND'S BAKERY

BOLAND'S MILLS

CLANWILLIAM HOUSE

No. 25 NORTHUMBERLAND ROAD

SANDBACH

CARLETON

REBEL FORCES

1 Headquarters Battalion

2 1st (City of Dublin) Battalion, Irish Volunteers

3 2nd (City of Dublin) Battalion, Irish Volunteers

4 3rd (City of Dublin) Battalion, Irish Volunteers

5 4th (City of Dublin) Battalion, Irish Volunteers

6 Irish Citizen Army

FRIDAY 28 APRIL –
THE BEGINNING OF THE END

At 2 a.m. on Friday morning, a small group of men disembarked from a British warship that had tied up against the North Wall Quay; ushered into three waiting motor cars, they were driven to Kilmainham Hospital. Gen Sir John Maxwell had arrived to assume his position as GOCinC (Irish Command). Maxwell quickly reaffirmed Lowe's existing dispositions and orders, and gave additional instructions for the 2/5th and 2/6th South Staffordshires to move across the Liffey to reduce the Four Courts area. The remainder of Carleton's 177th Brigade and the leading elements of 176th (Lincoln and Leicester) Brigade were to deploy to contain the area occupied by de Valera's men.

To some, dawn seemed to be a bit of an anticlimax. Few troops could be seen out in the open, however those with field glasses or telescopes could see small knots of khaki-clad men cautiously moving through the ruins to close in on the insurgent positions. At 9.30 a.m. both Pearse and Connolly addressed the GPO garrison and gave a version of events that was based on wishful thinking, claiming success on all fronts and a popular rising being enacted throughout the country. It may have been what Pearse wanted to believe but it was utterly divorced from reality.

Several thousand British soldiers now held cordons north of the river in order to prevent a breakout and reduce the area occupied by the rebels house by house, brick by brick. To emphasize this, one of the 18-pdrs was brought up to Great Britain Street from where it fired upon Arnott's drapery store, which butted onto the rear of the GPO. At the same time the guns in Westmoreland and D'Olier streets began again to engage targets along the quays and in Sackville Street over open sights.

It was at this stage that it dawned upon the Provisional Government that the British were not intent on making the anticipated frontal assault on the GPO, and it was therefore decided to evacuate the female members of the garrison under the protection of a Red Cross flag – despite this, several women, including Connolly's secretary Winifred Carney, were to stay until the end.

As the day progressed the fires that had taken hold on the upper floors began to burn out of control, and it was soon apparent that the numerous fire hoses that were being played across the inferno were simply delaying the inevitable. The British may not have chosen to attack the building but nevertheless it was doomed, and an alternative position needed to be found. At 6 p.m. the wounded were evacuated through a tunnel that led from the rear of the GPO to the Coliseum Theatre, and an hour later all prisoners that had been taken by the insurgents were brought downstairs and told to make a run for safety.

The wreckage of Sackville Street smoulders in the aftermath of the Easter Rising. (© Bettmann/Corbis)

Back in the GPO, O'Rahilly, the Irish Volunteers Treasurer, agreed to lead a party of men to secure the site of a new headquarters in the Williams and Woods factory in Great Britain Street. As he assembled his men he jokingly remarked, 'English speakers to the front, Irish speakers to the rear'. He himself took position in advance of his men.

In Moore Street O'Rahilly's party was fired on by British troops manning a barricade and he was hit several times. Minutes later, as he attempted to get across the street to Sackville Street, he was fatally wounded. Slumped in a doorway, he wrote a note to his wife and family before he died. Opposed to the Rising, O'Rahilly nevertheless gave it his unswerving support when it became a reality and he was the only senior member of the Volunteer movement to be killed in action.

Chaos now reigned as a last-ditch attempt to recall O'Rahilly's men turned into a fiasco as many of the garrison, believing it to be a breakout attempt, milled about in the streets only to be picked off by British riflemen. Sometime after 9 p.m. the surviving rebels began to tunnel their way from Cogan's Greengrocers in Moore Lane through neighbouring houses towards William and Woods, but by the early hours of Saturday morning they had only reached No. 16 Moore Street and it was here that the Provisional Government established its final headquarters.

Even as the insurgents were trying to establish a new headquarters the final nail was being driven into their coffin. Late in the evening the remaining battalions of 176th Brigade finally reached the city, as did Brig Gen Peel's artillery brigade. Had the fighting continued past Saturday afternoon the arrival of the 59th's batteries would have given Lowe and Maxwell the use of an additional 40 or so 18-pdr guns as well as a battery of howitzers.

However, in his diary Peel states that the 'guns arrived too late in the evening to be deployed for action' and that by the time that they could be brought into action 'the rebellion had fizzled out'. Thus, for the duration of the Rising, the mainstay of the British artillery deployed in Dublin was the four guns from Athlone.

Across the city it appeared that events were reaching their conclusion, but fate had one final card to play. Late on the Friday afternoon, the 2/6th South Staffordshires under Lt Col Henry Taylor were ordered to North King Street to complete the British cordon. Arriving in the area, Taylor received some valuable local intelligence from officers of the Sherwood Foresters who were operating in adjacent streets. Turning the enemy's own tactics against him, Taylor ordered his men to tunnel through the houses in order to keep casualties down but, despite the arrival of one of the armoured personnel carriers and the expenditure of thousands of rounds of ammunition, by midnight they had failed to make any tangible gains whatsoever and, as a result, frustration and anger began to set in.

At about 2 a.m. on Saturday morning, a party of the 2/6th South Staffordshires forced their way into No. 172 North King Street and began to abuse the occupants, many of whom had simply taken refuge in the building. Having been searched, the women were taken down into the cellar, while the men were taken upstairs. Sounds of scuffling were heard and then silence.

Elsewhere, the Staffordshires were making no progress against Daly's men and by 9 a.m. only the presence of the 2/5th South Staffordshires coming up through Smithfield forced the Volunteers to buckle and withdraw. Again, it was only the relentless pressure and numerical superiority of the British forces that turned the enemy positions.

SATURDAY 29 APRIL – SURRENDER

At the rebel headquarters, the situation was strained. Clarke, the lifelong revolutionary, wanted to carry on the fight irrespective of outcome or consequences, while his colleagues within the Provisional Government began to waver. The crux came when Pearse was faced with the unpleasant realities of war and witnessed a family being cut down by British fire while trying to escape their burning home under cover of a white flag.

Orders were then given for all insurgent forces to observe a ceasefire of one hour's duration while contact was made with the British commander, and at 12.45 p.m. nurse Elizabeth O'Farrell was sent to meet with the officer in charge of the area and was eventually taken to Lowe. Lowe's response was that he would not treat with the rebels unless they agreed to surrender unconditionally, and he gave Pearse's plenipotentiary half an hour's grace before hostilities would recommence. At first the Volunteer leader demurred but Lowe made his point more forcefully and at 2.30 p.m. Pearse, escorted by Nurse O'Farrell, met Lowe at the top of Great Britain Street, where he surrendered his sword to the British officer. Pearse and Lowe were then driven to Parkgate where, after a terse meeting with Maxwell, he signed the instrument of surrender:

> In order to prevent the further slaughter of Dublin citizens, and in the hope of saving the lives of our followers now surrounded and hopelessly outnumbered, the members of the Provisional Government present at Headquarters have agreed to an unconditional surrender, and the Commandants of the various districts in the City and Country will order their commands to lay down arms.

The note was countersigned by Connolly on behalf of the ICA and then taken to each of the battalions in turn. Although the final surrenders would not take place until the Sunday, the Rising was effectively over.

THE AFTERMATH

Once the rebels had surrendered, the next question that Maxwell had to face was the question of punishment and retribution. As far as he was concerned the ringleaders of the rebellion and their supporters were guilty of treason during time of war, and as Ireland was under martial law at the time they should receive the ultimate penalty – death.

Soldiers from the Royal Dublin Fusiliers search civilians visiting rebel prisoners. Ironically most of the men in the Royal Dublin Fusiliers had been members of the National Volunteers and were Redmondite Home Rulers. [Imperial War Museum, HU73487)

His problem was that such executions could not take place without at least some semblance of legal impartiality, and thus he instructed that all the prisoners be tried by a Field General Court Martial (FGCM), which could be held by as few as three officers. Ironically, the FGCM was designed to try cases involving troops on active service and by virtue of their trials the insurgents were given combatant status.

In his report to London, Maxwell wrote:

In view of the gravity of the Rebellion and its connection with German intrigue and propaganda, and in view of the great loss of life and destruction of property resulting therefrom, the General Officer Commanding in Chief Irish Command, has found it imperative to inflict the most severe sentences on the organisers of this detestable Rising and on the commanders who took an actual part in the actual fighting that occurred.

Patrick Pearse surrendering to Brig Gen Lowe at 2.30 p.m. in Moore Street, Dublin. The Rising was over. (National Museum of Ireland)

It is hoped that these examples will be sufficient to act as a deterrent to intriguers and to bring home to them that the murder of His Majesty's subjects or other acts calculated to imperil the safety of the Realm will not be tolerated.

The proceedings were pursued with an indecent haste that made a mockery of the court itself. When Eamonn Céannt was on trial, he was offered the opportunity to call a defence witness and named his senior officer, Thomas MacDonagh, only to be told that he was indisposed and could not testify. What was not admitted was that the prospective witness had been executed that morning.

As a result of the fighting more than 60,000 square yards of buildings were destroyed, with an estimated cost of some £2.5 million. To calculate the modern value this sum should be multiplied by a factor of about 30.

During the Rising it is estimated that the British forces suffered around 550 casualties, while up to 2,500 civilians were either killed or injured. For their part, the rebels are acknowledged to have incurred fewer than 200, to which must be added the following who were executed at Kilmainham Gaol:

3 May	Patrick Pearse, Thomas Clarke and Thomas MacDonagh
4 May	Joseph Plunkett, Edward Daly, Willie Pearse and Michael O'Hanrahan
5 May	Major John MacBride
8 May	Eamonn Céannt, Michael Mallin, Con Colbert and Seán Heuston
12 May	Seán MacDermott and James Connolly

In addition Thomas Kent was shot in Cork on 9 May and Sir Roger Casement was hanged in Pentonville Prison, London on 3 August 1916. Many of the rebels were sentenced to lengthy prison terms on the British mainland, where they learned techniques that would serve them in the Anglo-Irish War of 1919–21 and the Irish Civil War of 1922.

Irish rebels, however, were not the only ones placed on trial. Their fellow Irishman, Capt Bowen-Colthurst, was tried for the killings of Sheehy-Skeffington and several others. He was found guilty of two counts of murder, but was declared to be insane. He later retired to Canada on a military pension.

Coming from the cells through the gate on the left of the picture, Connolly's guards carried him a short distance to the far wall where, strapped to a chair, he was the last of the insurgent leaders to be executed. (David Murphy)

For the murders of the men in No. 172 North King Street, no member of the 2/6th South Staffordshires was ever charged. When an identity parade was called to offer witnesses the opportunity to identify the perpetrators, it was found that several members of the battalion had been transferred back to the British mainland.

A dramatic reconstruction of an unnamed Irish rebel being executed in Kilmainham Gaol after the 1916 Rising. (© Top Foto)

THE ANGLO-IRISH WAR

THE GATHERING STORM

The IRA's command structure had effectively been decapitated by the Rising's failure and the majority of militant Republicans found themselves behind bars in mainland Britain, but by June 1917 most of the Easter rebels had been released and were well placed to infiltrate Sinn Féin.

In 1916 the rebels had failed to gain the support of the Irish public and many Nationalists felt that Pearse and his cohorts had both betrayed and undermined their cause; however, their subsequent treatment made them Irish folk-heroes. Although the Defence of the Realm Act (DORA) gave the Army the authority to arrest, intern and try individuals without recourse to the civil judicial system the events that followed the Rising managed to alienate many ordinary Irishmen and women and drove a number into the arms of the Republican movement.

This was good for Sinn Féin as it capitalized on the IPP's declining fortunes and portrayed itself as the only true Nationalist party. Despite its monarchist beginnings, by 1917 Sinn Féin had been taken over by militant Republican survivors of the Easter Rising who were determined to gain control of every Nationalist organization in Ireland.

These personal links between the militant and political arms of Republicanism were so close that, despite not being responsible for orchestrating the 1916 rebellion, some British newspapers and officials began to refer to the 1916 Rising as the 'Sinn Féin Revolt' and its supporters as 'Shinners'. This perception was further reinforced when de Valera was elected President of Sinn Féin in 1917 and on 26 October called for Nationalist Ireland to unite against the British.

Sinn Féin's strategy was simple. They refused to recognize British rule and created an underground Irish Republic; acting as an alternative government, they encouraged and coerced people into boycotting British institutions. A direct consequence of this

The real mastermind behind IRA operations: despite his appearance being known to the security forces, Michael Collins travelled openly around Dublin on a bicycle. He was once stopped on O'Connell Bridge by Cadet Douglas Duff and another Auxiliary who decided that discretion was the better part of valour when Collins pointed out the dozen or so gunmen providing him with close protection. (Irish Military Archive)

82

Easter Rising veterans pose for a picture in Stafford Gaol. Then as now, prison acted as a 'Republican University' where inmates analysed past operations and worked out how to be more effective in the future. (Irish Military Archive)

policy was that the police, as local representatives of the Crown's authority, were directly targeted by Republicans. In addition, the Government was increasingly conscious that the Army's response to the Easter Rising had done more harm than good for their cause.

The British Government's public image was further dented when Republican prisoners refused to wear prison uniforms and those on hunger strike were force-fed. Things became even worse when Comdt Ashe died on 25 September 1917 after being force-fed, creating yet another rebel martyr.

The unpopular extension of conscription to Ireland in 1918 also handed Sinn Féin an effective weapon to further undermine both Dublin Castle and its police. Under a new generation of leaders like de Valera and Collins, Sinn Féin and the IRA used their time wisely to prepare for the struggle to come. Sinn Féin's appeal was also increased by the Government's ban on emigration and the extension of the franchise to all men over 21 and women over 30.

Ultimately, Sinn Féin managed to translate this support into overwhelming victory in the 1918 General Election on 14 December, by winning 73 out of 105 seats. They cut a deal with the Irish Labour Party and its candidates stood for election on the basis that they would not take their seats in Westminster but would convene an Irish Parliament, or Dáil Éireann, in Dublin, and felt that the election result was the mandate it required for rejecting British authority.

On 21 January 1919 the Dáil met in the Dublin Mansion House, claiming to be the first Irish national political assembly to meet since the Irish Parliament was dissolved in 1801. Every Irish MP, whether Nationalist or Unionist, was invited, although in reality only those 27 Sinn Féin MPs who were not in prison attended, while the Unionists and IPP boycotted it and attended the Westminster Parliament. The official constitution of the Dáil was read out along with the offices of state, although the names of their incumbents were not made public until later.

When the Dáil reconvened on 1 April 1919, de Valera, who had escaped from Lincoln Gaol on 3 February, was appointed President of the Dáil and Prime Minister of Ireland. The 2nd Dáil announced the names of the Republic's Officers of State: Arthur Griffith, Home Affairs; Count Plunkett, Foreign Affairs; Éoin MacNeill, Industry; Cathal Brugha, Defence; Constance Markiewicz, Labour; William Cosgrave, Local Government; and Michael Collins, Finance. All of them were either IRB or had had connections to it, as did Richard Mulcahy, a veteran of the Ashbourne ambush, who became COS of the Volunteers, or IRA, in March 1918.

Comdt Tom Ashe died whilst on hunger strike in 1917 and was buried with full military honours on the orders of Michael Collins. (National Museum of Ireland)

Despite winning the majority of the Irish vote in 1918, Sinn Féin and the Dáil were unable to gain recognition from the Westminster Parliament as the legitimate government of Ireland. The simple fact was that neither party was willing or able to recognize the other's authority in Ireland.

John Redmond's support for the war damaged the IPP's following in Ireland. Their failure to win the Roscommon by-election in February 1917 signalled the beginning of the end, and Redmond's death in March 1918 further hastened the decline of the party. The General Election in December 1918 saw the end of constitutional Nationalism as the IPP's 83 seats in Westminster were slashed to just six. By 1921 the IPP had ceased to contest elections in the South.

Sinn Féin was not the only Nationalist/Republican organization to change its tack after the Rising. The IRA realized that the age of glorious gestures, meeting to fight pitched battles against the British Army – as one rebel song had it, 'by the rising of the moon' – had passed for ever, and 1916 was to be the last time that Crown forces and Irish rebels would fight each other in anything resembling large-scale conventional military operations. Ironically, the next time the IRA would meet Government troops in the streets of Dublin would be the summer of 1922, and those troops would be the Irish Government's.

Although fewer than 64 rebels had been killed or wounded during the Rising, and only 15 out of the 112 sentenced to death were actually executed, the British had effectively destroyed the IRA's command structure. The collapse of the IPP, aggressive Sinn Féin propaganda and Britain's preoccupation with World War I allowed a new generation of hardliners to step forward into the vacuum that had been left.

The new men – de Valera, Collins, Brugha, Mulcahy, Boland and their ilk – were veterans of 1916 who shared a ruthless determination to end British rule by any means necessary and were determined not to repeat the mistakes of the Easter Rising. On 12 July 1917 the *Irish Independent* prophetically warned that their attempts to win independence would merely bring '… dire misfortune and untold horrors, and ruin and devastation, and the demon of civil strife'.

There were close personal links between Sinn Féin and the IRA; however the IRB infiltration of the IRA was more or less total, and in reality it was never fully under the control of the Sinn Féin-dominated Dáil, despite what de Valera may have claimed. Although Brugha became Minister of Defence in April 1919, he deeply resented that the real power behind the IRA was the 'Big Fellow', Michael Collins, who was a senior member of the IRB, and his patron Mulcahy. In fact the independence of the IRA from the Dáil was what sowed the seeds for civil war in 1922.

In 1917, however, the divisions in the Republican movement were still in the future and when the Easter rebels were released from Frongoch and elsewhere they were faced with that classic military debrief question – 'if you were to do it again how would you do it differently?'

In some respect greater urgency was added to this question when World War I ended on 11 November 1918 and effectively removed any hope of further German support.

Germany's defeat, however, was not such a great blow to the Republicans as it seemed – after all they had armed both the UVF and IVF, and had singularly failed to support the IRA during the 1916 rebellion. Consequently, the IRA decided to bide its time, lend support to Sinn Féin and concentrate on identifying other sources of weapons.

Nevertheless, the British firmly believed that Sinn Féin was behind the Rising and that the 'Shinners' were preparing to go again. In an attempt to pre-empt this action they arrested most of Sinn Féin's leadership on 17 May 1918 on the pretext of a largely fictitious German plot to start a second 'Easter Rising' in Ireland. Unfortunately the British failed to catch the IRA's key players, which allowed these militants to shape the Nationalist agenda.

Between 1917 and the winter of 1918 the IRA concentrated on stealing much-needed arms and ammunition from the British, and teaching its members how to use them. They were hindered by a serious lack of modern military firearms, which forced them to rely upon shotguns, hunting rifles and handguns commandeered from farmers and private households. These weapons were suitable for close-quarter assassinations, but did not convey the correct martial image and were unsuitable for engaging in combat with the Crown's forces. The IRA knew that the numerous sparsely manned RIC barracks, scattered across rural Ireland, represented a potential source of weapons, but it would be January 1920 before they felt confident enough to attack them directly.

Of course, the end of the war meant that not only were there hundreds of thousands of British soldiers demobilizing but also that there were millions of surplus firearms sluicing around the UK and the rest of Europe. Guns, however, cost money and, although it was expressly forbidden by GHQ, some Volunteers carried out armed robberies to obtain funds for the cause, while Collins (Minister for Finance) organized a Republican loan that raised more than £370,000 in Ireland alone. The Dáil insisted that the loan was purely voluntary, although many Unionists subscribed, which raises the question of how much intimidation was used to solicit this money. Refusal to subscribe could be construed as treason and invite bloody consequences.

Fundraising in the USA was not terribly successful, despite its Irish diaspora. The US Government was non-committal and appeared unwilling to upset the British. Ironically, the Irish community in mainland Britain seemed more willing to lend tangible support to the cause than their American cousins were, including carrying out attacks on the British mainland, especially in London, Liverpool and Manchester.

Such was the need for funds that de Valera, himself ambivalent to communism, even approached the fledgling Soviet Union for funds and military aid. This did nothing to improve his standing in America and simply served to reinforce an erroneous British perception that the Irish troubles were a Bolshevik plot stirred up by Comintern agents provocateurs.

When Sinn Féin won a landslide victory in the 1918 General Election it never crossed their minds that the result was anything less than a mandate to embark upon a war of independence against the British. Their manifesto did allude to using 'any means necessary' to end the Union but it made no mention of an insurgency, with all the chaos and bloodshed that entailed, and it is possibly stretching credibility a little to claim that the majority of Irishmen and women were voting for revolution. Undoubtedly the IRA campaign of 1919–21 enjoyed more support than that of 1916, but it is impossible to judge accurately how much.

THE FIGHTING: DYING FOR IRELAND

Although there is still some dispute as to when the Anglo-Irish War began, there is little doubt that the final and most violent phase of it started with two unconnected, albeit related, acts of defiance against British rule on 21 January 1919, when Republican politicians held the inaugural meeting of the Irish Republic's 1st Dáil, or Parliament, in the Mansion House, Dublin and members of the IRA carried out an attack at Soloheadbeg Quarry, outside Tipperary.

Soloheadbeg Quarry

By 1919 some Republican hardliners feared that the IRA would fall apart if it did not begin to act more aggressively. One such man, the Vice-Brigadier of the IRA's South Tipperary Brigade, Seán Treacy, believed that if his men forcibly took gelignite from an armed police escort it would boost their arsenal, prestige and confidence. No one knows whether Treacy planned to kill the police escort although it is unlikely that the prospect disturbed him.

The original plan was to ambush a consignment of gelignite being moved from the military barracks in Tipperary town to Soloheadbeg Quarry. On the morning of 16 January the IRA Volunteers took up position near the quarry, which was 3 miles from Tipperary outside the village of Monard on the road to Donohill. They lay up for several hours but the consignment did not appear until five days later, during which time his command shrank to nine men from the local South Tipperary Brigade: Seamus Robinson (Brigade OC), Treacy (Vice-Brigadier), Dan Breen (Quartermaster), Seán Hogan, Tim Crowe, Patrick McCormack, Patrick O'Dwyer, Michael Ryan and Jack O'Meara.

The two 'peelers' escorting the gelignite were both Irish Catholics. Constable James McDonnell was a 57-year-old married father of five from Co. Mayo, while Constable

Patrick O'Connell was 36 years old and from Co. Cork. Both men were typical village bobbies who happened to be in the wrong place at the wrong time.

Their task was to escort two county council employees, Edward Godfrey and Patrick Flynn, and a cartload of 168lb of gelignite. Flynn also had 38 detonators in his pocket. Masked and armed with a .22cal automatic rifle, Treacy stepped into the path of the constables and issued a challenge. Both policemen fumbled for their rifles and Treacy fired at them. As they fell his men opened fire, killing the two unfortunate officers.

The two policemen probably thought that they were caught up in an armed robbery and it is perhaps symptomatic of the RIC ethos that despite being surprised and outnumbered they had attempted to resist. With the exceptions of McDonnell and O'Connell, all of the participants in Soloheadbeg were local men, so when Breen's mask slipped either Flynn or Godfrey, who survived unhurt, recognized him, and by 29 January the Government was offering a reward of £1,000 – no mean sum in 1919.

Although Soloheadbeg was not sanctioned by GHQ it sent a clear message to the British that the IRA was willing and able to kill Crown servants to achieve its ends. The message was further reinforced when the IRA's newspaper, *An tÓglach* (The Volunteer), told its readers that it was their duty – 'morally and legally' – to kill soldiers and policemen. It was nothing less than a declaration of war by the IRA.

This development was not universally welcomed and both the press and the Catholic Church condemned their actions, rather naively believing that the Dáil would not

Pictured here are four of the nine men who carried out the attack at Soloheadbeg Quarry on 21 January 1919. From left to right: Seamus Robinson, Seán Treacy, Dan Breen and Seán Hogan. Treacy was killed in Dublin on 14 October 1920 and Breen and Robinson went on to become senior anti-Treaty IRA leaders during the Civil War. (National Museum of Ireland)

sanction such violence. De Valera, however, was less circumspect, and claimed in 1921 that the IRA, as the Army of the Irish Republic, had operated with the Dáil's approval since 1919, and as President he accepted full responsibility for its actions. The IRA was very sensitive about negative press and on 21 December 1919 Paddy Clancy led 20 to 30 men into the offices of the *Irish Independent* and smashed up its printing presses.

Despite the martial rhetoric the reality of IRA operations seems to have been a dozen or so local Volunteers ambushing a small group of policemen in quiet country lanes. They were local men who often knew the policemen they were ambushing and, more significantly, were probably known by them as well. Sometimes these ambushes resembled highway robbery, with masked men holding up bicycling 'peelers' in order to steal their weapons, while others degenerated into vicious close-quarter gun battles that the outnumbered policemen usually lost.

Throughout 1919 there were instances of the IRA shouting warnings before they opened fire, and of policemen giving up their service revolvers and Lee Enfield .303cal rifles without a fight and being sent on their way. Sadly, as the struggle progressed, these incidents became rarer as both sides became less inclined to act chivalrously.

As the majority of policemen were Irish, Sinn Féin knew that they needed to drive a wedge between the police and the public. They hoped to do this by portraying them as 'brave and trusting Irishmen', duped by the British 'to attain their ends', or 'England's Janissaries', and in April 1919 they ordered a boycott of all policemen, their families and friends. This was followed up by a further boycott of policemen and their friends and families in June 1920 that was ruthlessly enforced by the IRA.

People were forbidden all contact with policemen, and shops were vandalized for selling goods to the police. Mary Crean of Frenchpark, Co. Roscommon had three pig rings inserted in her buttock for supplying food to a policeman, while Michael McCarthy of Caheragh, Co. Cork, even had his hearse burned in July 1920 for burying one. Girls also had their heads shaved for walking out with 'peelers'.

The boycott was only effective in some areas, most notably the IRA strongholds of the south-west. Bizarrely, the unarmed DMP seemed to be excluded from the boycott and suffered relatively few casualties throughout the Troubles, with only nine men, six of whom were G-Men (G Division detectives), being killed by the IRA.

Sinn Féin hoped that by attacking the police they would encourage its members to resign, thus undermining the Castle's ability to impose its authority in rural communities. However, by ostracizing both serving and ex-policemen Sinn Féin's policy offered almost no prospects for alternative employment and so left many, and especially those with families, with little choice but to stick with the police.

Some policemen helped the IRA, and DMP G Division detectives Neligan, Broy, Kavanagh, MacNamara, Mannix and RIC Sgt McElligott were especially useful to

Michael Collins. Given that roughly 70 per cent of the 513 policemen killed were Irish there can be little doubt that they were singled out specifically by the IRA. Along with policemen, Irish civil servants, magistrates and even the Viceroy were potential targets. In all the IRA failed three times to kill Field Marshal Lord French, but succeeded in killing Sir Henry Wilson in 1922.

Although the military presented the IRA with a harder target, it managed to carry out several successful operations against them. In March 1919 the IRA raided the military aerodrome at Collinstown and got away with 75 rifles and 4,000 rounds of ammunition. On 16 June it ambushed a joint RIC–Army patrol near Rathclarin, wounding a policeman and a soldier before the remaining three men gave up their weapons and were sent on their way.

Despite a limited involvement in supporting the police, the Troubles were very much a sideshow for the Army in 1919. It was much more concerned with demobilization and overseas commitments to such an extent that on 27 August 1919

The funeral of RIC District Inspector James Brady in Glasnevin, Dublin 1920. Brady was an ex-Irish Guards officer. He was the son of Louis Brady, the Dublin Harbour Master, and nephew of P. J. Brady, the IPP MP for St Stephen's Green. He joined the RIC in March 1920, aged 21, and was killed in an IRA ambush on 30 September near Chaffpool, Co. Sligo. (National Library of Ireland)

the British GOCinC (Ireland), Sir Frederick Shaw, informed the RIC Inspector General (IG), Brig Gen Sir Joseph Byrne, that the Army would no longer be able to provide detachments to support police outposts.

Ultimately, the Army's intelligence network run by Brig Gen Winter in Dublin and men like Tom Barry's foil, Major Percival of the Essex Regiment in Cork, were their most effective contribution. Percival is probably better known for surrendering Singapore to the Japanese in 1942.

The sack of Fermoy, 8 September 1919

On Sunday 7 September members of the local IRA battalion led by their Brigadier, Liam Lynch, ambushed 18 men of the King's Shropshire Light Infantry (KSLI) en route to church in Fermoy, Co. Cork. Although the attack was well planned a soldier was killed in the ensuing scuffle and three wounded, while Lynch was accidentally injured by one of his own men. They got away with 13 rifles in waiting motor cars and although the Fermoy garrison reacted quickly, Lynch had also planned his escape; as the cars passed pre-designated spots, logs were thrown across the road to prevent further pursuit.

This was the first direct attack on the Army and Collins had personally authorized the raid on the condition that there would be no casualties – a difficult thing to guarantee under the circumstances. As a result Sinn Féin and the IRA were immediately banned in Co. Cork, which led de Valera in New York to state that 'the English are seeking to goad the people into open rebellion in the field'. Considering the Government's strategy had to date been completely reactive, the opposite was blatantly true and it was the IRA that was attempting to provoke an overreaction from the Castle. The inquest on 8 September did not help matters when it condemned the attack but failed to reach a verdict of murder, as the IRA had not intended to kill the unfortunate rifleman.

That night a mob of men from the Buffs (Royal East Kent Regiment), King's Shropshire Light Infantry and Royal Air Force (RAF) – many the worse for drink – ran amok in the town, smashing shop windows and those of the inquest jury's foreman, and instigating what Republican propagandists rather overegged as the 'sack of Fermoy'. Significantly, it heralded a new pattern of violence – the reprisal.

It would be another six months or so before reprisals became routine and 11 months before they became part of official Government policy. They were, however, counter-productive, being a blunt instrument that often alienated otherwise sympathetic civilians. Usually these reprisals were little more than drunken soldiers or policemen venting their spleen against property, but as the conflict progressed the murder of Sinn Féin/IRA supporters became more common. There is no evidence that the chain of command sanctioned reprisals, even if some officers privately condoned them, but by mid-1920 RIC reports constantly warned that discipline had declined to the point that reprisals were almost inevitable given the frustrations of trying to deal with an elusive enemy who increasingly attacked off-duty soldiers and policemen.

The day after the 'sack of Fermoy', RIC IG Byrne complained to the Irish Under-Secretary about the withdrawal of Army support and ordered his men to abandon the more isolated rural police stations. In all the RIC abandoned 434 of its 1,299 barracks. Most of them were left not because they were indefensible, but because the men who lived in them were too isolated to protect.

By the summer the IRA had successfully attacked and destroyed more than 351 vacated police barracks along with 15 occupied ones. On 14 February 1920 the IRA under Ernie O'Malley and Éoin O'Duffy managed to capture the RIC barracks at Ballytrain, Co. Monaghan. Ballytrain boosted IRA morale, even though no policemen were killed, as it was the first successful attack on a manned RIC barracks. Usually the RIC managed to fend off such attacks with relative ease, despite the fact that these buildings were not built for defence.

When the North Kerry IRA led by Humphrey Murphy failed to take the RIC barracks in Brosna on 5 June 1920, Sgt Coughlin and his 12 constables jeered at the fleeing Volunteers, calling them 'rainbow chasers'. To add insult to injury a policeman had provided a soundtrack to the bloodless firefight on a melodeon.

On 17 June the occupants of the RIC barracks in Listowel, Co. Kerry, were told that they were being reassigned to rural stations to assist the Army. Despite the best efforts of County Inspector Poer O'Shea, 14 of them refused to obey this instruction.

On 19 June the RIC Divisional Commissioner for Munster, Lt Col Gerard Smyth, and the then RIC IG, Maj Gen Sir Hugh Tudor attempted to defuse the situation. What happened next is remembered as the Listowel Mutiny, and it has passed into Nationalist legend.

The Listowel Mutiny

The only version of events to survive is that of RIC Constable Jeremiah Mee, the leader of the mutiny. His account was published in the underground Sinn Féin newspaper *Irish Bulletin*, which claimed that Smyth told them to shoot IRA suspects on sight.

Mee was so outraged that he said to Smyth, 'By your accent I take it you are an Englishman. You forget you are addressing Irishmen.' He then apparently took off his cap, belt and bayonet, and handed them to Smyth, saying, 'These too are English. Take them as a present from me, and to hell with you, you murderer.'

Ironically, Smyth was from Bainbridge, Co. Down and like many Irishman of his class spoke with an Anglo-Irish accent. He certainly advocated greater cooperation between the Army and the police, and was concerned with creating better defences for RIC stations.

It is also true that in Order No. 5, issued on 17 June 1920, he directed policemen to shoot armed IRA men who did not surrender 'when ordered to do so', in other words when challenged, not as Mee claimed 'on sight'. In paragraph four of that order he also specifically forbade reprisals as 'they bring discredit on the police … I will deal most severely with any officer or man concerned in them.' These were hardly the instructions of a man advocating murder.

Whether it was true or not, Mee's testimony was a death sentence for the one-armed Smyth, who was killed a month later, on 17 July, by six IRA men in the smoking room of the Cork Country Club. The mutiny may have been as high-minded and nationalistic as Mee implied, but it is also possible that neither he nor his compatriots fancied the risky business of rural policing and preferred dismissal. It is a little suspicious that the only version of events appeared in a Republican paper; however, Mee may have needed to establish his Republican credentials in order to avoid the all too common fate of ex-policemen – the assassin's bullet.

A British Army foot patrol sweeps an Irish street for IRA suspects in 1920. Few soldiers took the Irish Troubles seriously or enjoyed their posting there. (National Library of Ireland)

Direct assaults on police barracks were a new phenomenon and despite the belief that the RIC was some kind of paramilitary gendarmerie it had little or no experience of defending a building. In an attempt to 'buy in' this experience, on 8 May 1920 the RIC began recruiting ex-Army officers known as 'Defence of Barracks Sergeants', who would be paid £7 per week. They were not supposed to interfere with daily policing and had no authority over the constables they worked with unless the station was under attack – in other words, their role was purely military. In all, 33 men were recruited and RIC stations became better defended, with steel shutters over the windows and barbed wire around the grounds. It may have made the barracks safer but it also made them cramped and claustrophobic places to be.

The IRA's response was to increase its attacks on off-duty policemen, and according to police records just over half of the policemen killed were shot while at home, walking out with girlfriends, drinking in the pub or, as in the cases of RIC Sgts Gibbons and Gilmartin, while recovering from illness in hospital.

A circular issued by the RIC Acting Deputy IG, T. J. Smith, on 4 February 1920 warned of the dangers of moving about while off duty, especially at night, and advised that those living at home be escorted by armed men. Married policemen and their families were especially at risk. Not only were they being boycotted, but they were incredibly vulnerable when off duty at home. Many were faced with the stark choice of moving their families to safer areas and living in barracks, or continually placing both themselves and their families at risk by trying to live normal family lives. It was a difficult decision to make but, despite the dangers, the casualty rolls show that even at the height of the violence many policemen and army officers chose to live with their families or in rented accommodation rather than stay in barracks.

On 25 May 1921 the IRA carried out an operation against the Dublin Customs House, the HQ of the Local Government Board, on the insistence of de Valera. More than 100 men from the Dublin-based Active Service Unit (ASU) and Dublin Brigade seized the building and torched the archives. The ensuing fire destroyed thousands of irreplaceable documents, but Crown forces managed to surround the building and killed five Volunteers and captured a further 70. Arguably the raid had been a spectacular failure and severely damaged the Dublin IRA.

War in the shadows

Despite these attacks, the real war was fought in Dublin's shadows between the British intelligence services – Special Branch, RIC Crimes Branch Special, and G Division DMP – and the IRA.

G Division traditionally played a key role in policing Republicanism, running an extensive network of informers, despite in 1919 having only 18 detectives. Collins knew that defeating them was crucial if the IRA were to win, commenting that 'even when the new spy stepped into the shoes of an old one, he could not step into the old one's knowledge'.

Fortunately for Collins there were some G-Men who were willing to collaborate with the rebels, and on 7 April 1919 G-Man Eamonn Broy smuggled Collins into the Division's central archive in Brunswick Street. As a result Collins knew everything that the G-Men knew about the IRA. At first Collins tried to warn the G-Men off intelligence work but failed, so he decided to have them killed. In all the IRA killed six G-Men before the Truce in 1921, including its head, DMP Assistant Commissioner (AC) William Redmond.

Collins' instrument of choice for special operations, 'The Squad', was officially formed in September 1919 and it was answerable only to him. However, The Squad's first 'job' had already been the killing of Detective Sergeant (DS) Pat Smyth in Dublin on 30 July 1919, making him the first G-Man to die at the hands of Collins' men. The Castle was oblivious to the fact that at least four of its detectives were active IRA men and never worked out how Collins stayed one step ahead of them. Not only had Collins compromised the postal system, he also recruited at least one of the cipher clerks in the Castle, while RIC Sgt Gerry Maher supplied him with police codes.

Collins ran his network of agents from a string of Dublin safe houses and cycled openly around the city, confident that no one would sign their own death warrant by informing on him. But that does not mean that the British did not get close to Collins on occasion. One agent, an ex-soldier from Newcastle West, Co. Limerick by the name of John Byrnes (aka Jameson) met Collins several times. Some claim that Byrnes was supposed to assassinate Collins. However, the fact that he seemed to operate without any sort of back-up makes that unlikely. Whatever his actual mission was, his cover was blown before he could complete it and Paddy Daly executed him in Lovers Lane, Ballymun on 2 April 1920. According to Daly, Byrnes' last words were, 'God Bless the King. I would love to die for him.'

In August 1920, the Government passed the Restoration of Order in Ireland Act (ROIA), giving the police and Army draconian powers to crush the IRA. The Act certainly made life for Collins and his cohorts difficult, but despite the pressure he maintained his intelligence network.

Collins' greatest coup came on 21 November 1920, 12 days after the British Prime Minister Lloyd George had claimed to 'have murder by the throat' when he badly damaged British intelligence operations in Dublin by killing 11 members of a crack

Collins' hit team. These five members of 'The Squad' took their orders directly from Michael Collins. Left to right: Michael McDonnell, Tom Keogh, Vincent Byrne, Paddy Daly and James Slettery. (Gerry White and Brendan O'Shea)

undercover team known retrospectively in Republican circles as the 'Cairo Gang'. For the loss of one of Collins' men – Frank Teeling – the IRA had temporarily blinded the British intelligence operations in the capital.

Bloody Sunday

Later that day the Adjutant of F Company ADRIC, Maj Mills, led a mixed body of Auxiliaries and RIC to the Gaelic football ground, Croke Park, in north Dublin to search for IRA sympathizers who might be hiding in the crowd. Tension was high and tempers fragile, and within minutes of the RIC's arrival 12 civilians – including a woman, a child and one of the footballers – were shot dead.

The Auxiliaries especially were in an ugly mood and shot two of Collins' most valued Dublin IRA – Richard McKee and Peadar Clancy – along with an unconnected Gaelic-Leaguer called Conor Clune, in the guardroom of Dublin Castle 'whilst trying to escape'. By the next day the events of 21 November had already been dubbed 'Bloody Sunday'.

The Dáil was determined to substitute British justice with its own, and in June 1919 it established its own system of courts and Republican police. To promote this system it was vital to undermine the Castle's, and so magistrates and judges joined the police as IRA targets.

A wounded British cadet (foreground) and two of the three Irish Republicans killed in the 'Bloody Sunday' street battle, 21 November 1920, lie in the road as the other cadets take the remaining Republicans prisoner.
(© The Granger Collection/ TopFoto)

Although the IRA did establish a prison system of sorts, minor crimes were punished with beatings or exile. Many were tried *in absentia* and their bodies found dumped and labelled 'Spies beware – shot by the IRA', or words to that effect. Others simply disappeared without trace. Unlike the British system, there was no appeal system and few of those arraigned were ever acquitted.

Because the British did not view the IRA as soldiers, they were put on trial as criminals when they were captured. Perhaps the most famous and controversial IRA man to be executed was an 18-year-old medical student by the name of Kevin Barry in November 1920. Barry may have been the first rebel to hang since the end of the war but he was not the first Irishman. That honour went to RIC Constable 75719 William Mitchell, a fellow Irishman, who was executed for murdering a shopkeeper. Barry's death made him both a Republican hero and the subject of a stirring rebel ballad. Despite what the ballad says, Barry was not hanged for being Irish but for taking part in the cold-blooded killing of three unarmed soldiers collecting their unit's daily bread ration.

The rebel propaganda machine made much of Kevin Barry's tender age; however, the three dead soldiers – Pte Marshall (20), Pte Thomas Humphries (19) and Pte Harold Washington (15) – were not exactly elderly. Although there was no evidence that Barry actually shot any of them, he was captured at the scene of the killings with a loaded revolver, which would have convicted him in British, American and even post-independence Irish courts as an accessory if nothing else. On the grounds that the British had executed Constable Mitchell they had little alternative but to condemn him also to hang.

A mixture of British complacency and incompetence ensured that the IRA threat was completely underestimated in 1919. By 1920 the security forces had become quite hawkish towards the Republicans, while the civil authorities in the Castle were prepared to be conciliatory. Both groups felt that dithering politicians in Whitehall were undermining their efforts.

By 1921 the IRA campaign was beginning to put pressure on the RIC and in 1921 3 per cent of its men left the force. While Nationalists tend to argue that these losses were as a result of the boycott and IRA activity, a significant number of them were

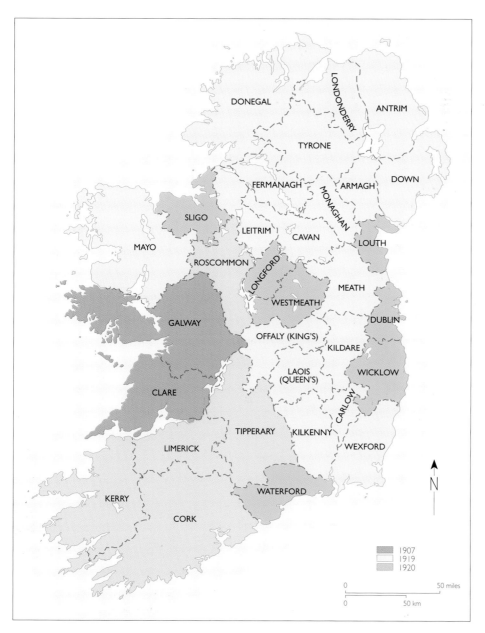

Between 1907 and 1920 several counties were placed under emergency measures to deal with political unrest. At no point was all of Ireland ever placed under martial law.

retirees. (The London Metropolitan Police lost 3.1 per cent of its strength in the same year without having to deal with the same problems.) Although much has been made of these statistics, over 63 per cent of RIC serving in 1919 were still on-strength when the force was disbanded in May 1922. In reality the highest turnover of personnel was not from the ranks of the Regular RIC but from among the Temporary Constables and Auxiliaries, who had few emotional ties to Ireland.

In March 1920 the RIC began recruiting the men remembered as the Black and Tans to bolster the ranks of the police. It is true that there were tensions between the 'Tans' and the Regular RIC, in part because of their lack of proper training, but they were not the monsters of legend. According to one IRA veteran there was even an unofficial ceasefire in Co. Mayo where they sometimes drank together until Collins sent some men to restart the war in the county.

It would seem that the Tans' real crime was that most were ex-soldiers 'from over the water' who brought the mentality of the trench-raid to policing. Although the majority of Tans came from Britain, one-fifth were Irish-born and a significant number were the children of Irish émigrés. Incidentally, the children of émigrés who returned to fight for the Republicans have never been similarly condemned as foreign

A rare photograph of an RIC–Army patrol in contact with an IRA flying column in Co. Clare. Motorised patrols and armour support were vital elements of the British counter-insurgency strategy. (Imperial War Museum, IWM 107751)

mercenaries. While many, like Matthew Gallagher from Glasgow, joined to escape unemployment, others like the budding music-hall comedian Stanley Holloway – an ex-Connaught Ranger – did so because they believed in what they were doing.

In addition the 2,200 men of the Auxiliary Division brought another violent edge to the conflict. Again, some of its most effective members, like Capt Hervey de Montmorency, were themselves Irish. The Auxiliaries, or Auxies, were meant to take the fight to the IRA, and operated in the worst trouble spots.

Although they disliked ex-soldiers the IRA needed their expertise. Some, like Tom Barry – the son of a policeman and ex-Royal Artillery Sergeant – helped train and then led the West Cork Brigade Flying Column. Barry was a ruthless guerrilla leader who prosecuted a merciless war against the Essex Regiment and the RIC.

On 28 November 1920 the IRA – in retribution for the deaths of three Volunteers – executed a successful ambush against two truckloads of Auxiliaries from C Company based in Macroom Castle, leaving 16 of them dead and one so badly injured that he was paraplegic for the rest of his life. One man, Cadet Guthrie, escaped but was later captured and shot by the IRA, who hid his body in a bog. As a result C Company was moved to Dublin and later disbanded.

The Kilmichael ambush, 28 November 1920

The ambush that took place on the afternoon of Sunday 28 November 1920 on a quiet country road near Kilmichael, Co. Cork is perhaps one of the best-known and most controversial incidents of the Irish War of Independence. It is impossible to know exactly what actually happened, as several contradictory accounts survive. Even the man who commanded the IRA at Kilmichael, Tom Barry, produced different accounts of the event in his after-action report and in his memoirs.

Compared to the losses suffered by Britain in World War I, or even Iraq in the 1920s, the loss at Kilmichael of some 17 men was militarily trivial. What was deeply significant, however, was that the IRA's No. 3 (West) Cork Brigade managed to defeat an Auxiliary patrol in a conventional operation, thus undermining the Auxiliaries' reputation as 'super fighters'. It was a classically simple and ruthlessly executed ambush employing cut-offs and killing groups to eliminate the police patrol.

Although the Auxiliaries who died at Kilmichael were all war veterans and many had been decorated for bravery, they were killed because they had become complacent, letting down their guard and failing to vary their patrol routes.

Barry claimed that he knew on the previous Monday that the policemen would use the Kilmichael road and that it was only a matter of time before he was able to spring his trap. The trap was a lethal one and it is likely that Barry intended to eliminate the

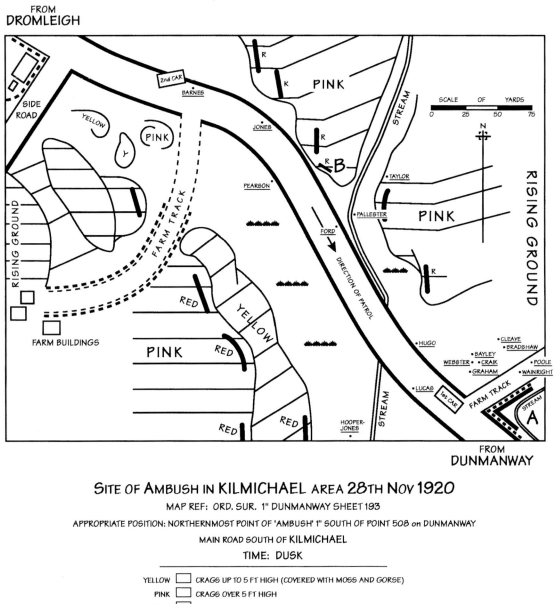

FROM
DROMLEIGH

SIDE
ROAD

2nd CAR
BARNES

YELLOW

PINK

Y

PINK

RISING GROUND

FARM TRACK

FARM BUILDINGS

RED

YELLOW

PINK

RED

RED

RED

RED

HOOPER-
JONES

R

R

PINK

JONES

R

PEARSON

FORD

DIRECTION OF PATROL

R

B

TAYLOR

PALLESTER

PINK

RISING GROUND

N

SCALE   OF   YARDS
0   25   50   75

R

HUGO

CLEAVE
BRADSHAW
BAYLEY
WEBSTER CRAIK
GRAHAM
POOLE
WAINRIGHT

LUCAS

1st CAR

FARM TRACK

STREAM

A

STREAM

STREAM

FROM
DUNMANWAY

SITE OF AMBUSH IN KILMICHAEL AREA 28TH NOV 1920

MAP REF: ORD. SUR. 1" DUNMANWAY SHEET 193

APPROPRIATE POSITION: NORTHERNMOST POINT OF 'AMBUSH' 1" SOUTH OF POINT 508 on DUNMANWAY

MAIN ROAD SOUTH OF **KILMICHAEL**

TIME: DUSK

YELLOW ☐ CRAGS UP TO 5 FT HIGH (COVERED WITH MOSS AND GORSE)

PINK ☐ CRAGS OVER 5 FT HIGH

BLUE ∿∿∿ BOG

RED ▬ POSITIONS OF REBEL TROOPS

THESE POSITIONS WERE EXCEPT **A** AND **B** ENTIRELY
NATURAL AND WOULD IN EACH CASE ACCOMMODATE 4 TO 6
REBELS LYING IN WHICH POSITION THEY WOULD BE
VERY WELL CONCEALED. SMALL QUANTITIES OF CUT GORSE
WERE FOUND IN SOME POSITIONS. PRESUMABLY THE REBELS
HAD USED IT TO COVER THEIR HEADS.

A A STONEWALL HEIGHTENED 1" 6" AND LOOPHOLED

B ENTIRELY ARTIFICIAL A SMALL STONE WALL LOOPHOLED
FOR 2 RIFLES (MACHINE) OR LIGHT MACHINE GUN

•— POSITIONS OF CARS AND BODIES AS FOUND BY SEARCH
PARTY ON MORNING OF 29TH NOV 1920

E FLEMING LIEUT.
D.I.B.

entire patrol; after all, as an ex-soldier he was well aware that well-executed ambushes rarely leave survivors.

The patrol's elimination would undoubtedly send a message to both his men and to the Auxiliaries. Barry was the son of a policeman and an ex-soldier so he needed to prove his Republican credentials to his comrades-in-arms. He also had to break the psychological hold that the Auxiliaries had over many rebels, by showing that they could be defeated. Nothing could more graphically serve that purpose than annihilating an ADRIC patrol. The British later claimed that some of the policemen had been shot after they had surrendered, and that others had been mutilated with axes after they had been shot. There is, however, no evidence to support these claims.

In his memoir *Guerilla Days in Ireland*, Barry claimed that some of the Auxiliaries had pretended to surrender in order to lure his men into the open and then fired on them, killing Volunteers Michael McCarthy, Jim Sullivan and Pat Deasy, and wounding Jack Hennesy, causing his men to ignore further pleas for mercy.

What is perplexing is that Barry did not mention the false surrender in his report, nor do some of the other survivors of the attack. Another contradiction in *Guerilla Days* is Barry's claim that Cadet Cecil Guthrie was wounded and crawled off into a bog where he drowned. In reality he did escape the killing ground only to be captured and shot two days later by the IRA. It is hard to believe that one of the most active and effective IRA leaders in West Cork would have been unaware of Guthrie's fate and unclear why he might have felt compelled to lie about it.

Although the truth will never be known as to what exactly happened at Kilmichael, there is a rough consensus on the course of events.

Barry's scouts spotted the patrol, consisting of two lorries carrying men of No. 2 Section, C Company, ADRIC, at about 4.05 p.m. coming from the direction of Macroom. Shortly afterwards the two vehicles entered the killing zone and a man dressed in full Volunteer Officer's uniform, possibly Barry, stepped into the road and flagged them down. This ruse was

Tom Barry, commander of the 3rd West Cork Brigade Flying Column learned his soldiering as a sergeant in the British Army in Iraq and led the ambush at Kilmichael. He was one of the IRA's most successful column commanders and fought against the *Saorstát* in the Civil War. (Dara McGrath/Cork Public Museum)

intended to force the lorries to brake so that they could be engaged with hand grenades. It is possible that the Auxiliaries mistook the man in the road for a British officer; regardless, the ruse worked and the lead vehicle slowed down.

The blast killed the driver and the passenger in the cab, and a hail of gunfire quickly dealt with the remainder in the back. Lt E. Fleming's map clearly shows where each of the policemen died, indicating that, unlike those in the lead vehicle, the men in the second lorry had the chance to put up much more of a fight.

Cadet Guthrie, driving the second vehicle, attempted to manoeuvre out of danger but was prevented from doing so by one of the cut-off groups. A brisk firefight developed, and it was during this engagement that the false surrender is said to have taken place. The fight ended at close quarters and it is likely that claims of post-mortem mutilation were in reality the bayonet and bullet wounds caused during hand-to-hand combat. In many respects Kilmichael was a typical ambush fought at short range, concluded in minutes and leaving no survivors.

In the lull that followed the storm, many of the IRA were visibly shaken by what they had just done. Unlike Barry, most of them had never been in combat nor seen the detritus of battle before. In a move seen as callous by some, Barry berated his men for the loss of four men and then drilled them for five minutes among the British dead. According to Barry he did this to snap them out of their torpor by making them do something as familiar as drill. He was not alone in believing that routine mundane activity can help men cope with the trauma of combat. After removing the Auxiliaries' weapons and documents, Barry formed his men up and marched them away. By 11 p.m. that night they were 11 miles away and they spent the night in a cottage at Granure.

Kilmichael was heralded as a great victory because it was the single greatest loss of life caused in one incident. Barry's attack was extremely aggressive and his dispositions such that if his initial onslaught had failed he would have had great difficulty in extracting his men.

In short, he had created a situation where his men had no choice but to kill or be killed. Although the action was well executed and made Barry a rebel hero, it did little to change the course of the conflict and it would take another year of bloodshed before a negotiated settlement brought Irish independence.

Martial law and reprisals

Although it would be an exaggeration to claim that the IRA did not enjoy support right across Ireland its real heartlands were in parts of Dublin, Munster and sections of Connacht. Consequently, the war passed much of Ireland by and only eight of Ireland's 32 counties were ever placed under martial law.

There was almost no IRA activity in Queen's County and Leitrim, which would indicate that policing and everyday life changed little throughout the Troubles. Counties Meath, Kildare, Wexford and Wicklow were also relatively unaffected. In essence the struggle for Ireland focused around the Munster counties of Cork, Limerick, Kerry and Tipperary, where the bulk of Army, police, IRA and civilian casualties were suffered.

In disturbed areas the Army operated in conjunction with the RIC, and under ROIA IRA men could be tried by military courts rather than by civilian ones. Not only did this prevent juries being intimidated but it was also easier to convict IRA suspects. ROIA also permitted Crown forces to carry out reprisals against property, and many felt that, in the words of one report of 1920 in the *Morning Post* 'Whatever we may think of these reprisals in theory, in practice they are found to be the most effective way of causing murders to cease.' But if anything they were counter-productive.

However, other papers, such as the *Daily Mail*, agreed. When the Army demolished several houses in Midleton, Co. Cork on 1 January 1921 it wrote that 'this is of course martial law. It is legal and disciplined. It is, we must believe, necessary. But it is horrible.' The reprisal was in response to an IRA ambush by members of the 4th Battalion, 1st Cork Brigade, when it killed three policemen and wounded

A British tank demolishes a building at Dillon's Cross, Co Cork as part of a reprisal in January 1921. (Imperial War Museum, L107756)

five others on Midleton High Street on 29 December 1920. Not all the press was convinced about reprisals, however, and the *Galway Express* commented that 'when they throw petrol on a Sinn Feiner's house, they are merely pouring paraffin on the flames of Irish nationality'.

The Times believed that 'the name of England is being sullied throughout the Empire … however much they may seek to disclaim responsibility'. This paper was deeply uncomfortable with British soldiers and police using 'methods inexcusable even under the loose code of revolutionaries'.

While official reprisals were an attempt to control the anger and frustration of the thousands of policemen and soldiers who endured attacks by an elusive enemy, the Government's habit of releasing convicted gunmen in its frequent amnesties created a frustrating 'revolving door' and a sense of betrayal among many soldiers and policemen.

Increasingly anti-Sinn Féin societies began to appear, sending masked men – in all probability policemen and soldiers rather than Irish Loyalists – to liquidate Republican sympathizers in revenge for IRA killings. The Castle never condoned these attacks and on 28 September 1920 the RIC Deputy IG C. A. Walsh issued a warning that anyone found taking the law into their own hands would be punished. In all, 766 policemen were dismissed for disciplinary offences and two, including the erstwhile Constable Mitchell, were executed for murder.

When Cadet Chapman was killed at Dillon's Cross, Co. Cork on 11 December 1920 an angry mob of policemen burned down Cork City Hall and most of St Patrick's

A joint British Army–RIC motorised patrol hunting for the IRA near Limerick. (National Library of Ireland)

Street, killing two suspected IRA men and wounding five civilians. Many Auxiliaries tactfully took to wearing half-burned corks in their caps to 'celebrate' this act of retribution. Threats, however, were not enough for the men whose lives were now becoming dominated by the spectre of violence.

As the number of murders by 'Loyalists' increased, the IRA began to hit out at anyone they suspected of complicity. Irish Protestants increasingly became the targets of IRA murder and intimidation, as they were seen by many not as Irishmen of a different faith, but as English settlers who were acting as a fifth column for the Crown.

Much to the Castle's disappointment Ireland's Protestants played little part in the South's Troubles, while the breakdown of policing in parts of Ireland became an excuse for sectarian violence. Ultimately many Protestants died not because of their Unionism but because of the resentment of poorer Catholic neighbours.

Loyalist and Republican gunmen alike fuelled the bloody cycle of violence. When the IRA killed Constable Joseph Murtagh on 19 March 1920, masked men burst into Tomas MacCurtain's home at about 1.00 a.m. on the following day and shot him dead. MacCurtain was the local IRA commander and also the Lord Mayor of Cork. The lack of witnesses, despite the proximity of a police station, reinforced the widely held belief that the RIC had carried out the killing. In revenge, the IRA gunned down District Inspector Oswald Swanzy on 22 August 1920 as he left Christ Church Cathedral, Lisburn, in the mistaken belief that Swanzy had shot MacCurtain.

The IRA, however, lacked support in Ulster, and Swanzy's murder sparked off rioting in Lisburn and Belfast that left 22 people dead and several houses burned out. The rioting forced the authorities to enrol Special Constables on 24 August. It was the first use of Special Constables in the Troubles, and presaged the creation of the Ulster Special Constabulary (USC) or 'Specials' on 1 November 1920.

Arch-Unionist and CIGS Sir Henry Wilson disliked the fact that most Specials were UVF members but in a similar vein to the adoption of 'official' reprisals, their use was probably the only chance that the Government had of controlling the forces that had been unleashed by the Troubles.

IRA operations in mainland Britain

It was perhaps inevitable that Ireland's troubles spilled over into Britain, and IRA activists sought to bring the 'war' home to the British public. The IRA's British command may have numbered more than 1,000 men, but only a couple of hundred at most were ever active.

During 1920–21 a total of six people were killed and 19 wounded in bombings and shootings in Britain. Several thousand Irish men and women were detained but only about 600 were formally arrested and charged. Collins, who joined the IRB in London, viewed his British forces as 'the auxiliaries of our attacking forces' and in reality the IRA outside of London and Liverpool was relatively inactive, although the Manchester battalion was responsible for 16 per cent of IRA activity in England.

In December 1920, Collins sent Paddy Daly (not The Squad's Paddy Daly) to London to head up the IRA campaign. Until Daly's arrival British IRA units had little real idea of Collins' strategy and as a result missed several opportunities while awaiting orders.

Between February and July 1921 revenge attacks on farms and factories for British reprisals against creameries and farms in Ireland intensified. Most attacks were arson rather than bombings, and despite the abundance of firearms they rarely seemed adequately prepared to confront the police. In Liverpool and Tyneside, IRA men cut telephone and telegraph lines and there were several skirmishes with the police on Merseyside. As in Ireland, the IRA was a police matter and even though the Army played a supporting role, Special Branch and MI5 adopted a proactive policy based on counter-espionage.

The British were convinced that the IRA was a Bolshevik-inspired conspiracy, and this gave the Government the excuse to extend DORA into a permanent Emergency Powers Act (1920), giving it extensive powers of arrest and detention. On 4 May 1921 two policemen were killed during an attempted rescue of the commander of the Sligo Brigade from a prison van in Glasgow. Ten days later the IRA attacked 15 houses belonging to Auxiliaries or their relatives, burning several out and killing one person.

VICTIMS OF IRA VIOLENCE IN MAINLAND BRITAIN, 1920–1922

K = killed W = wounded	Police		IRA		Civilians		Total	
	K	W	K	W	K	W	K	W
1920–July 1921	1	7	2	6	3	6	6	19
July 1921–1922	–	2	3	1	1	2	4	5
Total	1	9	5	7	4	8	10	24

Compared to the bigger IRA organizations in Carlow, Westmeath and Waterford, the relatively small British IRA with 400–500 activists was much more aggressive. It burned out 149 buildings and caused significant disruption to the Royal Mail, railways, roads and communication system, costing the British taxpayer more than £1.5m. The cost to the IRA was five dead, seven wounded and hundreds arrested.

The IRA had a vague idea that attacks in Britain would focus attention on the Irish Troubles and undermine British public support, thus putting pressure on the Government.

Although Ireland did feature regularly in the news and took up a significant amount of police effort, the campaign played second fiddle to Britain's other post-war problems, to the extent that the Cabinet rarely received reports on Ireland.

Portrait of a Soldier: David Neligan

It is difficult to know accurately what the experience was like for the ordinary foot soldiers that fought the Anglo-Irish War. However, some survivors did write down their experiences, and one of the most unusual and credible sets of memoirs is probably that of David Neligan.

Neligan's experience of the violence between 1919 and 1923 was unique, as during this period he served as a Volunteer, G-Man, IRA intelligence officer, British Secret Service agent, National Army intelligence officer and founder of the *Garda Siochána* Detective Branch. His book, *The Spy in the Castle*, is highly readable and it is difficult not to like Neligan. Although his narrative appears to be frank and starkly honest in places, it is worth remembering that it is a subjective account of his time as a G-Man and IRA informer.

Considering that he knew or worked with many of the men killed in his story, Neligan usually dismisses their deaths in the surprisingly bland factual statement 'he was shot by the IRA', without any emotional exposition. Equally Neligan was undoubtedly a ruthless man whose work for Collins led directly to the deaths of several men, and whose conduct of intelligence operations in Kerry during the Civil War earned him the hatred of the anti-Treaty IRA.

Born in Templeglantine, Co. Limerick in 1899 he was the youngest of eight children. He grew up in a happy, middle-class Catholic household and his book paints a picture of a rural Ireland more interested in labour shortages and foot and mouth than the climactic battles on the Western Front. Interestingly, Neligan never indicates that he had any intention of enlisting in the Army to fight, and World War I hardly features in his account at all.

Regardless of how honest or otherwise Neligan's revelations are, they give some interesting insights into the life of both ordinary policemen and IRA activists at the time and although two of Neligan's uncles and several of his father's friends were policemen he joined the IVF when he was 15, some time before the Redmond–MacNeill split.

He never knew which side of the schism his unit was on, which was in his words 'following the usual Irish pattern'. His unit was poorly equipped and 'had no arms except wooden guns', which seems to have been typical

A rare photograph of Col David Neligan, Collins' 'Spy in the Castle' taken while he was serving in the National Army during the Civil War. (Jim Herlihy)

of many Volunteer units. Even though he was a Volunteer, Neligan decided to join the police in 1918 and even got a glowing reference from his parish priest.

In 1915 the Government had passed the Emergency Provisions (Police) Act, halting police recruiting in order to keep the Army up to strength. Interestingly neither this act nor his Volunteer membership prevented Neligan from joining the DMP in 1918. His account also indicates that he could have just as easily joined the RIC but being stuck at some 'strategically placed crossroads' with three or four other 'peelers' just did not appeal to him, despite the pay being better than the DMP.

Neligan tells us that promotion 'in both forces was as a result of examinations and open to Irish Roman Catholics' but that 'the top brass was reserved for English or Irish Protestants and Freemasons'. There were some Catholic senior officers, like DMP Assistant Commissioner Fergus Quinn, but they were rare. In Neligan's estimation 'religious and racial discrimination were rife' – as indeed they were in the rest of the UK at the time. Overall he paints a sympathetic picture of the police, and despite Sinn Féin's calls for a boycott of the police Neligan tells us that in 1918 the public still supported the police force, and it was seen as a good job with good prospects.

Neligan felt that the rebels missed a trick by killing policemen rather than trying to win them over. Resignation records show that most of those who resigned were single men with little service. Married men needed to look after their families and – as the IRA invariably prevented them from getting jobs or, worse still, killed them when they resigned – they had few options other than to stick it out in the police or face starvation.

Neligan paints an affectionate picture of the DMP as full of decent men doing a thankless task for very little money. They knew their 'patch' intimately and stuck together to the extent that 'the police would lie like devils inside and outside court to save a comrade'. Such was the close-knit world that Neligan entered in 1918 and ultimately betrayed.

He joined the DMP mostly because, like so many country boys, the lure of the city as 'an unknown entity' was too much for him to resist. When he got to Dublin he discovered that much of it was squalid and overcrowded and in his estimation the DMP Depot in Kevin Street was little better.

Neligan's training was fairly uneventful, but his book gives a fascinating insight into life in the DMP and some of its characters, such as the elderly but dapper Constable Denis 'Count' O'Connor who was reputably the best-dressed copper in Dublin. He also explained how the DMP was divided into six uniformed divisions, A to F, and the infamous G Division.

G Division was a cross between the CID and Special Branch, and dealt with civil as well as criminal investigations. It relied on 18 detectives to keep tabs on Dublin's political and criminal underworld. Its members, who were known as G-Men long before the name was popularized in American gangster films, operated in plain clothes and, unlike the rest of the DMP, were armed. They carried notoriously unreliable .38cal automatics, and Neligan's went off in his pocket on one occasion. One thing that stands out in Neligan's account is that all of the G-Men were very snappy dressers.

After a brief period working out of College Street Police Station and as a clerk in the G Division archives in Brunswick (now Pearse) Street, Neligan volunteered to become a G-Man at the end of 1919 because he was 'heartily tired of uniform and beat duties'. Neligan tells us that before the Troubles G Division was difficult to get into, but casualties had made it unpopular.

While in uniform Neligan had been among the party who had found the body of DMP DS Daniel Hoey after Collins' Squad had shot him outside the Central Police Station in Brunswick Street on 13 September 1919. Neligan also knew another victim of the Squad, DMP DS John Barton, killed by Seán Tracey on 29 November 1919. He probably even knew DMP DS Patrick Smyth who was killed on 30 July 1919. Neligan is very matter-of-fact about these killings but there is no evidence to suggest that he was behind the deaths.

The men who were probably guilty of these murders were three other G-Men: DS Eamonn 'Ned' Broy, DC James McNamara and DC Kavanagh, who had worked for Collins since at least 1917. In fact, Broy even smuggled Collins into the G Division archives in Brunswick Street where he was able to assess just how much the Castle knew about his organization. Between them these men were responsible not only for the deaths of a number of British intelligence agents but also for damaging the Castle's efforts to contain the IRA.

Despite being a G-Man, Neligan appears to have remained acquainted with several Sinn Féin activists, including de Valera's secretary, Paddy Sheehan. How and why Neligan knew Sheehan is never explained, but he does mention that he recognized DS Hoey from a Sinn Féin meeting without explaining why he was there himself.

Neligan's brother Maurice was a trade union activist, and along with Sheehan they convinced Neligan to resign, which he did on 11 May 1920. Before he did so, he offered his services to the rebels but Sheehan declined to accept. When Collins heard of this he was furious that the opportunity to turn another G-Man had been squandered and not long after his resignation Neligan was contacted by the IRA and eventually met Collins in Dublin.

It was the beginning of an association that would come to an end only when the IRA shot Collins in 1922. On Collins' instructions Neligan made his way back to the Castle and told his old boss, DCI Bruton, that the IRA had threatened to kill him. Neligan always felt that Bruton did not really believe him, but he was reassigned to G Division nonetheless.

Neligan proved to be a valuable asset and was soon passing Collins high-grade intelligence. It was Neligan who told Collins that an ex-RIC District Inspector and Resident Magistrate, Alan Bell, was investigating how the rebels were funding their operations. Neligan betrayed Bell's address, movements and security arrangements and within days he was dead.

By 1921, G Division had been rendered more or less ineffective against the IRA. Five G-Men, including AC William Redmond, had been murdered and at least four were IRA activists. Both the RIC Crimes Branch Special and the Secret Service knew that something was wrong with G Division and marginalized it.

According to Neligan the division's parlous state was simply a symptom of a 'demoralized state practically finished'. Despite his IRA activities no one suspected Neligan of 'working for the enemy', and much to Collins' delight he managed to join the Secret Service in May 1921.

Neligan was extremely complimentary about the Secret Service, whom he claimed 'sent some of their crack operators here. I must say they were brave men who carried their lives in their hands.' Despite obvious admiration and a degree of empathy for them he provided much of the information that led to the mass killing of British agents in Dublin on 21 November 1920, which is perhaps a comment in itself about their efficiency. When the Civil War broke out, Neligan became a colonel in military intelligence and earned a fearsome reputation in Co. Kerry, where he was allegedly involved in the torture and execution of several anti-Treaty IRA men in February 1922.

After the Civil War ended, Neligan returned to the DMP as a chief superintendent heading up its post-war G Division, and eventually headed the *Garda* Detective Branch. By the time he retired he was in receipt of a pension from the British Government for his time in the DMP and Secret Service, and from the Irish Government for his time in the *Garda*. When asked in later life if he would do any of it again his answer was an unequivocal no: '…revolution devours its own children'.

CIVILIAN LIFE DURING THE TROUBLES

Like the millions of other people in post-World War I Europe who found themselves citizens of new ethnic-based states, millions of Irish men and women ended this period as citizens of a state that had simply not existed when they were born.

The trauma of the war and the political violence that followed it inevitably had a considerable impact upon the lives of ordinary Irish people. World War I left tens of thousands of Irish women dependent upon Army allowances while their husbands were away fighting. In addition, the appalling casualties of Gallipoli, the Somme and four years of war left thousands of widows and orphans whose financial security was dependent on Britain, their losses virtually ignored by the Irish State.

Just as it would be a sweeping exaggeration to say that every Irishman was a Nationalist who aspired to an independent Irish Republic, so it would be a gross oversimplification to portray all people, in all parts of the country, as being affected by the Troubles.

In 1916 the Easter Rising had been played out almost exclusively in Dublin and, except in an emotional sense, had little effect upon the everyday lives of the Irish. In fact, the Rising had been deeply unpopular and many Irish people, including some who later took up arms in 1919, saw it as a betrayal while the country was at war.

Although the violence of 1919–23 was far more widespread than in 1916 it was still quite localized and the drama was played out predominantly in Munster and – to a lesser extent – in Dublin. There was virtually no meaningful IRA activity in Co. Leitrim in 1919, 1920 or 1922 and their only significant act in 1921 was the killing of 35-year-old RIC Constable Wilfred Jones while he was walking with his girlfriend near his barracks in Ballinamore on 15 April. Queen's County (now Co. Laois) was also quiet during 1919, 1920 and 1922. Similarly, the only major act of IRA violence was the killing of 26-year-old RIC Constable William Vanston from Belfast as he left his father's house in Maryborough (now Port Laois) on 2 February 1921.

Even among the IRA's veterans there was a feeling that the burden of the war had not been evenly distributed and in 1933 Éoin O'Duffy (who took over from Richard Mucahy as Chief of Staff of the IRA in May 1921) even quipped, albeit

A Lancia armoured car supports an RIC/USC cordon on the junction of May Street and Joy Street, Belfast after the murder of Special Constables Thomas Cunningham and William Chermside in 1922. (RUC GC Foundation)

RIC Constable 70979 Patrick Joseph Larkin, one of the thousands of Irishmen who joined the RIC after the end of the Great War. (Jim Herlihy)

inaccurately, that the Kerry IRA's entire contribution to the war had been shooting an unfortunate soldier on the day of the Truce.

Of course, the tempo of violence in the south-western counties was far higher, as was the instance of reprisals. Not only did more soldiers, policemen and IRA members become casualties in counties Cork, Limerick, Tipperary and Kerry, but the numbers of civilians caught in the crossfire was significantly higher as well. It is difficult to calculate exactly how many civilians were killed between 1919 and 1923, although estimates range from 300 up to around 1,000. The historian Peter Hart suggests that at least 198 civilians were killed and 189 wounded between 1919 and 1921 in Co. Cork alone.

At the centre of the struggle between the Castle and the rebel Dáil was the struggle for the hearts and minds of the Irish population, as each side vied to establish itself as the legitimate government of Ireland. The Castle had the distinct advantage of being the *de facto*, and arguably *de jure*, government in 1918, with a functioning legal system and an effective police service. To supplant this, the Dáil needed to dismantle the British system and replace it with its own. This was the logic behind the IRA attacks on policemen and police stations.

Although the rebels did attempt to create an alternative judicial system and a 'Republican' police force led by IRA GHQ staff officer Simon Donnelly, they also managed to create a climate of lawlessness in some areas that simply allowed rebels and Loyalists alike to commit arson, theft and murder with little chance of apprehension. The general breakdown of law and order was most marked in Munster and especially in Co. Cork. In the affected counties the civil population had a hard choice to make. If they refused to recognize the Crown's authority they were likely to fall victim to Government reprisals. The police and Army singled out Republican sympathizers and destroyed their homes and goods with impunity. Alternatively, if they refused to recognize the authority of the Dáil they were likely to receive a midnight visit from the IRA who would deal with them as traitors to the Republic.

Such treatment ranged from being tarred and feathered and subjected to public ridicule, to exile and even execution. It is impossible to estimate how many 'collaborators' the IRA killed, but the bodies of men and women were found dumped on country roads on most days.

Despite their paranoia about informers, evidence for Co. Cork suggests that of the 122 people shot as spies by the IRA between 1919 and 1923, only 38 actually passed information to the British. That means that 84 of those killed were entirely innocent of having done anything except attracting the suspicion of the IRA. Vagrants or 'tinkers' were also frequent victims, although few people missed them and many communities were glad to be rid of them. Statistically 27 per cent of those the IRA suspected of being informers were tramps. In reality they were only 14 per cent of the RIC's sources, yet they made up 67 per cent of the non-combatants murdered in Co. Cork. Protestants also fell victim to IRA violence. Twenty-five per cent of those suspected of passing information to the British were Protestants, but they made up 64 per cent of those killed for allegedly doing so.

In reality, the Protestant population, rather than being a Loyalist fifth column, proved to be a deep disappointment to the Castle. One vocal Cork Protestant Loyalist by the name of Tom Bradfield commented that he was 'not like the rest of them round here', indicating that most Munster Protestants were painfully aware of their vulnerability and were unwilling to put their heads above the parapet. The IRA killed Bradfield for his vocal Unionism. Some tried to weather the storm, while others simply moved to safer ground in Ulster or mainland Britain.

Between 15 April and 8 June 1920 Arthur Griffith managed to establish shadow Republican courts under Austin Stack and Volunteer police in 21 of Ireland's 32 counties. Their influence was non-existent in Ulster and strongest where the IRA had managed to supplant the Castle's authority. The *Irish Bulletin* reported that rebel police had arrested 84 people in the first two weeks of June 1920.

Of course, punishment was always an issue and investigative procedures were questionable at times. There is one recorded occasion when the RIC attempted to rescue men imprisoned by the IRA on an island off the west coast, but they refused to be rescued. Legend has it that their refusal was because they were loyal citizens of the Republic, although it is equally likely that they were afraid of what the IRA would do to them if they accepted help from the British.

Several county councils declared openly for the Republic and withheld funds that were intended for the Castle administration. This was a two-way street, and the Castle withheld Central Government funds intended for these areas. Ultimately this created the bizarre phenomenon of two alternative judicial and policing systems jockeying for position with each one attempting to undermine the power of the other, causing confusion, uncertainty and chaos.

Maj Arthur Percival, on the right of this picture, arrived in Co. Cork in 1920 as Intelligence Officer of 1st Bn The Essex Regiment. He was an energetic enemy of the IRA. Tom Barry wrote of him that he 'was easily the most viciously anti-Irish of serving British officers. He was tireless in his attempts to destroy the spirit of the people.' (Imperial War Museum, L71730)

Despite its obvious limitations, the Sinn Féin legal system did attempt to conduct its affairs in a recognizable and responsible fashion. As the British legal system broke down, people increasingly turned to the Republican courts for want of an alternative. For the civilians caught in the middle it must have been an awful situation. Unemployment in post-war Ireland was high, with ex-soldiers being among the worst affected. During the war the British had banned emigration in the hope that Ireland's young men would enlist, and after it was lifted Sinn Féin promptly banned it again, making any attempt to leave Ireland an offence punishable by the IRA.

Most traditional histories of the Troubles emphasize the transition of *de facto* authority from the Castle to the Dáil while ignoring the fact that in many places nothing much really changed. RIC Constable Patrick Larkin, a native of Oranmore, Co. Galway, accompanied by a group of Black and Tans, was once called out to deal with the unwarlike activity of cattle and horses wandering around on the roads outside Rathdrum, Co. Wicklow, in August 1920.

Normally a man may have thought himself extremely fortunate to be able to afford a motor car in the 1920s. During the Troubles, however, he was likely to have his vehicle commandeered by either the police or the IRA and if he was lucky he might see it again in one piece. More often than not such vehicles were never seen again.

The IRA dragged some men from their beds to dig trenches across the roads to disrupt the police's superior mobility. By day the same men could find themselves being compelled by the RIC to fill in the same trenches to re-open the roads, and so it went on. Ultimately, most ordinary people tried to get on with their lives despite the upheaval all around them.

This was, of course, made extremely difficult in some areas where the IRA and Crown forces were in competition for control. One activity that seems to have been utterly unaffected by the violence of 1916–23 was the 'sport of kings' – horse racing. Gen Macready had warned that if there was any trouble at race meetings or if any of his men were killed at them he would enforce a universal ban, ending the sport in Ireland.

Horse racing was extremely popular among both sides in the struggle and the IRA realized that any action on their part to precipitate a ban would have serious consequences as far as popular support was concerned. As a result, racecourses became almost neutral ground where both rebels and Loyalists rubbed shoulders, and they even offered some the opportunity to discover whether they were on an IRA death list or not.

By 1922 the majority of the population of Great Britain and Ireland were tired of the seemingly endless hostilities, and in June the British offered a solution. They suggested that Nationalists should be granted a degree of independence in 26 of Ireland's 32 counties and that six of the nine counties of Ulster should form a province that would remain Protestant and part of the United Kingdom.

The result of this June 1922 Southern Irish General Election, or Partition Election as it is sometimes known, was a resounding 78 per cent in favour of the Treaty and, by implication, partition. This does not mean that the majority of ordinary Irish people wanted partition, but rather that most were so sick of the violence that they preferred any sort of peace to continued war.

If partition did not come easily to Nationalist Ireland it would be wrong to see it as being welcomed by the Unionists either. The Unionist leader Sir Edward Carson was a Dubliner by birth and would have preferred to see all of Ireland remain within the UK. As it was the Unionists cut their losses and settled for what they could.

Ulster may have been the heartland of Unionism but not all its population was Protestant or Ulster-born. Because Belfast was the only industrial centre in an essentially agricultural country it drew Northern as well as Southern Catholics to it in much the same way as Glasgow and Liverpool. This helped swell the Catholic ghettos within the city, storing up potential problems for the future. Although Loyalist gunmen carried out sectarian killings in the North, not every Catholic who went to Belfast was a rebel at heart, and many moved there to gain both employment and sanctuary from the violence in the South.

The view from mainland Britain

The British public had some sympathy for Home Rule but very little for the IRA's campaign of violence. In fact, the Troubles 'over the water' probably reinforced anti-Irish prejudice in some quarters. However, much of the British press was uneasy with the methods employed by British police and soldiers to suppress the rebels. As early as 13 May 1918 the *Manchester Guardian* reported that the appointment of Lord French as Viceroy meant that 'the government is preparing for some very evil work in Ireland'.

Many in the British Government saw the Troubles in Ireland as an irritating sideshow in comparison to their other problems. The Army was heavily involved in suppressing a bloody revolt in Iraq as well as trying to cope with the demobilization of millions of war-service soldiers. Sinn Féin was not alone in increasing its vote in 1918; the Labour Party also gained support, while many feared that Britain was on the verge of a communist revolution.

Ultimately there was a war-weariness in 1919 that was absent in 1914, which allowed the Irish rebels to push the country down the road to independence. For Lloyd George, the 'Irish question' threatened to destroy the delicate balance of his Liberal–Conservative coalition, and eventually it saw his ultimate downfall and tore apart the Liberal Party. Once again England's adversity was Ireland's opportunity.

Portrait of a civilian: Thomas Hornibrook

In 1891, 10 per cent of the population of the 26 counties that now constitute the Republic of Ireland was Protestant. By 1991 Protestants constituted a mere 3 per cent. Although this process of decline began in 1911, when the spectre of Home Rule began to rear its head, it had levelled off by 1926. It is not surprising that the most rapid period of decline was 1921–23, when the country was experiencing the most turmoil.

In many respects the Protestant population of Southern Ireland were the real losers in the Anglo-Irish War. For the most part they were Irish-born and their families had been in Ireland for hundreds of years, yet in the eyes of some Republicans, like the West Cork Republican activist Kathleen Keys McDonnell, they were 'foreigners'. To many Irish Catholics they were merely strangers in a strange land. One such alien in the land of his birth was Thomas Hornibrook of Ballygroman House, in the Bandon district of Co. Cork.

In 1861 only Kilkenny had a population less than 6 per cent Protestant. Dublin was 20 per cent Protestant, as was Monaghan and Cavan. In many respects, the Dunmanway area of Co. Cork was the Ulster of the South. County Cork's Protestant population numbered 8.3 per cent on average, but in Dunmanway it was higher than the national average at 16 per cent, and for several hundred years the Protestants and the Catholic majority had an uneasy coexistence.

Unlike the Protestants in Ulster, most of Cork's Protestants were English by descent and were Anglicans rather than Scots Presbyterians. However, like their Ulster brethren there was a deeply ingrained fear of sectarian violence if law and order ever broke down, which engendered a siege mentality more usually associated with the Northern Protestants. In their cultural collective memory the massacres of 1641 and 1798 were as fresh in their minds as if they were in Ulster.

Thomas Hornibrook was a landowner who lived at Ballygroman, halfway between Bandon and Cork, and was typical of his caste. He served for at least ten years as a

Mr Ian MacPherson, Chief Secretary of Ireland and Field Marshal Viscount French of Ypres and High Lake (Co. Roscommon), Lord Lieutenant of Ireland. (National Library of Ireland)

magistrate in Ballincollig and only resigned the bench under pressure from the IRA in 1921. He was a man of very strong Unionist convictions and, unlike most Cork Protestants, he was unafraid of voicing his support for the Union. He had a reputation for being a hard man, as did his son Sam.

Many Republicans viewed the Protestant community as a fifth column in their midst. Although there were plenty of Irish Catholics who worked for the Castle regime it was Ireland's Protestants who made up the bulk of the political and social elite. In many Nationalists' eyes it was the Protestant landlords, big business and Freemasons who kept the British regime operating in Ireland. Some Catholics did reach senior positions in the police, Army and civil service but the perception was that the Castle positively discriminated in favour of the Protestants.

The Republicans had a special dislike for Freemasons, whom they viewed as particularly pro-British. As a result, the IRA killed several Irishmen – like Tom Nagle and Francis Fitzmaurice, both from Dunmanway – who were Protestant Freemasons. This dislike was probably reinforced because policemen were barred from being members of any 'secret' societies except the Freemasons. It is strange that Republicans should have been so hostile towards the Freemasons when one considers that most of the founders of the United Irishmen, the spiritual ancestors of the IRA, were not only Protestants like Wolfe Tone, but also Freemasons themselves.

It is not known for certain that Hornibrook was a Mason, but it is extremely likely as both Nagle and Fitzmaurice were neighbours of his and members of the same Church of Ireland congregation. In the eyes of the rebels most landowners were Freemasons, and most landowners were pro-British, which meant that all Freemasons must be pro-British as well. By a similar train of logic all Freemasons were Protestant so all Protestants were Loyalists. This was most definitely not the case with James Buttimer of Dunmanway, who was a dedicated supporter of Home Rule. This did not stop the IRA from killing him in April 1922.

The West Cork IRA was convinced that the county's Protestants were behind the 'Protestant Action Group' that was responsible for the assassination of several Republicans. In reality, the Protestant Action Group was probably a front organization for a Loyalist death squad drawn from the ranks of the RIC or Auxiliaries. However, the Protestant community was a disappointment to the British security forces. James McDougall, a Scottish businessman in Cork, accused the county's Protestants of being 'spineless'.

As the RIC was driven out of its more isolated stations in West Cork, and law and order began to break down, the Protestant community became fair game for robbers and land-grabbers. One Protestant, Joe Tanner, was forced out of his home by armed men who told him that 'as there is no law in the county now I will have to get back what belonged to my forefathers'.

Despite their families having been resident in Co. Cork for a few hundred years, men like Hornibrook, Tanner, Nagle and the rest were seen as outsiders by many Cork Catholics who referred to them as 'English' and one of the IRA men who attempted to assassinate Tom Bradfield's brother Henry is alleged to have boasted that they would 'soon have the English out of the county'.

As the Anglo-Irish War developed, Co. Cork also experienced a crime wave. In 1918 there were only two armed robberies in Cork City, but RIC records show that in the following three years 41 took place and the situation was worse in the countryside. Tom Hornibrook was robbed several times of weapons and cattle and while his robbers usually claimed to be acting 'in the name of the Republic', much of this activity, especially that involving cattle, was simply theft.

As an ex-magistrate and well-to-do farmer, Hornibrook was a figure of envy for many of his Catholic neighbours, and several people claiming to be evicted ex-tenants sought a share of his land. Evictions were always a very emotive issue and one that was bound to elicit sympathy for evictees in Republican circles. We will never know what the outcome of this dispute was, as IRA gunmen killed Hornibrook and his son in April 1922 and his estate became the property of the State.

On the night of 26 April 1922 a group of anti-Treaty IRA officers led by Michael O'Neill, the acting commander of the Bandon Battalion, broke into Ballygroman House.

They had attempted to rouse the occupants but with no success and so had forced entry. O'Neill was shot in the chest by Hornibrook's son-in-law, Capt Herbert Woods.

Charlie O'Donoghue, one of the IRA men, left by car for Bandon to get reinforcements. After a standoff lasting several hours Woods, along with Tom and Sam Hornibrook, agreed to surrender if their lives were spared. Woods was beaten unconscious and all three were bundled into a car and driven into the south Cork hills. All three were tried by an impromptu IRA court martial and sentenced to death for the 'unlawful' killing of O'Neill. Woods was shot on the 26th and his body dragged behind a car for several miles in an act of revenge for the same thing being done to an IRA man, Walter Murphy, by British officers in 1921.

Tom and Sam Hornibrook were taken out the next day and forced to dig their own graves. After he had finished digging, Tom Hornibrook tossed his shovel into the hole, turned to his assassins and apparently said, 'Go ahead'. Neither man's grave was ever found. Ballygroman House was burned to the ground, the fences were torn down and no Irish newspapers reported the murders of Woods and the Hornibrooks. It was almost as if they had never existed.

Local Protestants were horrified, not at their killing by the IRA, but at their utter foolishness in trying to resist armed intruders in the middle of the night. At the inquest all the blame for what happened on 26 and 27 April was firmly placed upon the shoulders of Woods and the Hornibrooks. Even though the IRA men never explained why they were there, or even announced to the occupants of Ballygroman House that they were IRA, at O'Neill's inquest the conclusion was that he had been brutally murdered by Woods.

Charlie O'Donoghue later claimed that they had stopped at Ballygroman House because their car had run out of petrol, but that did not explain why he was able to drive to Bandon for help after O'Neill was shot. It was likely that they had gone there to kill Hornibrook, as O'Neill was convinced that he was involved in Loyalist paramilitary activity. In 1921 an IRA officer had informed another Cork Protestant, William Jagoe, that regardless of the Truce there were a number of Protestants who were going to be shot.

The incident at Ballygroman House sparked two further nights of violence as armed gangs raided Protestant households in the Dunmanway area, killing ten men. Both the Irish and British papers were outraged at the killings, and Seán Hales, a senior Cork IRA officer, condemned the murders and promised to protect the Protestant community.

However, by April 1922 the pro-Treaty Dublin Government had lost control of Co. Cork and was in no position to help. Several of the IRA who carried out the killings were heard to shout, 'Take that, you Orange Free Stater!' as they shot their victims. In the minds of the anti-Treaty IRA it was logical that if the Protestants had been Loyalists under the British then they would be pro-Treaty, and thus still their enemies. Seán Moylan, an anti-Treaty member of the Dáil and an IRA leader in north Cork, commented that 'if there is a war of extermination on us by God no Loyalist in North Cork will see its finish'.

Many Republicans were convinced that the Protestant community was working against them. British records, however, indicate that only a minority of Protestant civilians ever passed information to the security forces. During the Civil War the number was even less. Because of Protestant attacks on Catholics in Northern Ireland Protestants in the South knew they were vulnerable and tried to keep their heads down.

Their caution did not do them much good, however, as 64 per cent of those executed as spies by the IRA in Co. Cork were Protestants. Of the 122 people executed in Cork between 1919 and 1923, only 38 were actually British spies; most were executed because of what they represented rather than what they had actually done. Like the Hornibrooks, they did not 'fit in' in the 'New' Ireland and were effectively eliminated from it. Many more left for Northern Ireland or Britain to escape intimidation, which in the eyes of many rebels merely confirmed their guilt.

THE TRUCE

In order to try to end an increasingly squalid conflict, the British had attempted a constitutional settlement by passing the Government of Ireland Act (1920), which provided for two separate Irish Parliaments: one in Belfast to govern Ulster and one in Dublin for the rest of Ireland, with the intention that they would eventually unite into one. Neither the rebels nor the Unionists were happy with this solution, which, like so many British attempts to solve Irish problems, was a fudge.

When King George V opened the Belfast Parliament on 22 June 1922 he appealed for peace. However, he did not attend the opening of its Dublin counterpart, which had a far less auspicious start. Only the four Unionist MPs for Trinity College and the 15 senators appointed by the Viceroy put in an appearance when it convened on 28 June. Facing the reality of the situation the Parliament adjourned indefinitely.

When de Valera returned from America on 23 December 1920 it was apparent to him that the IRA was not winning – but neither were the British. The British began to explore the possibility of coming to terms with the rebels, and in June started to ease off the pressure in order to facilitate the peace process. In spite of this, IRA violence escalated and British casualties rose as a result from roughly 30 casualties per week in March to 67 in the first week of June 1921. The Army continued to hit back but in military terms neither side had the upper hand. Demoralized and frustrated, Gen

Macready and the Southern Unionist leader the Earl of Middleton secretly met with Dáil representatives and agreed an informal ceasefire on 8 July 1921.

When the Anglo-Irish Truce came into force on 11 July 1921 the war was effectively over. Both sides claimed victory, although the British were finding it extremely difficult to sustain operations, while in 1922 the then IRA Chief of Staff, Richard Mulcahy, told the Dáil that the IRA was incapable of defeating the British Army in the field and was effectively beaten.

Between the Easter Rising and the Truce over 2,000 people had lost their lives. Of the 3,000–5,000 active IRA who took part in the struggle, approximately 650 were killed and several thousand arrested. The British had approximately 66,000 troops and policemen of whom around 555 had been killed and 1,027 wounded. In addition, at least 300 civilians had been murdered or simply vanished. However, although the Truce had effectively ended the Anglo-Irish War it did not signal the end of political violence in Ireland.

The Changing of the Guard: British troops march out of Richmond Barracks, Dublin (renamed Keogh Barracks by the Irish Government) while the new National Army marches in. (National Library of Ireland)

THE WARRING SIDES

THE CROWN FORCES

The British Army

Throughout Ireland's period as a part of the UK it was administered from Dublin Castle by a notoriously inefficient and incompetent civil service, headed by a member of the British Cabinet called the Chief Secretary of Ireland. The last incumbent was a Canadian called Sir Hamar Greenwood, who held the office from 1920 to 1922.

Although Scotland also had a Secretary of State sitting in the British Cabinet, Ireland differed from the other member states of the Union in that it had a Lord Lieutenant or Viceroy to represent the monarch, making it appear more of a colony than an integral part of the UK. As elsewhere in the UK the Crown relied upon the police and the Army to enforce the 'King's Writ' and the rule of law and, despite efforts to show otherwise, the vast majority of civil servants, policemen and soldiers who made Ireland's membership of the UK work were Irish Catholics.

Ireland was a major recruiting ground for the British Army and in 1914 more than 22,000 of its Regular soldiers were Irishmen, with 33,000 in the reserves, and by 1918 over 200,000 had fought for King and Country. During World War I tens of thousands of British Army recruits from Great Britain also trained at the Curragh in Co. Kildare, and Southern Ireland remained a recruiting ground for the British Army after the Treaty.

The British Army in 1918 was radically different from that of 1914. It was war-weary, battle-hardened and utterly unprepared for counter-insurgency operations in Ireland. Lack of a coherent doctrine also ensured that while some soldiers did not take the IRA seriously others were prepared to apply solutions more appropriate to a trench-raid rather than to a civil emergency within the UK. Unsurprisingly, its officers tended to be rather conservative and harboured Unionist sympathies.

Auxiliaries search an IRA suspect. These war veterans proved successful against the IRA but their reputation for brutality caused an uproar in Ireland, Britain and the USA. (Topical Press Agency/Getty Images)

Until 1919 Ireland was divided into three military districts: Northern (Belfast), Midland (Curragh) and Southern (Cork), while Dublin was a separate sub-district. However, during the Anglo-Irish War this structure was re-organized drastically. The Northern District ceased to be a separate command and came directly under the Army's GHQ and the direct control of the British GOCinC (Ireland). Midland District became 5th Divison, with its HQ in the Curragh, while Southern District became 6th Divison, based in Cork.

By November 1919 there were 34 infantry battalions stationed in Ireland undergoing a process of demobilization, training and reorganization and during the Troubles six Irish-based battalions were disbanded. War service conscripts and volunteers were far more concerned with being demobbed rather than fighting the IRA and a lack of a unified civil–military command structure also ensured that both the police and Army were unsure of how to deal with the Republican threat. In reality the military tended to play second fiddle to the civil authorities even in the 25 per cent of Ireland that was placed under martial law.

By July 1921 more than 66,000 troops were scattered across Ireland to support the police. It is worth noting that in August 1920 14 infantry battalions (about 14,000 men) fulfilled the same role in mainland Britain and about 200,000 were in Iraq.

The British order of battle in January 1922 was as follows:

A British propaganda postcard showing all the branches of the RIC. From left to right: an RIC Regular, a Black and Tan, and Auxiliary and a Regular advancing arm in arm. (Jim Herlihy)

GHQ Troops (Dublin): Gen Sir Nevil Macready

3 Bn Royal Tank Corps

5 Armoured Car Company

1 Mobile Searchlight Group RE – Dublin

2 Mobile Searchlight Group RE – Fermoy

'B' Mobile Searchlight Group RE – Limerick

Special Signal Company

'K' Signal Company

3rd Cavalry Brigade (Curragh)

3 Dragoon Guards

12 Lancers

15 Hussars – Dublin

B & M Batteries RHA

Non-Brigaded Cavalry Regiments

Royal Dragoons – Ballinasloe

10 Hussars – Curragh

13 Hussars – Longford

17 Lancers – Galway

Coast Defence Artillery

15 Company RGA – Londonderry

R, W & X Coast Batteries RGA – Queenstown

U & V Coast Batteries RGA – Berehaven

Y Coast Battery RGA – Lough Swilly

15th Infantry Brigade (Belfast): under direct command of GHQ

1 Bn Royal Norfolk Regiment

1 Bn Somerset Light Infantry

1 Bn Seaforth Highlanders

1 Bn Duke of Cornwall's Light Infantry – Ballykinlar

1 Bn King's Royal Rifle Corps – Ballykinlar

1 Bn Dorsetshire Regiment – Londonderry

2 Bn Rifle Brigade – Finner

5th DIVISION (Curragh) – Maj Gen Sir Hugh Jeudwine

XXX Brigade RFA-128, 129 130 Field Batteries – Kildare

XXXVI Brigade RFA-15, 48, 71 Field Batteries – Newbridge

17 Field Company RE – Curragh

59 Field Company RE – Curragh

5 Division Signal Company– Curragh

Galway Brigade

4 Bn Worcestershire Regiment – Galway

2 Bn Border Regiment – Castlebar

1 Bn King's Own Yorkshire Light Infantry – Tuam

2 Bn Argyll & Sutherland Highlanders – Claremorris

13 Infantry Brigade (Athlone)

1 Bn East Yorkshire Regiment – Mullingar
1 Bn Bedfordshire & Hertfordshire Regiment – Sligo
1 Bn Leicestershire Regiment– Sligo
1 Bn Royal Sussex Regiment – Carrickshannon

14 Infantry Brigade (Curragh)

1 Bn Northumberland Fusiliers – Carlow
2 Bn Suffolk Regiment – Curragh
1 Bn Royal Scots Fusiliers – Tullamore
1 Bn Cameronians – Curragh
1 Bn Duke of Wellington's Regiment – Curragh
2 Bn King's Shropshire Light Infantry – Curragh
2 Bn Gordon Highlanders – Maryborough

6th DIVISION (Cork): Maj Gen Sir Peter Strickland

I Brigade RFA-98, 136, 146 Field Batteries – Kilkenny
II Brigade RFA-45, 53, 87 Field Batteries – Fermoy
XXXI Brigade RFA-131, 132, 133 Field Batteries – Fermoy
VII Medium Brigade RGA - Medium Batteries – Fermoy
12 Field Company RE – Limerick
38 Field Company RE – Fermoy
6 Divisional Signal Company – Cork

16 Infantry Brigade (Fermoy)

1 Bn Queen's Regiment – Kilworth
1 Bn Buffs – Fermoy
1 Bn Lincolnshire Regiment – Tipperary
1 Bn Devonshire Regiment – Waterford
2 Bn Green Howards – Tipperary
2 Bn Oxfordshire & Buckinghamshire Light Infantry – Tipperary
1 Bn York & Lancaster Regiment – Clonmel

17 Infantry Brigade (Cork)

1 Bn King's Liverpool Regiment – Bantry
1 Bn West Yorkshire Regiment – Kinsale
2 Bn King's Own Scottish Borderers – Bere
2 Bn Hampshire Regiment – Cork
2 Bn North Staffordshire Regiment – Cork
1 Bn Dorsetshire Regiment – Kinsale
1 Bn Sherwood Foresters – Skibbereen
1 Bn Manchester Regiment – Ballincolig
2 Bn Cameron Highlanders – Queenstown

18 Infantry Brigade (Limerick)

2 Bn Royal Scots, Ennis
1 Bn Royal Warwickshire Regiment – Newcastle West
3 Bn Royal Fusiliers – Killaloe

2 Bn Royal Welch Fusiliers – Limerick
1 Bn Oxfordshire & Buckinghamshire Light Infantry – Limerick
2 Bn Loyal North Lancashire Regiment – Tralee
1 Bn Northamptonshire Regiment – Templemore
2 Bn North Staffordshire Regiment – Nenagh

Kerry Brigade (Buttevant)

1 Bn Royal Fusiliers – Killarney
2 Bn Cheshire Regiment – Ballynovcare
1 Bn Gloucestershire Regiment – Kanturk
2 Bn East Lancashire Regiment – Buttevant
1 Bn Machine Gun Corps – Ballynovcare

DUBLIN DISTRICT – Maj Gen Gerald Farrell Boyd

XXXIII Brigade RFA-137, 138, 139 Field Batteries – Dundalk
V Medium Brigade RGA-15, 17, 20, 21 Medium Batteries – Tallaght
1 Works Company RE
14 Survey Company RE
24 Provisional Brigade
1 Bn Lancashire Fusiliers
2 Bn East Surrey Regiment
2 Bn Royal West Kent Regiment
1 Bn Wiltshire Regiment
3 Bn Rifle Brigade
1 Bn South Wales Borderers – Dunshaughlin
2 Bn Duke of Wellington's Regiment – Collinstown

Summer 1921 – 1 Essex's new 'flying column' takes a smoke-break in West Cork: Maj Percival decided to try and beat the IRA at its own game and formed flying columns of his own from 1 Essex to try to deny the rebels the freedom to manoeuvre in rural areas. (Imperial War Museum, IL71695)

25 Provisional Brigade

1 Bn King's Own Royal Regiment

2 Bn Worcestershire Regiment

2 Bn Duke of Cornwall's Light Infantry

1 Bn South Lancashire Regiment

2 Bn Welch Regiment

2 Bn Royal Berkshire Regiment

1 Bn Cheshire Regiment – Raithdrum

26 Provisional Brigade (Dundalk)

2 Bn King's Own Yorkshire Light Infantry

2 Bn King's Royal Rifle Corps – Clonagh

1 Bn Middlesex Regiment – Cootehill

Spectators run when trouble breaks out in Dublin for a convoy of Black and Tans and British soldiers. Irish War of Independence, 1921. (© Sean Sexton Collection/Corbis)

While there were few conventional military operations during the Troubles, British Army intelligence was not only active but also relatively successful in combating the IRA. Brig Gen Sir Ormonde de l'Epee Winter was appointed by Churchill to be head of the Army's intelligence branch and deputy chief of police in Dublin, where he was known as 'O'. He was a strict disciplinarian and reorganized British intelligence operations in Ireland. One Castle civil servant, Mark Sturgis, commented that 'O is a marvel, he looks like a wicked little white snake, he can do anything'.

Even though Winter's intelligence network was badly damaged in November 1920 when most of the members of a Dublin-based intelligence team known as the 'Cairo Gang' were killed by The Squad on Bloody Sunday, his agents were remarkably successful against the IRA. He also established other plain-clothes police, like the 'Igoe Gang' commanded by RIC Head Constable Eugene Igoe, who successfully conducted covert operations against the IRA in Dublin.

Winter cultivated a network of informers on both sides of the Irish Sea and even set up a confidential address in England for people to pass information anonymously to the British. Although the bulk of the letters sent were either hoaxes or abuse, some useful intelligence was also gathered.

Winter also set up 'The Raid Bureau' to analyse captured IRA documents. Because Mulcahy generated vast amounts of paperwork, the Bureau was able to identify the locations of arms caches and the identities of IRA members and rebel sympathizers in the RIC without having to rely on informers. There was also at least one agent operating within the upper echelons of Sinn Féin.

Army intelligence also compiled photomontages of known rebels and actively sought to recruit them as informers. Winter's operations successfully turned at least three leading IRA members and an unknown number of junior ranks. He also conducted a vigorous psychological warfare campaign, publishing forgeries of Republican newspapers, like *Irish Bulletin*, skilfully edited to undermine the IRA cause. After the Treaty British intelligence organizations continued to conduct covert operations in Southern Ireland and maintained close links with the *Saorstát*'s nascent intelligence service known as G2.

The Anglo-Irish Treaty of 1922 provided for an Irish defence force formed from the IRA and there was even talk of transferring the existing Irish regiments into it. Consequently, the British Army began to withdraw from Southern Ireland immediately after the treaty was signed and handed over their barracks to the IRA.

The only exceptions were the six infantry battalions that became the Northern Ireland garrison – 1st Bn Royal Warwickshire Regiment and 1st Bn Royal Sussex Regiment (both in Ballykinlar), 1st Bn Essex Regiment (Carrickfergus), 1st Bn Lincolnshire Regiment (Enniskillen), 2nd Bn East Lancashire Regiment (Londonderry) and 4th Worcestershire Regiment (Belfast) – and a force of some 5,000 men under the command of Gen Macready based in Dublin that finally left in December 1922.

When the Civil War broke out only the British had conducted any contingency planning and it was the threat of armed intervention during the Four Courts occupation by IRA Irregulars that finally galvanized the *Saorstát* into action. When Collins and de Valera announced their electoral pact in the summer of 1922 the British suspended all troop withdrawals with an explicit threat of renewed conflict if the Provisional Government failed to honour the Treaty.

The Police

As the Crown's representatives in the community, the police bore the brunt of IRA violence from 1918 to 1922; 513 were killed, 682 wounded and their friends and families were also intimidated and ostracized by Republicans. There were two constabularies in Ireland: the Royal Irish Constabulary and the Dublin Metropolitan Police.

The 1,202-strong DMP was responsible for the greater Dublin area and its men were indistinguishable from their mainland colleagues. Although most of the senior

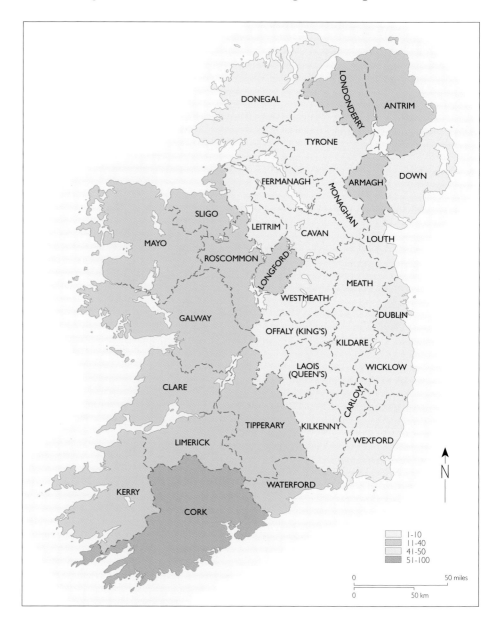

The majority of police casualties occurred in the RA heartlands of the south-west and Dublin. Police casualties were lowest in Queen's County.

officers were Protestants, some, like Assistant Commissioner Quinn, were Catholics. With the exception of G Division the DMP played almost no part in combating the IRA and survived until 1925 when it was absorbed by the *Garda*.

The DMP relied on the 18 armed, plain-clothes detectives of G Division to monitor political dissidents and investigate ordinary crimes. Charged with policing a population of 304,000 Dubliners it had an unsatisfactory working relationship with both the RIC Special Branch and the Secret Service because of its poor track record during the Troubles, and by 1921 six so-called G-Men had been killed. Of course, unbeknown to either organization, its failings were mainly because four of its detectives were active members of the IRA.

Despite accusations that the RIC was a foreign gendarmerie imposing colonial rule, the overwhelming majority of the 10,000 or so RIC Regulars and a significant number of its Auxiliaries and Temporary Constables were Irish or of Irish descent. About 70 per cent of the other ranks were Catholics, while 60 per cent of the officers were Protestant, and in 1913 the constabulary was seen as a legitimate force even if its involvement in evictions did nothing for its popularity.

Despite being called barracks their stations were in reality ordinary houses rather than military installations, accommodating up to half a dozen men, and resembled rural police houses elsewhere in the UK. RIC and DMP ranks are given in the table below.

The most controversial elements of the RIC were the Temporary Constables and the Temporary Cadets of the ADRIC (or 'Auxies'). Because of initial kit shortages the Temporary Constables wore a mixture of RIC green and army khaki uniforms, and were soon dubbed Black and Tans after a famous pack of hunting hounds. Despite their folk-myth image, the Tans were never a separate organization but short-service policemen who served alongside the Regular RIC.

UK Constabularies	RIC/RUC (until 1969)	DMP
Chief Constable	Inspector General (IG)	Chief Commissioner
Deputy Chief Constable	Deputy IG	Assistant Commissioner
Assistant Chief Constable	Assistant IG	2nd Assistant Commissioner
Chief Superintendant	County Inspector	Chief Superintendant
Superintendant	District Inspector	Superintendant
Chief Inspector		Chief Inspector
Inspector	Head Constable	Inspector (1st, 2nd & 3rd class)
		Station Sergeant
Sergeant	Sergeant	Sergeant
Constable	Constable	Constable

GALLANTRY AWARDS HELD BY THE ADRIC	
Award	**Number**
Victoria Cross	2
Conspicuous Gallantry Medal	2
Distinguished Service Order	22
Military Cross	130
Distinguished Conduct Medal	23
Military Medal	63
Foreign Awards	40
Order of Merit	1
Mentioned in Dispatches	350

Although Republicans considered these men to be foreigners, it should be remembered that they were serving inside the borders of what they regarded as their country – the UK – and at no point did the British public consider the 26 per cent of mainland British policemen who had been born in Ireland as foreigners.

The Auxies are often confused with the Tans and erroneously treated as one and the same. They were not. The ADRIC were mostly ex-officers recruited specifically to form 14 companies (A–Q and a Depot) that would operate against the IRA independently of the rest of the RIC. Irish folk-myth remembers them as brutal foreigners recruited from English gaols, but in reality the 2,200 men of the ADRIC were ex-Army officers rather than ex-convicts and between them they held 632 gallantry awards; Cadets George Onions and James Leach had each won the VC; Cadet Bernard Beard MC had been a brigadier general. Onions had fought against the Easter rebels in 1916 and undoubtedly believed in the cause that he fought for as an Auxiliary.

It is also easy to forget the long shadow that World War I cast over the young men who joined the RIC, or even the IRA, after coming of age in the trenches. Disillusioned and brutalized, they brought a degree of ruthlessness to the conflict that was probably unthinkable before 1914.

Another controversial police force was the Ulster Special Constabulary, raised on 26 August 1920. The USC was independent of the RIC and organized into a full-time element called the 'A Specials' and two part-time groups – the 'B' and 'C Specials'. What made the USC radically different from the RIC, DMP or even the Army was that it was essentially raised from one of Ireland's paramilitary groups – the UVF. Although they were both Irish Protestants, Field Marshal Sir Henry Wilson and General Sir Nevil Macready had reservations about using the UVF as policemen, and controversy surrounded the USC until it was disbanded in 1970.

The USC was absorbed into the Royal Ulster Constabulary (RUC) when it was created in June 1922. The RUC was effectively a repackaging of the RIC in Northern Ireland right down to its green uniforms, ranks and insignia, and initially around 40 per cent of its members were Catholics.

Some Catholics, like County Inspector William Atteridge who was Assistant Commissioner of Police in Belfast in 1922, even rose to senior rank in the new force. In Northern Ireland the IRA was seen very much as a police matter and the RUC and USC bore the brunt of internal security operations until 1969.

The Loyalists

Towards the end of the nineteenth century an Irish Unionist Party (IUP) emerged under the leadership of Col Edward James Saunderson from Co. Cavan. In March 1905 Ulster-based Unionists formed the Ulster Unionist Council (UUC) to unify Northern opposition to Home Rule. The UUC was strongly supported by the Orange Order (initially 50 per cent of the council's 500 delegates were Orangemen) and in 1920 the UUC evolved into the Ulster Unionist Party. Under the leadership of Sir Edward Carson both the Ulster Unionist Council and Party enjoyed the support of the majority of Northern Protestants and were at the forefront of Ulster's resistance to Home Rule.

On 13 January 1913, Sir Edward Carson and Sir James Craig founded the Ulster Volunteer Force by unifying several existing Protestant militias to resist Irish Home Rule, by force if necessary. Theoretically, the UVF consisted of 100,000 men aged 17–65 organized into locally based companies and battalions along British Army lines. Much to the consternation of Irish Nationalists, both the Army and the Government tolerated the UVF and, despite its overt threat to plunge the country into civil war, turned a blind eye in April 1914 when it illegally landed 30,000 German Mauser rifles with 3,000,000 rounds at Larne, Co. Antrim and openly drilled under the instruction of both retired and serving Army officers. During World War I the UVF formed the 36th (Ulster) Division and suffered heavy casualties on the Somme. Even though it was not the only region to suffer in the war, many Ulstermen believed that this loss was a 'blood tax' that had placed Britain in their debt.

The upsurge in IRA violence revitalized the post-war UVF and it was in an attempt to keep them under control that the Government formed the USC. The 'B Specials' later earned a place in Republican folk-myth that had previously been reserved for the Black and Tans, and they are still the subject of much debate today. Although Loyalist death-squads operated in Southern Ireland during the Anglo-Irish War there is little evidence to support the premise that they were part of a Southern Irish equivalent to the UVF, and most evidence suggests that they were really a front for policemen and soldiers acting illegally against Republican sympathizers.

The Nationalists

In November 1913 more than 7,000 men attended the inaugural meeting of the Irish Volunteer Force at the Rotunda Rink in Dublin and 3,000 enlisted on the spot. Thereafter, a series of meetings were held throughout the country and by the end of August 1914 more than 180,000 had volunteered to 'secure and maintain the rights and liberties common to all the people of Ireland'. This ideology attracted recruits from all shades of Nationalist opinion, with members of existing organizations such as the Gaelic Athletic Association (GAA), the Gaelic League and the *Fianna Éireann* youth movement all viewing the Volunteers as the vehicle to promote their own cultural causes. Equally, supporters of Redmond and the IPP also saw the Volunteers as the perfect mechanism to secure Home Rule.

When the Volunteers split in 1914 the majority supported Redmond and went on to form the bulk of the 10th and 16th Irish divisions of the British Army while the minority Irish Volunteers under Éoin MacNeill resolved to oppose participation in 'England's war'. Unbeknown to most Irish Volunteers, however, their organization had been thoroughly infiltrated by the secretive Irish Republican Brotherhood, which had its own agenda.

Periodicals such as *The Irish Volunteer* were used to publicize the aims of the Irish Volunteers and public parades proved successful in attracting recruits. Those wishing to enlist then had to sign the following enrolment form:

I, the undersigned, desire to be enrolled for service in Ireland as a member of the Irish Volunteer Force. I subscribe to the Constitution of the Irish Volunteers and pledge my willing obedience to every article of it. I declare that in joining the Irish Volunteer Force I set before myself the stated objects of the Irish Volunteers and no others.

1. To secure and maintain the rights and liberties common to all the peoples of Ireland.
2. To train, discipline, and equip for this purpose an Irish Volunteer Force which will render service to an Irish National Government when such is established.
3. To unite in the service of Ireland Irishmen of every creed and of every party and class.

POLICE NOTICE

£1000 REWARD.

WANTED FOR MURDER IN IRELAND

DANIEL BREEN

(calls himself Commandant of the Third Tipperary Brigade).

Age 27, 5 feet 7 inches in height, bronzed complexion, dark hair (long in front), grey eyes, short cocked nose, stout build, weight about 12 stone, clean shaven ; sulky bulldog appearance ; looks rather like a blacksmith coming from work ; wears cap pulled well down over face.

The above reward will be paid by the Irish Authorities, to any person not in the Public Service who may give information resulting in his arrest.

Information to be given at any Police Station.

Members of the West Mayo Flying Column during the Anglo-Irish War. Their appearance is typical of IRA guerrillas during this conflict and the subsequent Civil War. The column commander, Comdt Michael Kilroy, is standing on the left of the back row in his Volunteer uniform. (Irish Military Archive)

Much work has been done, especially by Peter Hart, on what sort of men joined the Volunteers. The overwhelming majority were Roman Catholic, aged between 20 and 30, and from a working- or middle-class backgrounds. Officers, on the other hand, tended to be slightly older, better educated and more financially secure. Later, as the Anglo-Irish War progressed, the average age of those enlisting dropped slightly and the difference in background largely disappeared.

Although recruitment became less visible after the Easter Rising it did not cease and was boosted by the UK Government's threat to extend conscription to Ireland in 1918. Recruiting continued throughout the Anglo-Irish War, the only significant change being that from June 1920 onwards new recruits were required to swear an oath of allegiance to Dáil Éireann and the Irish Republic.

The signing of the Truce in July 1921 brought in more Volunteers, some of whom had been too young to take part in the war, while others now joining for the first time could certainly have taken part in the fighting had they wished to do so. Veterans of the war contemptuously dismissed the latter as 'Truciliers'.

The Irish Volunteers were governed by a 50-man General Council and a nine-man Executive Committee. On 5 December 1914 a GHQ was also established to direct Volunteer operations. The GHQ staff consisted of a chief of staff, quartermaster-general and directors of operations, organization, training, arms, communications and a chief of inspection. This structure remained extant until in 1922 the IRA split over the Treaty.

The main tactical unit was a company of 103 men divided into two half-companies. Companies were grouped into battalions and battalions into brigades. In April 1921 GHQ decided to group brigades into regional divisions. These units were locally based and it was very rare for a Volunteer from one district to operate in another during the Anglo-Irish War, or indeed the Civil War.

Although the Volunteers did not officially adopt the name IRA until 1919, Pearse had referred to himself as the Commandant-General of the IRA during the Easter Rising and unofficially they were increasingly known by this name after 1917. It is difficult to know exactly how large the IRA was but in July 1921 its paper strength was about 100,000, theoretically under the control of the rebel Dáil. The reality was somewhat different as most played little or no significant part in the struggle – it is likely that there were fewer than 3,000 active guerrillas. This hard core, bound by local loyalties and often beyond effective control, were at the heart of IRA operations, forming 'flying columns' of 20–100 men. Dublin Brigade's equivalent of a flying column was called the 'Active Service Unit'.

Although the Volunteers had a grey-green uniform and a rank system very loosely based on that of the British Army it was rarely worn after the Easter Rising and the majority of IRA wore civilian clothes during the Anglo-Irish War. From 1915 to 1922 the Irish Volunteers/IRA rank structure was as in the table below.

The majority favoured trench coats, soft hats and leggings (gaiters) as the most suitable garments for guerrilla warfare in the countryside, and for survival in Ireland's

Rank	Insignia	Position
Commandant General	Three 'wheeled crosses' and four dark green bands	Cuffs
Vice Comdt General	Two 'wheeled' crosses' and four dark green bands	Cuffs
Commandant	Two 'wheeled' crosses' and three dark green bands	Cuffs
Vice Commandant	One 'wheeled' cross' and three dark green bands	Cuffs
Captain	Two trefoils (Shamrocks) and two dark green bands	Cuffs
1st Lieutenant	Two trefoils and one dark green band	Cuffs
2nd Lieutenant	One trefoil and one dark green band	Cuff
Company Adjutant	Three dark green stripes	Left breast of tunic
Section Commander	Two dark green stripes	Left breast of tunic
Squad Commander	One dark green stripe	Left breast of tunic

notoriously inclement weather. In most cases the officers could be identified only by the Sam Browne belts they wore and the fact that generally they also sported a collar and tie. However, when the Truce came into effect in July 1921 some old Volunteer uniforms reappeared, as it was safe once again to wear them in public, but when recruitment began for the NA in 1922, an entirely new uniform was authorized.

For the first six years of their existence, with the exception of Easter week 1916, the Irish Volunteers were essentially part-time soldiers who, in addition to pursuing their military commitments, also maintained full-time employment, education and normal family life. The average Volunteer received no pay and committed himself to a code of discipline that had as its ultimate sanction an ignominious dismissal. Advancement within this 'territorial force' was not rank-based *per se* but depended instead on a spirit of democracy that was completely out of keeping with contemporary mainstream military thought. Initially Volunteer officers were elected by the membership and from time to time also de-selected if they proved to be ineffective. This overt democracy was destined to diminish once GHQ had established effective control but it served its purpose in the early days by empowering the rank and file, which in turn facilitated the selection of some fine officers.

During the Anglo-Irish conflict the IRA concentrated on conducting a guerrilla war and many Volunteers were forced to go on the run to escape arrest. For food, shelter and a change of clothing they often had to rely on a network of safe houses established in each brigade area.

By 1920 the IRA had a comprehensive network of safe houses, and GHQ directed all units to form full-time units. Strengths varied considerably, with some comprising no more than a dozen, while the flying column that fought at Crossbarry in Co. Cork was over 100 strong.

Life was severe and Tom Barry described the conditions under which his men were expected to serve: '... they had to live rough, sleep in their clothes, and be expected to march by day and march by night'. But not all Volunteers were involved with flying columns or urban ASUs, and many more were tasked with other duties.

In June 1922 the IRA's ORBAT and paper strength was as follows:

1st Northern Division (Comdt Gen Joseph Sweeney) (5,000 men)
Donegal

2nd Northern Division (Comdt Gen Charles Daly) (2,800 men)
Tyrone and Derry

3rd Northern Division (Comdt Gen Seamus Woods) (1,200 men)
Antrim and north Down

4th Northern Division (Comdt Frank Aiken) (2,300 men)
Armagh, Louth and west and south Down

December 1922 – Not everyone was pleased to see the last of the British garrison withdraw from Dublin. (Corbis)

5th Northern Division (Comdt Gen Dan Hogan) (2,200 men)
Monaghan and east Cavan

1st Eastern Division (Comdt Sean Boylan) (3,700 men)
Meath, Kildare, south Louth, south-east Cavan and east Westmeath

2nd Eastern Division (Gen Thomas Ennis) (5,100 men)
Dublin and Carlow

3rd Eastern Division (Patrick Flemming) (3,100 men)
Wexford

Midland Division (Comdt Sean MacEoin) (6,600 men)
Longford, Westmeath, the east Leitrim, mid-Cavan, and east Fermanagh

1st Western Division (Comdt Gen Frank Barrett) (8,500 men)
Clare and south Galway

2nd Western Division (Comdt Thomas Maguire) (4,000 men)
North-east Galway, south Roscommon and south-east Mayo

3rd Western Division (Comdt Liam Pilkington) (7,700 men)
Sligo, west Leitrim and west Fermanagh

4th Western Division (Comdt Gen Michael Kilroy) (8,400 men)
West Mayo and west Galway

1st Southern Division (Comdt Gen Liam Lynch) (33,550 men)
Waterford, Cork, Kerry and west Limerick

2nd Southern Division (Ernie O'Malley) (12,500 men)
Kilkenny, east Limerick, south and mid-Tipperary

3rd Southern Division (Comdt Gen Seamus Robinson) (6,000 men)
Offaly (King's), Laois (Queen's) and north Tipperary

During the Anglo-Irish War the IRA were hostile to ex-British soldiers and killed more than 180 in what the *Irish Times* referred to as 'The Campaign Against Ex-Servicemen'. Inevitably, however, Nationalists like Emmet Dalton MC, Martin Doyle VC MM and Tom Barry, who had served in the British military during World War I, did end up in the IRA and supplied much-needed expertise and combat experience.

As Director of Intelligence Collins controlled the IRA Intelligence Department (IRAID) and ran an extensive network of spies consisting of sympathetic G-Men, policemen, civil servants, soldiers, the Castle's classified cipher clerk and even a few Auxiliaries. Collins' 'special operations' unit, The Squad, allowed him to wage a vicious war of terror and counter-terror against Britain's security apparatus. Led by Comdt Paddy Daly, it emerged from the conflict with an almost mythical status in Republican circles and originally consisted of Mick McDonnell, Ben Barrett, James Conroy, Seán Doyle, Joe Leonard, Pat McCrae, Jim Slattery and Bill Stapleton.

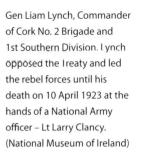

Gen Liam Lynch, Commander of Cork No. 2 Brigade and 1st Southern Division. Lynch opposed the Treaty and led the rebel forces until his death on 10 April 1923 at the hands of a National Army officer – Lt Larry Clancy. (National Museum of Ireland)

They were later joined by Dublin IRA men Mick Love, Gearóid Ó'Sullivan, Charlie Dalton (Emmet's brother), Mick O'Reilly, Vincent Byrne, Seán Healy, Francis Healy, Tom Keogh and Tom Cullen, who all went on to fight for the *Saorstát* during the Civil War. Seán Lemass and the writer Brendan Behan's father, Stephen Behan, are also believed to have been members. The Squad was informally known as the 'The Twelve Apostles' and merged with the Dublin Brigade ASU to form the Dublin Guards after the abortive attack on the Customs House.

Liam Mellows photographed at the graveside of Wolfe Tone in 1922. He was one of de Valera's strongest supporters and was executed on the orders of Richard Mulcahy on 8 December 1922. Mellows believed that Britain was the only enemy of Ireland. (Corbis)

In addition the rise in militant Socialism before World War I, and its growing influence over the emerging working classes in both Dublin and Belfast, saw the creation of the ICA. While Socialism did not quite manage to rise above the sectarian mire in Ireland, and it had more influence in Dublin during the dock strike and lockout of 1913 than it did in the Protestant North, violent clashes between the DMP and strikers led Irish-Glaswegian ex-soldier James Connolly along with fellow Irish Socialists James Larkin and Capt Jack White to found the ICA as a workers' defence force rather than a Republican revolutionary militia. Connolly was persuaded to involve the ICA in the Easter Rising and afterwards its remnants were absorbed by the IRA, bringing an element of Socialist politics to what was ultimately a rather conservative Catholic organization.

THE CIVIL WAR

During the Civil War the military forces on both sides were the offspring of the IRA that had fought the British. The pro-Treaty forces became the National Army (NA) and the anti-Treaty element continued to refer to itself as the IRA even though the Irish and British Governments and press called them Irregulars. For convenience the opposing forces are referred to as the NA and IRA.

Republican forces – the IRA

While the Republican movement split over the Anglo-Irish Treaty, the majority of IRA units declared against, and the Republicans utilized the existing IRA battalion, brigade and divisional organization as well as the rank structures of the Anglo-Irish War.

Despite adopting the IRA's organization the Irregulars did not inherit most of its equipment or many of its key personnel as the majority of GHQ staff, including Collins, backed the Treaty. This caused Rory O'Connor, Liam Mellows, Seán Russell and Seamus O'Donovan to break away from GHQ and in March 1922 Liam Forde, OC Mid-Limerick IRA Brigade, declared that he no longer recognized GHQ's authority.

A banned IRA Army Convention voted that the organization 'shall be maintained as the Army of the Irish Republic under an Executive appointed by the Convention'. Liam Lynch was elected head of an anti-Treaty Executive and was IRA COS until he was killed on 10 April 1923, when he was replaced by Frank Aiken from Armagh.

The fact that the IRA did not feel bound to obey the Dáil's decision over the Treaty served to emphasize how little control elected officials had over it. Just as the IRA had never really been under the Dáil's control during the Anglo-Irish War, so its anti-Treaty namesake paid little heed to the Republican 'Government' during the Civil War.

Despite his nominal position as President of the Irish Republic de Valera was marginalized and Republican policy was so disjointed that in July 1922 Lynch's Assistant Chief of Staff Ernie O'Malley asked him to 'give me an outline of your military and national policy as we are in the dark here with regard to both'.

Because the Treaty was accepted by the overwhelming majority of the Irish electorate in 1922 the IRA did not enjoy the same levels of popular support that it had during the Anglo-Irish War, and when anti-Treaty West Cork IRA leader Tom Barry was on the run in the winter of 1922 he admitted that he had to be careful not to fall into 'the wrong hands' as the majority of the population were hostile.

The IRA had three major difficulties to overcome if they were to win. First, they needed safe areas to operate in, secondly they required arms, and thirdly they needed money. South-west Ireland was the heartland of anti-Treaty resistance until an NA offensive in August 1922 deprived them of this key ground. Ironically, some areas that had played little or no part in the rebellion against the British became hotbeds of IRA activity.

In Northern Ireland and Britain the split threw the IRA into disarray and allowed the British to keep them firmly under control. In addition the *Saorstát* sent undercover teams into these areas to keep tabs on Republican activists. Some British and Northern IRA units did participate in the Civil War but, deprived of coherent direction, their activities were limited.

In June 1922 the IRA had some 6,780 rifles to equip 12,900 men and throughout the war they never broke their dependence upon arms captured from the NA, although they did try to supplement this by smuggling guns from overseas. To do this they needed money and in the spring of 1922 more than 650 armed robberies took place on the IRA Executive's orders, with almost £50,000 being stolen on 1 May 1922 alone.

Initially anti-Treaty forces attempted to destabilize the *Saorstát* by seizing key points in central Dublin. Instead they managed to replicate the failures of the Easter Rising but without gaining the sympathy vote that that Rising had elicited. Between July and August 1922 the IRA attempted to defeat the NA in the field but this strategy failed and it was forced to revert to the methods used during the Anglo-Irish War, forming small flying columns and ASUs.

Although effective, their attacks on the railway network led de Valera to complain that if they continued 'the people will begin to treat us like bandits'. Assassinations and arson did nothing to further their cause and simply prompted a wave of reprisals and executions by the *Saorstát* that overshadowed anything done by the British.

By May 1923 the military situation was hopeless; outgunned by the NA Aiken ordered his men to dump their arms and wait until 'our time will come' – *Tioclaidh ar la*. De Valera was also consigned to the political wilderness until 1932, when he became the first *Fianna Fáil Taoiseach* (Prime Minister).

Saorstát Éireann forces – the National Army

The Defence Forces Temporary Provisions Act passed on 3 August 1923 provided a legal basis for the National Army and was retrospectively dated to 21 January 1922 when its first unit, the Dublin Guards, was formed. In Irish the army was called *Oglaich na hÉireann* after the Irish Volunteers and the Provisional Government sought to portray the NA as the true inheritors of the IRA. The NA went on to form the foundations of the modern Irish Army.

It was perhaps inevitable that the NA organization was heavily influenced by that of the British Army but until January 1923 it retained the ranks used by the Volunteers. The revised rank titles bore closer resemblance to those used by other armies although the IRA title 'Commandant' was retained in preference to the more commonly used rank of Major. By 1923 the NA rank structure was as the table on p148.

Unlike the Republicans the *Saorstát* was able to draw on British resources to equip its forces. The British Government was willing to supply arms and equipment in large

General Richard Mulcahy (centre) flanked by two senior National Army officers. Mulcahy made his name in the 1916 Easter Rising and became COS of the IRA. He was appointed COS of the NA and became C.-in-C. after Collins' death. He was also Minister of Defence and set out to create a professional and apolitical Irish Army. (Donal MacCarron)

Rank	Insignia	Position
General	Three gold bars	Shoulder strap and collar
Lt General	Two gold bars	Shoulder strap and collar
Maj General	Two gold bars and one red bar	Shoulder strap and collar
Colonel	Three red bars	Shoulder strap and collar
Commandant	Two red bars	Shoulder strap and collar
Captain	Three blue bars	Shoulder strap and collar
Lieutenant	Two blue bars	Shoulder strap and collar
2nd Lieutenant	One blue bar	Shoulder strap and collar
Sergeant Major	Three green bars	Left sleeve
Sergeant	Two green bars	Left sleeve
Corporal	One green bar	Left sleeve
Private	-	

quantities and was even prepared to loan troops if asked. When NA troops shelled the Four Courts they did so using borrowed British guns firing borrowed ammunition. Even the NA's uniforms were manufactured in Britain.

Although the NA pre-dated the Civil War it was during this conflict that its expansion was most rapid. In July 1922 the Dáil authorized an establishment of 35,000 men but by May 1923 it had grown to 53,000. This in itself created major problems as the NA lacked the expertise necessary to train and fight with a force of that size. After the Civil War demobilization became another headache for the Irish Government and the problems of reducing the size of the NA and how to deal with ex-servicemen would dog Irish politics well into the 1930s.

Approximately 20 per cent of its officers and 50 per cent of its soldiers had served in the British Army and men like Henry Kelly, Martin Doyle, W. R. E. Murphy, and Emmet Dalton brought considerable expertise to it. Others, however, were not so useful and one of the first courts martial was of an ex-British NCO, Sgt Maj Dixon, who was charged with mutiny and insubordination. Ill discipline plagued the NA as half-trained troops were thrown into fighting that most taxing of operations – a counter-insurgency campaign.

Although there was considerable combat experience in the NA, there was very little in the way of administrative, logistical and training experience to accompany it. Some units were of course better than others and the Dublin Guards became the shock troops of the *Saorstát*. The Dublin Guards were an eclectic mix of IRA veterans loyal to Collins and ex-Royal Dublin Fusiliers who earned a fearsome reputation in Co. Kerry for brutality that persists to this day. Their commander, Brig Paddy Daly, one-time OC of Collins' special unit, The Squad, once commented that '... nobody had asked me to take kid gloves to Kerry so I didn't'.

The NA proved both willing and able to execute prisoners and carry out reprisals. In all 77 men were executed under the Public Safety Act, while many others were shot out of hand. The worst atrocity took place at Ballyseedy, Co. Kerry in March 1923, when nine Republicans were tied to a mine and blown up.

As the NA grew, the Provisional Government attempted to create a command structure to manage it. Only General W. R. E. Murphy had higher command experience, having been a British Army brigadier general during World War I. Maj Gen Dalton had been a major in the British Army while Lt Gen J. J. 'Ginger' O'Connell and Maj Gen John Prout had both fought in the US Army.

Originally GHQ created three Military Districts (Eastern, Western and Southern) but in July 1922 these expanded to eight regional commands that were reorganized again in January 1923 into nine. Collins was NA Commander-in-Chief until his

September 1922: an Irish Air Corps gunner practices his aim from the back of a British-supplied Bristol F2B Fighter during the Civil War. Air support played a key role in most major NA operations. (Getty Images)

Soldiers of 1st Bn, Dublin Brigade land at the Cork Shipbuilding Co. Dock, Passage West, Co. Cork on 8 August 1922. Given the secrecy of the entire operation the two men in civilian clothes are probably G2 (National Army Intelligence) agents. (George Morrison)

death in August 1922, when he was replaced by his Chief of Staff, Gen Mulcahy. Mulcahy was also the *Saorstát* Minister of Defence and this dual role as politician and soldier created a degree of unease among several TDs, including Home Affairs Minister Kevin O'Higgins.

The NA was dominated by the infantry and by January 1923 it had more than 60 battalions. The British supplied armoured cars, armoured personnel carriers, artillery, and aeroplanes, which allowed the NA to create separate cavalry, artillery and air corps. An air corps Bristol Fighter flown by an RAF veteran provided close air support during the NA attack on Blessington, Co. Dublin in July 1922 and by mid-1923 the NA had 27 machines supporting ground operations from bases at Baldonnel, Co. Dublin and Fermoy, Co. Cork.

Collins also established a special plain-clothes intelligence unit, the Criminal Investigation Department (CID), to carry out the sorts of operations conducted by the DMP G Division, Special Branch and Army Intelligence during the Anglo-Irish War. However, it was more commonly known as Oriel House after its Dublin HQ. Its personnel were drawn from the NA and ex-policemen, like Neligan, and during the Civil War they arrested over 500 Irregulars and compiled files on 2,500 others. Commanded by Capt Pat Moynihan, Oriel House gained a reputation for brutality and killing Republican suspects. In all, four of its members were killed by the IRA during the Civil War.

Oriel House operated exclusively within the *Saorstát*, while officers from the NA intelligence branch, G2, carried out operations in the UK as well. G2 had close links with Britain's MI5 and Alfred Cope, the British Assistant Under Secretary in Dublin, even obtained firearms permits for G2 agents operating in Britain. On 22 August 1922 the police element of Oriel House split from NA control and became the Civic Guards' CID.

The Civic Guard

Thanks to the efforts of the IRA during the Anglo-Irish War and the withdrawal of the RIC after the Treaty, law and order had broken down in much of Ireland. The situation was further aggravated by the competing ambitions of the Republicans and *Saorstát* to be recognized as the legitimate Government. As a result the *Saorstát* established the Civic Guard in February 1922. From the start the influence of the RIC on the new force was apparent, despite its adoption of more conventional blue police uniforms; even its first recruit, P. J. Kerrigan, was an ex-RIC constable and Irish Guardsman.

The Civic Guard was, like its predecessor the RIC, a national police force commanded by a Commissioner based in the old RIC depot in Phoenix Park, Dublin. While the DMP continued to police Dublin, the Guard was given the task of policing the rest of the *Saorstát* and, where local circumstances allowed, the Guard occupied vacated RIC barracks.

Administratively the Guard adopted the divisional structure of the RIC, with the obvious exception of Ulster, and between February 1922 and August 1923 more than 180 ex-members of the RIC joined, including 14 who were given the rank of Superintendent or higher.

Although initially armed, the Civic Guard played little part in the Civil War, being overshadowed by the NA, and in September 1922 it was disarmed and renamed *An Garda Síochána* – the Irish police's current title – in August 1923. The DMP was absorbed by the *Garda* on 5 April 1925.

THE IRISH CIVIL WAR

OUTBREAK: THE ANGLO-IRISH PEACE AND THE REPUBLICANS

Although the ceasefire of July 1921 effectively brought to an end the phase of hostilities known as the Anglo-Irish War, few realized it at the time. Both the British security forces and the IRA saw it as a breathing space to re-arm, gather intelligence and limber up for the next round.

During the London peace negotiations in the autumn and winter of 1921 the British Prime Minister, Lloyd George, continually pressured the Irish negotiators with threats of renewed violence on a scale hitherto unseen. Lloyd George wanted a swift resolution to the peace talks and did not really seem to care how Ireland was governed as long as it retained the monarchy and remained within the Empire, supporting British strategic interests in the Atlantic.

Collins and Griffith had to gamble that Lloyd George was bluffing about renewing hostilities. At best the IRA had achieved a military stalemate and Collins admitted that he 'recognized our inability to beat the British out of Ireland'. If the British were bluffing then so were the Irish. Lloyd George gave Collins no opportunity to refer the document back to Dublin for approval.

The choice was simple: was it to be war or peace? Lloyd George, ever the consummate politician, had called Collins' bluff and Collins had no choice but to fold. Consequently, outclassed and outmanoeuvred, the Irish delegates signed the Anglo-Irish Treaty at 2.10 a.m. on 6 December 1921. Prophetically Collins even quipped that he was signing his own death warrant.

In essence the Treaty confirmed the partition of Ireland enshrined in the 1920 Government of Ireland Act and its provisions applied almost exclusively to the

Kevin O'Higgins TD. Sinn Fein activist during the Anglo-Irish War and Provisional Government Minister for Home Affairs. He was a bitter enemy of the anti-Treaty Republicans and a fierce critic of the National Army's conduct of military and policing operations. He was assassinated by the IRA in 1927. (Corbis)

26 counties of what is now the Irish Republic. As far as Northern Unionists were concerned the 1920 Act was the final settlement of the issue of Home Rule and, much to de Valera's chagrin, they refused to take part in the negotiations, despite Lloyd George's efforts.

The Treaty also ensured that the new Irish Free State or *Saorstát Éireann* retained the King as head of state. Erskine Childers, the Anglo-Irish secretary to the Irish negotiators and ardent Republican, was horrified that '... Irish Ministers would be the King's Ministers' and worse still for Republicans, the *Saorstát* would be a Dominion within the British Empire and Commonwealth. Famously Collins said that it might not be '... the ultimate freedom that all nations aspire and develop, but the freedom to achieve freedom'.

Republicans objected to the oath of allegiance contained in the Treaty. Ironically, both Collins and de Valera had been involved in drafting the oath and as oaths of allegiance went it was fairly innocuous. It required '... allegiance to the constitution of the Irish Free State' and to be '... faithful to HM King George V' whereas Britons swore '... by Almighty God that I will be faithful and bear true allegiance to HM King George' alone. Loyalty was primarily to the constitution of the *Saorstát* and Collins had even gained the approval of the IRB before accepting it.

Ultimately the Treaty was a compromise and Collins and its supporters knew it. De Valera was furious when he heard that it had been signed without his consent. Both the Irish historians and commentators Ryle Dwyer and P. S. O'Hegarty have claimed that de Valera's objections had much more to do with wounded pride than his Republican beliefs. According to Irish historian Ronan Fanning, his objections were more about it being someone else's compromise rather than his own.

The Treaty also left the British in control of three naval bases within the Free State. Childers thought that this was 'the most humiliating condition that can be inflicted on any nation claiming to be free'. It also left British troops in Dublin as insurance in case anything went wrong.

The Dáil began debating the Treaty on 14 December and finally voted by a narrow margin of 64 to 57 in favour of it. In many respects the Dáil was probably not the best place for the debate as virtually all its members were dedicated Republicans. That is no doubt why the debates were so bitter and personal rivalries soon bubbled to the surface. Many opponents to the Treaty felt that the Republic's Minister of Defence, Cathal Brugha's vitriolic attacks on Collins cost them key votes, while similarly bitter exchanges also ensued between Childers and Griffith.

De Valera claimed that if he 'wanted to know what the Irish people wanted I only had to examine my heart', ably demonstrating what historian Charles Townshend described as a Robespierrist tendency to tell people what they were thinking rather than ask them. He also claimed that regardless of the debate the Dáil had the authority to dissolve neither itself nor the Republic, which was what would effectively happen if the Treaty were accepted.

Some believed it a betrayal of everything they had fought for since 1916 and Liam Mellows, the IRA's Director of Supplies during the war, was adamant that the delegates '… had no power to sign away the rights of Ireland and the Irish Republic'. In the minds of many, Irish independence and the Irish Republic had become one and the same thing and they could not conceive of one without the other.

The problem faced by Republicans was that not all their countrymen felt as passionately about 'the Republic' as they did. Sinn Féin's landslide victory in the 1918 General Election had been as much about protests against the introduction of conscription and the lack of a credible Nationalist alternative after the collapse of the IPP as it was an endorsement of the Irish revolution.

Michael Collins speaks to a throng at College Green on the day of the official launch of the Irish Free State. (© Hulton-Deutsch Collection/Corbis)

It is important to remember that Sinn Féin in 1918 was not the same unitary party as its modern namesake but an umbrella organization for a whole host of constitutional Nationalist as well as 'physical force' Republicans. Its main unifying factor had been the process of undoing the 1801 Act of Union, so, while these differences had been relatively contained during the Anglo-Irish War, within days of the Treaty's signature the threads that bound it together began to unravel.

By Christmas 1921 24 Southern county councils had passed resolutions in support of the Treaty. Nevertheless, between the Dáil vote and the General Election in June 1922 opponents of the Treaty attempted to prevent any sort of plebiscite on the issue. Rory O'Connor even implied that the IRA should stage a *coup d'état* and impose its own authority if the politicians failed to defend the Republic. None of this did anything to reassure the British Government of the stability of the fledgling *Saorstát*.

Nor did it reassure the Unionists in Northern Ireland. Many Northern Protestants saw Northern Catholics as the enemy within and according to Peter Hart sectarian violence forced at least 8,000 people from their homes in Belfast alone. Meanwhile the IRA's campaign continued in what some Republicans called the 'occupied six counties' of Ulster. There was also sectarian violence in the South but not to the same degree as in the North.

In response to the anti-Catholic violence taking place in the North, Sinn Féin and the IRA instigated a boycott of Northern businesses known as the 'Belfast Boycott'. Sir Edward Carson had once commented that 'Ulster might be wooed by sympathetic understanding – she can never be coerced.' The boycott and attacks on Southern Protestants did nothing to reassure Northern Loyalists and simply reinforced their fears of becoming subsumed in a Catholic Irish state.

In January and March 1922 Collins and the Unionist leader Sir James Craig made a series of deals that became known as the 'Craig–Collins Agreements', which sought to end the boycott in the South and sectarian violence in the North. The agreements failed to achieve their goals and Unionist obfuscation of the boundary commission established under the Treaty ensured that many issues surrounding the border were unresolved until the 1998 Good Friday Agreement.

Northern Unionists had not wanted devolution in 1914 or 1920 but if Britain was imposing a local Parliament on them then Loyalists were determined that it would make reunification with the South impossible and serve as a '...Protestant Parliament for a Protestant people'.

Some even saw Dominion status for 'Ulster' as the answer and in December 1922, at the height of the Southern Civil War, Northern Ireland formally voted to reject membership of the *Saorstát*, as the Anglo-Irish Treaty offered them the opportunity to do.

For the IRA the truce was a mixed blessing. Some Republicans had convinced themselves that they had taken on the British Empire and won; however, both Collins and Mulcahy knew how weak the IRA's military capability really was and how close they had come to defeat. They were also well aware that Britain's commitment of more than 200,000 troops to suppress an insurgency in Iraq ensured that Ireland was a sideshow for the War Office.

Once hostilities ended IRA ranks swelled with what veteran guerrillas sneeringly called 'truciliers' who did not share their dedication to the Republic they had fought and suffered for. On the whole this hardcore of the IRA opposed the Treaty and some, like Tom Barry, saw renewal of hostilities as the only way to save Republican unity.

Shortly before de Valera resigned as President of the Dáil in January 1922 as a protest against the Anglo-Irish Treaty, GHQ had reassured him that the IRA would support the Government; but in reality it was as divided as Sinn Féin. Collins and Mulcahy supported the Treaty along with Éoin O'Duffy (Deputy Chief of Staff), J. J. O'Connell (Assistant Chief of Staff), Diarmuid O'Hegarty (Director of Organization), Emmet Dalton (Director of Training) and Piaras Béalsaí (Director of Publicity).

Fortunately for the *Saorstát* those staff officers who declared against the Treaty – Rory O'Connor (Director of Engineering), Liam Mellows (Director of Purchases), Seán Russell (Director of Munitions) and Seamus O'Donovan (Director of Chemicals) – did not head the operations and training branches of the IRA. This lack of expertise would become apparent as the Civil War progressed.

8 May 1922 pro- and anti-Treaty IRA officers meet at the Mansion House to attempt to avert the looming civil war. Left to right: Gen Seán MacEoin, Seán Moylan, Gen Éoin O'Duffy, Liam Lynch, Gearóid O'Sullivan and Liam Mellows. (George Morrison)

Seán MacEntee, a Belfast-born anti-Treaty Republican politician, warned the Dáil that 'We are now upon the brink of civil war in Ireland. Let there be no mistake about that.' Even opponents of the Treaty like Seán Hegarty came to believe that civil war simply gave the British an excuse for 'coming back in'. Michael Hayes TD was convinced that Collins' and Mulcahy's influence in the IRA was crucial and many men went pro-Treaty simply because it was 'good enough for Mick'.

With pro- and anti-Treaty elements of the IRA facing each other in an uneasy peace the Provisional Government's solution to the rift in the IRA was to create the National Army. On 16 January 1922 it made its first public appearance, when men of what would become the Dublin Guards paraded in Dublin Castle and Collins received the keys from the Catholic Lord Lieutenant, Edmund Bernard FitzAlan-Howard, 1st Viscount FitzAlan of Derwent, formally ending 800 years of 'British' rule.

Meanwhile the British were handing over their bases across Southern Ireland to IRA units regardless of their allegiances. Consequently the Dublin-based Provisional

In the north, sectarian violence plagued relations between Ulster's Catholic and Protestant communities. British troops guard a barricade on the Newtownards Road in an attempt to separate the two communities and curb further rioting. (© Bettmann/Corbis)

Government did not control large areas of Ireland 'beyond the Pale' and low-level IRA violence continued in some areas, with more than 52 RIC members being killed in the first half of 1922. Of more concern was the fact that some IRA units began publicly to reject the authority of GHQ and Griffith's Provisional Government in Dublin.

The split in the IRA was exacerbated when in March and April 1922 a series of anti-Treaty Army Conventions voted to establish a new Executive and Army Council headed by Liam Lynch as Chief of Staff. Beyond a desire to launch an IRA offensive against the North (which would in fact be launched in May), it seemed there were no unifying factors left.

On 13 April 1922, 180 men from the 1st and 2nd Battalions, Dublin No. 1 Brigade IRA under Comdt Patrick O'Brien occupied the Four Courts in central Dublin accompanied by most of the members of the Republican Executive. The British saw the occupation as a breach of the Treaty and began planning to remove O'Brien's men even if such action ran the risk of reuniting the IRA.

The following month, in a vain attempt to paper over the cracks in the Republican movement and maintain unity, Collins and de Valera made a pact in the run-up to the 1922 General Election. They agreed that a panel of pro- and anti-Treaty Sinn Féin candidates would stand with the aim of creating a coalition government after the election.

The British declared that the pact was a breach of the Treaty and demanded that the Irish should stop trying to avoid implementing it. In the end Collins repudiated the pact two days before the 16 June election and the Provisional Government published its constitution on polling day. The result was an overwhelming vote in favour of the Treaty and by implication the new *Saorstát* constitution.

Of the 26 counties, 78 per cent voted to accept a flawed peace rather than see a continuation of the Troubles, with only 22 per cent of the vote going to anti-Treaty candidates. The majority of the Irish diaspora within the British Empire and more crucially the USA were also happy to accept the Treaty as an end to the war. The loss of Irish-America was a critical blow to the Republican movement's ability to overturn the Treaty by force.

In March de Valera had warned that if the electorate ratified the Treaty then the IRA would 'have to wade through Irish blood' to achieve freedom. The election results therefore reinforced the pro-Treaty position. The situation was made worse by the

JUNE 1922 IRISH GENERAL ELECTION RESULTS					
Party	Sinn Fein	Labour Party	Farmers' Party	Independents	Total
Pro-Treaty	58	17	7	10	92
Anti-Treaty	36	-	-	-	36
Total number of seats in the 3rd Dáil					128

assassination of Field Marshal Sir Henry Wilson MP by the London IRA on 22 June. Although there is no evidence linking Collins to the shooting it was widely believed by many IRA that he, not the Executive, had authorized the slaying. The truth is that we will probably never know who ordered the attack as his killers, who had anti-Treaty sympathies, insisted at their trial that they had acted on their own initiative.

The British chose to blame the Executive for killing Wilson because as a Unionist MP and military adviser to the Northern Government many Republicans blamed him for the sectarian violence in Belfast. Nothing could have been further from the truth, however, for despite being an Irish Protestant Wilson was very critical of the USC and felt that sectarian violence undermined the Unionist cause.

His death placed Griffith's Provisional Government under increased pressure to act if British intervention was to be avoided, and they finally made the decision to clear the Four Courts. NA troops under Brig Paddy Daly cordoned off the Courts, capturing Leo Henderson on 27 June in Dublin. This provoked the Executive to order the kidnapping of J. J. 'Ginger' O'Connell as a reprisal.

The kidnapping backfired, as the Executive underestimated O'Connell's popularity with NA troops. Mulcahy had, however, already decided on 26 June to attack the courts and O'Connell's kidnapping simply provided a pretext. At 4 a.m. on 28 June 1922 the occupants of the courts were given an ultimatum to surrender. Thirty minutes later the Civil War began.

THE FIGHTING: CONFLICT IN DUBLIN AND THE PROVINCES

The period formally remembered as the Irish Civil War began at 4.30 a.m. on 28 June 1922, when 1916 veteran and now NA officer Capt Johnny Doyle, after one misfire and a hefty kick to the breech of his 18-pdr gun, fired the first shell at the Four Courts. However, tensions had been mounting for several months. This shot was not the first to be exchanged between rival members of the IRA since the signing of the Treaty and an uneasy standoff had developed in Limerick in March after inconclusive skirmishes.

Despite low-level violence outside Dublin, many believed that war could be avoided and, according to anti-Treaty IRA Army Council member Florrie O'Donoghue, 'no plans existed on either side for conducting it'. Mulcahy had hoped that by creating an army loyal to the *Saorstát* he could draw the teeth of the IRA, while Republicans believed that as long as the 'Ulster Question' remained unresolved their former comrades could be won over, especially if the British could be provoked into action.

Only the British seemed to believe that conflict was possible and planned accordingly. In the first six months of 1922 they had supplied more than 3,504 grenades, 11,900 rifles, 4,200 revolvers and 79 machine guns to the NA, with sufficient ammunition to service them, and maintained 5,000 troops in Dublin. Unbeknown to the British, Collins redirected many of these weapons to ensure that the IRA in Northern Ireland was sufficiently equipped to prosecute operations against the Stormont regime.

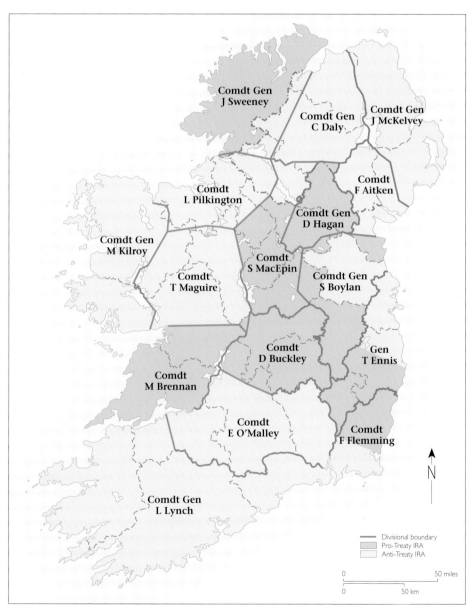

Ireland was divided up into divisional areas by the IRA. Whether the division declared for or against the Treaty depended heavily upon the loyalties of the divisional and brigade commanders and their relationship with Michael Collins.

An Anti-Treaty IRA patrol on Grafton Street during the early stages of the Dublin fighting in the summer of 1922. Their appearance is typical of the Irregulars during the civil war. (Hulton-Getty Library)

Despite upping the ante by occupying the Four Courts and several other locations in Dublin, Republican forces failed to seize the initiative, squandering the only opportunity they had to win a war against the *Saorstát* and their British backers. To win they needed a quick victory, one that would rapidly neutralize the NA and its long-term materiél advantage. In short, nothing less than a *coup de main* against their former comrades would suffice.

Instead they chose to virtually replicate the militaristic gesture of Easter 1916 and seize key points in Dublin, then simply sit back and await the consequences. With most of the rebel Executive's members holed up in the Four Courts they were unable to direct operations in Munster or any other Republican stronghold. It was a failing that characterized the strategic direction of their operations throughout the war.

In essence the military conduct of the Irish Civil War can be divided into three distinct phases. The first, from 28 June to 5 July 1922, was almost a rerun of Easter week 1916. The second, from 5 July until 19 August 1922, was dominated by *Saorstát* assaults on Republican strongholds in the west and south of Ireland, while the third and final phase, which ended in May 1923, saw the IRA revert to the guerrilla tactics used against the British.

Unlike the IRA of 1919–21 the Civil War IRA lacked popular support, which eventually led its COS, Frank Aiken, to issue an order on 24 May 1923 for his men to dump arms and go home. Although this would mark an effective end to the Irish Civil War, few realized it at the time – much as with the Truce of 1921. Although the pro-Treaty faction had won, it was a far from decisive victory and, to misappropriate the words of T. S. Eliot's poem 'The Hollow Men', the conflict had ended 'Not with a bang but a whimper'.

Dublin, 28 June–5 July 1922

The Republicans' lack of strategic thought was exemplified by the presence of 12 of the Executive's 16 members in the Four Courts, including COS Joe McKelvey, Rory O'Connor and Liam Mellows abrogating their command responsibilities and acting as common soldiers. Contained within a small area of Dublin they were unable to direct operations elsewhere.

Comdt O'Brien worked out plans for the defence of the Four Courts with Ernie O'Malley (OC 2nd Southern Division) and Oscar Traynor (OC Dublin No. 1 Brigade). Since April they had been fortifying the complex with sandbags, trenches and mines but O'Malley knew that he needed at least another 70 men to defend it properly.

Equipped with a number of automatic weapons as well as rifles and a Rolls-Royce armoured car, 'The Mutineer', the Republicans sat back and waited. The NA negated much of The Mutineer's value by blocking the exits to the Four Courts with two disabled Lancia armoured cars. Outgunned, O'Brien planned to hold the Four Courts and some of its neighbouring buildings, while sympathizers from outside Dublin surrounded the encircling Provisional Government troops.

The flaw in the plan was that in order to maintain the moral high ground no coherent orders for a Republican offensive on Dublin were issued. The Executive wanted the Provisional Government's forces to fire the first shot and thus bear the blame for starting the war. In the end all this course of action achieved was to give the NA a free hand to clear Republican forces out of the capital.

To counter the Republican threat in Dublin the Provisional Government had roughly 4,000 troops, drawn from Daly's Dublin Guards and Gen Tom Ennis' 2nd Eastern Division. Their cordon around the Four Courts took in the Four Courts Hotel, Chancery Place, Bridewell Prison, Jameson's Distillery and St Michan's Church. In addition two field guns borrowed from the British were deployed south of the Liffey on Winetavern Street under the command of Maj Gen Dalton.

Dalton's experience in World War I had taught him that 'the use of these guns would have a very demoralizing effect upon a garrison unused to artillery fire'.

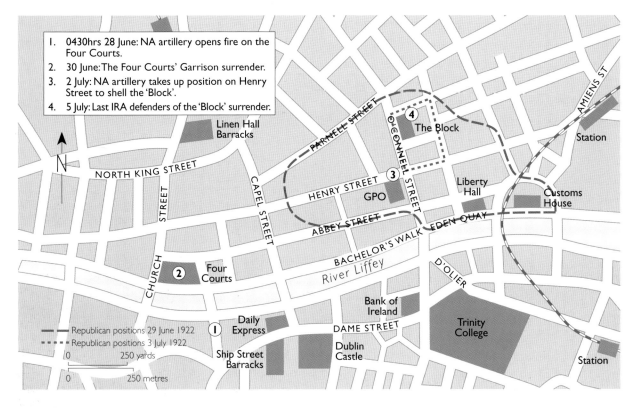

1. 0430hrs 28 June: NA artillery opens fire on the Four Courts.
2. 30 June: The Four Courts' Garrison surrender.
3. 2 July: NA artillery takes up position on Henry Street to shell the 'Block'.
4. 5 July: Last IRA defenders of the 'Block' surrender.

Republican positions 29 June 1922
Republican positions 3 July 1922

The battle for Dublin bore some marked similarities to that which took place in 1916.

His gunners, however, lacked training and the meagre supply of shrapnel shells from the British made him conclude erroneously that 'as a destructive agent against the Four Courts building [the guns] would be quite insignificant'. He also saw the guns as a morale booster for his own men and dreaded running out of ammunition.

As the fighting that had started with Doyle's first shot on 28 June progressed, every effort was made to locate ex-British gunners to service the guns and at one point Dalton, an ex-infantryman, was reduced to laying and firing one of the guns himself. Admittedly this was not too difficult a task as they were being fired over open sights across the Liffey into the Four Courts. Unfortunately this meant that his gunners were well within rifle range of the enemy and on occasion shells punched their way through the building and landed in the grounds of the British HQ just outside Phoenix Park. During the fighting Dalton met regularly with the British commander, Gen Macready, and petitioned him for additional guns and ammunition.

Alfred Cope believed that if the NA failed to clear the Courts then the *Saorstát* would be finished. The British feared that the longer the indecisive assault on the Republicans continued, just as in 1916, the greater the likelihood that the public would begin to sympathize with them. Churchill knew that direct British military intervention would be fatal for the Provisional Government and issued instructions to 'tell Collins to ask for any assistance he requires and report to me any difficulty that has been raised by the military'.

From the start the NA attack on the Four Courts did not go well and according to Cope it was 'not a battle. Rory is in the Four Courts. Free Staters are in the houses opposite each firing at the other hundreds of rounds with probably remarkably few hits. A few hundred yards away the people carry on their ordinary business.'

Although the southern wing of the Four Courts had sustained damage it was insufficient to break the defenders, causing the British to offer heavy artillery and close air support sporting Irish colours to finish the job. Machine-gun fire from The Mutineer was a constant nuisance to Dalton's gunners and they were forced to take cover behind a couple of parked Lancia armoured cars.

A crowd gathers on the O'Connell Bridge to watch the fighting in O'Connell Street in July 1922. 'The Block' is in the distance on the right-hand side of the street. (Corbis)

In the end a supply of British shells from Carrickfergus improved the effectiveness of Dalton's guns. The British had initially supplied 20 shrapnel shells per gun and Dalton was worried that he would run out of ammunition. Macready duly handed over two more guns and 50 extra shrapnel shells which he insisted were 'all we had left, simply to make noise through the night', as Dalton was afraid that his men would lose heart and drift off if the guns fell silent.

Elsewhere in Dublin there were attempts to mobilize IRA units sympathetic to the Executive's cause. Traynor's Dublin No. 1 Brigade mobilized on the evening of 27 June but disbanded later that night. This was not really such a surprise when the best officers in the brigade were either pro-Treaty or already holed up in the Four Courts. When fighting did break out IRA veteran Emmet Humphreys recalled that 'there seemed no question of coordinating our operations with adjoining companies or with the battalion as a whole.'

Not all the Executive's members were bottled up with O'Connor, however. Tom Barry was in custody, having been arrested while trying to join him in the Four Courts disguised as a woman. Lynch had set up his headquarters in the Clarence Hotel and on 28 June made his way to Kingsbridge Station, where he was arrested by NA troops but inexplicably released on Mulcahy's orders. He headed west and set up a Republican HQ in Limerick.

Despite envisaging a guerrilla campaign, Traynor had been convinced by his supporters in Tipperary and Belfast that holding part of central Dublin was the best course of action. On 29 June, while Lynch was establishing his HQ in Limerick, Traynor occupied the Gresham, Crown, Granville, and Hammam hotels on the east side of O'Connell Street, which became known as 'The Block'.

Republican elements of Dublin No. 1 Brigade also occupied Barry's Hotel in north Dublin and several buildings on the South Circular Road, York Street, the Kildare Street Club and Dolphin's Barn. There was no military logic to the positions and, as Humphreys pointed out, little mutual support. It was at this point that de Valera, Brugha, Stack and Seán T. O'Kelly came out in favour of the Executive and joined those occupying O'Connell Street.

De Valera rejoined his old unit, 3rd Battalion, as an ordinary volunteer and issued a statement that '… at the bidding of the English Irishmen today are shooting down, on the streets of our capital, brother Irishmen. In Rory O'Connor and his comrades lives the unbought indomitable soul of Ireland.' The *Irish Times* reported that de Valera 'has associated himself openly with the men firing on Irish homes'.

Privately de Valera, the sole surviving leader of the 1916 Rising, had grave concerns about the fighting and was in favour of a peace initiative proposed by the Lord Mayor of Dublin and the Labour Party. Brugha and Stack were not so keen, while de Valera's

30 June 1922, a National Army 18-pdr gun on the junction of Winetavern St and Merchant's Quay fires on rebels occupying the Four Courts. Although the NA had few guns, its use of artillery significantly undermined the moral of anti-government troops during the Civil War. (© Bettmann/Corbis)

refusal to take a leading role ensured that his views were marginalized. Throughout the Civil War the Republican political and military leaderships failed to coordinate their efforts, leading ultimately to disaster.

The piecemeal nature of the Republican defence allowed the NA to concentrate its efforts against the Four Courts almost unhindered by the IRA stationed elsewhere in the city even though, according to Gen MacMahon, the NA troops outside the Four Courts were exhausted. Within the complex the situation was even worse. O'Malley, who was inside the Four Courts, later wrote that '... it seemed a haphazard pattern of war. A garrison without proper food, surrounded on all sides, bad communications between their inside posts, faulty defences, girls bringing ammunition from attackers, relieving forces on our side concentrated on the wrong side of the widest street in the capital.' Cut off and without support, their position was increasingly hopeless.

By 30 June the NA troops had recovered from their initial failure to storm the Four Courts and, bayonets fixed, forced their way into the complex. In the end it was a short sharp fight that culminated in what Tim Pat Coogan described as one of the greatest acts of vandalism ever perpetrated in Dublin, when Republicans detonated two pre-planted mines under the Public Records Office – although Hopkinson blames NA shelling for detonating the mines.

NA soldiers use a charabanc bus as a barricade during the battle of Dublin.(© Hulton-Deutsch Collection/Corbis)

A column of smoke rose over 200ft in the air as the ensuing fire consumed centuries-old papers. For hours fragments of ancient documents floated over Dublin and the event led Churchill to write to Collins after the fighting saying that, 'The archives of the Four Courts may be scattered but the title-deeds of Ireland are safe.'

Even faced with a hopeless situation Mellows and O'Connor wanted to fight on in the spirit of Patrick Pearse's 1916 call for a blood sacrifice. Heroic though it may have been, the defence of the Four Courts had been poorly planned and organized from the start. Seán Smith later claimed that even though they could plainly see *Saorstát* soldiers taking up positions around their own in the Four Courts they did nothing, as 'we had no orders to fire on them'.

According to Ben Doyle, another Republican survivor, 'the whole thing was taken in a half-hearted slipshod manner'. The tidal ebb and flow of the Liffey made escape through the sewers impossible and in the end Traynor overruled the Executive's insistence upon a last stand and ordered his men in the Four Courts to surrender. Only O'Brien seemed to realize that it was vital to get the members of the Executive out of the Four Courts. O'Malley and Seán Lemass managed to get out through Jameson's Distillery but O'Connor and Mellows surrendered.

With the battle for the Four Courts over, the Provisional Government shifted its main effort to isolating O'Connell Street. Republican efforts in the rest of the city proved to be of little value and by 3 July most of their positions south of the Liffey had fallen. Thus, free from the danger of being attacked in the rear the *Saorstát's* forces massed around the Republican positions in 'The Block' to administer the *coup de grâce*.

Fighting in a built-up area is one of the most complicated, manpower-intensive and bloody operations that any soldier can be called upon to perform and requires levels of discipline, determination and training that neither the NA nor Republican forces possessed. Instead of fighting from house to house and room to room with grenade, bayonet and rifle butt, both sides settled down to sniping and inconclusive firefights.

Time, however, was on the side of the Provisional Government and as Republican manpower and ammunition dwindled that of the NA increased and, much as the British had done in 1916, they relied upon artillery to shell the Republicans into submission. For the second time in six years the guns of its own government's army flattened central Dublin. One by one the Republicans evacuated their positions as concentrated artillery and machine-gun fire rendered them untenable. The IRA was accused of using Red Cross vehicles as fire positions and Daly, no shrinking violet himself, claimed they were the 'dirtiest lot of fighters he ever saw'. The situation was made worse when NA Comdt O'Connor was fired upon while attempting to accept the surrender of the forces in the Hammam Hotel on 5 July.

Free State troops fight
through a building during the
street battle for Dublin in July
1922. (National Library of
Ireland)

In many ways it was a sign of things to come. Even before the end came, Republicans trapped in O'Connell Street knew it was only a matter of time before they would have to accept defeat. Several Republican leaders, including de Valera, were smuggled out across the river to Mount Street, which is a fair indication of how lax the cordon was and how poor the discipline of the NA soldiery was. Those who could do so began to leave Dublin and seek shelter in the Republican heartlands to the south-west.

By 5 July one side of O'Connell Street was in flames from St Mary's Pro-Cathedral to Findlater Place. By late afternoon the only Republican troops left were under the command of Cathal Brugha. Faced with a hopeless situation he ordered his remaining 15 men to surrender and then with suicidal courage ran into the street, gun in hand. The outcome was inevitable and he died of his wounds later that evening in Mater Hospital.

It was estimated that £3–4m of damage had been done to central Dublin, with a butcher's bill of 65 killed and 281 wounded, which compared to the casualties of Easter week 1916 meant that both Dubliners and the combatants had come off lightly. The capture of several key members of the Executive also ensured that the Republican leadership was severely weakened at the start of the Civil War.

Lynch was the only major Republican military leader still at large and he swiftly abandoned the Dublin-centric strategy of O'Connor and the others now languishing in Mountjoy Gaol. Having established his HQ in Limerick he reasserted himself as the COS of Republican forces and ordered his divisional commanders to return to their formations rather than converge on the capital. From here on in the Republicans' war effort would be quite literally beyond the Pale.

5 July–19 August 1922

Again there are parallels between IRA activity outside Dublin in the events of Easter 1916 and June 1922. As in 1916 the forces were divided and confused orders were issued and countermanded. In response to an appeal from Traynor, Mick Sheehan and more than 100 men from south Tipperary occupied Blessington, Co. Dublin on 1 July 1922 with the intent of marching on the capital 15 miles away.

More than 200 men from the South Dublin Brigade and Kildare IRA as well as escapees from the fighting in Dublin soon joined them. Traynor had confused the issue by telling Sheehan 'neither to march on Dublin nor defend Blessington if attacked'. By the time he and O'Malley arrived in Blessington on 6 July he was convinced that a counter-attack on Dublin was impossible with the troops at hand and ordered them to revert to guerrilla tactics. His orders were probably recognition of a degenerating situation and on 8 July a Republican report recommended that the men dump arms. O'Malley took some men with him to occupy towns in Co. Wexford but many others simply went home. The NA response to Sheehan's seizure of Blessington was to dispatch columns from the Curragh, Dublin and the coast to converge on the town.

IRA Irregulars begin building barricades in Carrick-on-Suir, Co. Tipperary, 20 July 1922 in anticipation of Gen Prout's assault. (George Morrison)

Major engagements, June–
August 1922. The fighting
was concentrated in Dublin
and the south-east.

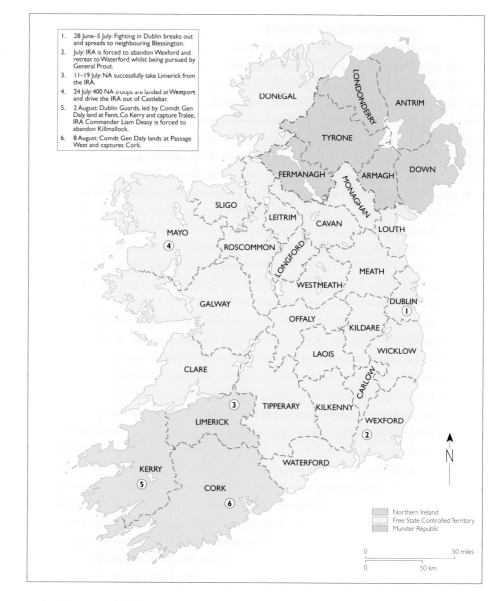

1. 28 June–5 July: Fighting in Dublin breaks out and spreads to neighbouring Blessington.
2. July: IRA is forced to abandon Wexford and retreat to Waterford whilst being pursued by General Prout.
3. 11–19 July: NA successfully take Limerick from the IRA.
4. 24 July: 400 NA troops are landed at Westport and drive the IRA out of Castlebar.
5. 2 August: Dublin Guards, led by Comdt Gen Daly land at Fenit, Co Kerry and capture Tralee, IRA Commander Liam Deasy is forced to abandon Killmallock.
6. 8 August: Comdt Gen Daly lands at Passage West and captures Cork.

Northern Ireland
Free State Controlled Territory
Munster Republic

0   50 miles

0   50 km

At Brittas and Ballymore Eustace they captured 73 Irregulars with barely a shot fired and by the time they reached Blessington the fight had gone out of its defenders. Traynor believed that many of his men were 'completely out of their element'. The town was abandoned and Brig Andy McDonnell, Gerry Boland and around 100 others were taken prisoner.

The Republican failure to defend Blessington sapped the morale of its fighting men and virtually became the template of their efforts in other towns. Again and again they would abandon strategically vital towns, almost without a shot, when faced with an NA attack. Perhaps the experience of guerrilla warfare against the British made many of the IRA temperamentally unsuited to positional warfare, while a complete lack of strategic guidance from the Executive could not have helped.

For the NA, Blessington also provided a template for what was to come. Each of the columns dispatched to retake the town was supplied with artillery, armoured cars and automatic weapons. The nascent Irish Air Corps even flew sorties in support of the offensive and although the British supplied the NA with only nine field guns, artillery support featured in almost every major attack.

In fact the Republicans' lack of artillery vexed Lynch, who spent a disproportionate amount of effort in attempting to source guns and instructors from Germany. He even made contact with an obscure German politician by the name of Adolf Hitler in his pursuit of such weapons. Lynch's fixation with artillery betrayed his failure to grasp the realities of the situation. While the NA lacked trained gunners they had at least access to British assistance and both Collins and Dalton actively sought to recruit British Army veterans.

The Republicans, however, did not enjoy such expertise and when Aiken finally captured a field gun at Dundalk on 14 August he was forced to abandon it because no one knew how to operate it. Even if they had retained it, it is difficult to imagine what useful purpose it would have served in a guerrilla war.

O'Malley's activities in Co. Wexford lacked strategic vision and proved of little value when he abandoned towns in the face of Government troops sent to confront him

NA troops in Claregalway, Co. Galway, 20 July 1922. Supply problems ensured that during the early stages of the conflict the Provisional Government's soldiery lacked the appearance of a regular army. (George Morrison)

under the command of Maj Gen Prout. The IRA made a brief stand in Waterford but when Capt Ned O'Brien secured the quays on 20 July, allowing Prout to ferry men and artillery into the town, the Republicans surrendered.

Despite their inability to hold static defences, on 9 July Liam Deasy, the anti-Treaty OC 1st Division IRA, claimed that Republican forces were establishing a defensive line from Waterford to Limerick; however, as Hopkinson points out, this never really existed except on paper. Its dubious value was further undermined when Dan Breen and 400 Republicans lost Carrick-on-Suir to Prout's 600-man column on 3 August, effectively abandoning Co. Tipperary to the Government.

In his analysis of the conventional phase of the Civil War, Paul V. Walsh observed that, with the notable exception of NA Maj Gen Murphy outside Kilmallock, none of the commanders on either side attempted to replicate the trench warfare that typified World War I. That is perhaps what makes the Republican emphasis on a defensive line so strange, especially as they would have been incapable of holding such a line even if they had managed to construct one.

The fact that few of the World War I veterans on either side had been professional soldiers may also have contributed to their willingness to embrace new technology and adopt innovative tactics. Consequently extensive use was made of mobile forces to impose authority quickly upon areas that indicated a willingness to look forward rather than back for operational solutions.

That does not mean that the Irish forces were blessed with military visionaries whose ideas augured *Blitzkrieg* with its mobile all-arms battlegroups. The Republican use of armoured vehicles to attack Bruree, or the NA amphibious attacks on Munster, were products of expediency rather than of coherent doctrine and the lessons identified were rapidly forgotten after the war.

Lack of a coherent Republican strategy beyond trying to re-ignite the Anglo-Irish War and poor leadership ensured that the Provisional Government seized the initiative. Both Collins and Mulcahy knew that the British would only withdraw their troops from Southern Ireland if they believed that the Provisional Government had the situation under control. To that end Collins needed a rapid victory and that dictated the tempo of NA operations. Even before the outbreak of violence in Dublin it was obvious that Limerick would be strategically vital in any future conflict. Lynch established his GHQ there on 29 June and the NA commander in the city, Comdt Gen Michael Brennan, OC 1st Western Division, believed that 'whoever held Limerick held the south and the west'.

When the local IRA commander Comdt Liam Forde repudiated GHQ's authority on 18 February, Mulcahy ordered Brennan to occupy the city with his pro-Treaty IRA. Shots were exchanged and it was only the intervention of Lynch and Traynor that

National Army troops occupy Millmount Fort, Drogheda. The fort was originally built by Anglo-Norman invaders in 1172, and after a week of ferocious fighting it fell to the National Army, suffering significant damage.
(© Underwood & Corbis)

The fall of the Munster Republic Army, August 1922. Emmet Dalton's amphibious assault on Co. Cork destroyed the Republican hold on south-west Ireland and made the rebels' defeat inevitable. Sadly, Dalton's brilliant campign has been largely forgotten by the Irish Army and the Irish public in general.

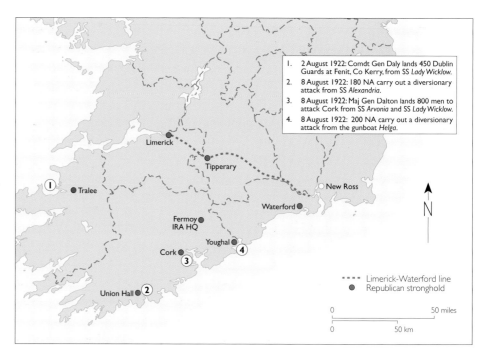

1. 2 August 1922: Comdt Gen Daly lands 450 Dublin Guards at Fenit, Co Kerry, from SS *Lady Wicklow*.
2. 8 August 1922: 180 NA carry out a diversionary attack from SS *Alexandria*.
3. 8 August 1922: Maj Gen Dalton lands 800 men to attack Cork from SS *Arvonia* and SS *Lady Wicklow*.
4. 8 August 1922: 200 NA carry out a diversionary attack from the gunboat *Helga*.

Limerick-Waterford line
● Republican stronghold

averted civil war at that time. The Republicans occupied four barracks and most of the town, while *Saorstát* troops, drawn mostly from Comdt Gen O'Hannigan's 4th Southern Division, occupied the Customs House, the courthouse, the gaol and Williams Street RIC barracks.

Brennan established his HQ in Cruise's Hotel and secured the strategically important Athlunkard Bridge outside the city, deploying his troops to defend the road that led across it into Limerick. If the situation degenerated he would be able to feed troops into the city via the bridge without hindrance from Republican forces.

As a result of the outbreak of violence in Dublin both Brennan and Lynch made some attempts to defuse the situation in Limerick. On 7 July they negotiated a truce, much to the chagrin of Republicans in Munster who believed that it would give the pro-Treaty forces time to consolidate their positions in the city. At 7 p.m. on 11 July the truce broke down when 150 fresh NA reinforcements arrived in the city and Brennan ordered his men to attack the IRA forces garrisoning the Ordnance Barracks.

Lynch withdrew to Clonmel and ten days later Gen Éoin O'Duffy, with a further 1,500 men, four armoured cars and a field gun, arrived to reinforce Brennan. By 19 July the Republicans had been driven out of their positions and Limerick was in Government hands. Casualties had been light with only eight NA soldiers killed and 20 wounded, and 20–30 Republicans killed. More importantly several hundred IRA had been captured and the road to Munster lay open.

The Provisional Government faced similar problems to the British when it came to Republican prisoners, and in order to cope with the sheer volume of captured rebels they were forced to open internment camps at the Curragh, Gormanstown and Kilmainham Gaol. By November Limerick Gaol had more than 800 inmates in a complex designed to hold only 120.

Like the British before them, the Provisional Government decided that internment was counterproductive and on 10 July it released prisoners as part of an amnesty. The Government was resolved to keep captured Republican leaders in prison but it believed that there was little value in keeping the rank and file locked up and was willing to release anyone who signed a pledge not to take up arms against the *Saorstát*.

Although the NA was making considerable headway in counties Dublin, Waterford and Limerick, the Republicans did enjoy limited military success. By 4 July they had effectively cleared pro-Treaty troops out of Co. Cork when they took Skibbereen and Listowel. County Cork had been the heartland of the Republican struggle against the British and although the local IRA was ambivalent about fighting their former comrades they bitterly opposed the Treaty.

This area of south-west Ireland became known as the 'Munster Republic' and it was this area that the vaunted Waterford–Limerick Line was meant to defend. The fall of Limerick was a blow to the Republican cause but Deasy's successful defence, with 2,000 men, against O'Duffy's southward thrust towards Kilmallock helped secure the area and stabilize the situation.

The respite was, however, only temporary and on 23 July the NA launched a fresh offensive. Despite taking Bruff, Murphy was quickly dislodged by the Republicans and 76 of his men surrendered. A swift counter-attack retook the town and on 30 July the Dublin Guards stormed Bruree. These were the NA's best troops and after a five-hour firefight with close artillery support they managed to force Deasy's men out.

On 2 August the Republicans attempted to retake Bruree using three armoured cars but the assault failed. Faced with a degenerating situation Deasy decided to break contact and withdraw towards Kilmallock, pursued by more than 3,000 NA troops supported by armoured cars, artillery and aircraft. His situation was made worse when the NA landed troops on the Kerry and Cork coasts.

By the time Murphy entered Kilmallock on 5 August all that remained was the remnants of Deasy's rearguard and the only major set-piece battle of the war was over. Waterford had fallen to Prout on 17 July and Col Comdt Christopher O'Malley had cleared Co. Mayo of Republicans after landing 400 men, a gun and an armoured car from the SS *Minerva* near Westport on 24 July. The Republicans had abandoned the town without a fight and O'Malley was able to link up with MacÉoin's forces in Castlebar, Co. Mayo. By the end of the month MacÉoin was able to report to Collins that 'in the Midlands Divisions all posts and positions of military value are in our hands'.

Although the Provisional Government wanted a swift victory it knew that it needed to prepare for a protracted struggle. A call to arms was issued on 6 July that put the NA on a formal footing with an establishment of 20,000 men, finally breaking its links with the 'Old' IRA. This would rise to over 58,000 officers and men before the war was over.

In addition Mulcahy abandoned the old IRA divisional boundaries and created five new commands under Dalton (Eastern), MacÉoin (Western), Prout (South-East), O'Duffy (South-West) and O'Connell (Curragh). On 13 July a War Council was established with Collins as Commander-in-Chief and Mulcahy as Minister of Defence and Chief of Staff. Cosgrave became Chairman of the Provisional Government and Minister of Finance while Griffith remained President of the Dáil, which effectively left two pro-Treaty administrations in charge of the state. In fact the confusing situation of who actually was the government of the *Saorstát* was not fully resolved until the Dáil and the Southern Irish Parliament finally merged in September 1922. The blurring of jurisdiction suited Collins, who until his death was effectively the head of the Irish Government.

The fortunes of the Republicans were further dented on 16 July when the NA arrested Frank Aiken, OC 4th Northern Division in Dundalk. Despite his objections to the Treaty he had hoped to avert a split in the IRA by staying neutral and focusing attention on the situation in Northern Ireland. When he finally escaped he reluctantly threw in his lot with the Republicans and eventually succeeded Lynch as IRA Chief of Staff.

Traynor was also captured on 27 July, while Harry Boland was fatally wounded outside the Grand Hotel in Skerries on the 30th. Boland had written earlier in the month to Joe McGarrity of *Clan na Gael* in the United States asking him, with a degree of irony, if he could, 'imagine, me on the run from Mick Collins?' Despite Republican setbacks, Boland had been optimistic about the chances of victory, telling McGarrity that 'I am certain we cannot be defeated even if Collins and his British guns succeed in garrisoning every town in Ireland'.

August saw a renewal of the Provisional Government's offensive in the south-west and a series of victories that were effectively to end the Republicans' conventional military capability. Much as the use of armoured cars and artillery in Waterford and Limerick were to become hallmarks of NA tactics, the amphibious landing in Clew Bay, Co. Mayo, which led to the fall of Westport, was also to act as a template for later, and decisive, NA operations.

Dalton, NA Director of Operations, believed that a frontal attack on the Munster Republic would be a bloody grinding match and suggested to Collins that a series of amphibious landings in counties Kerry and Cork should secure victory. In modern military terms Dalton was suggesting what would now be called a 'manoeuvrist' approach to the situation, as Republican defences faced inland not seaward. By doing something that was unexpected Dalton was able to overrun the 'Munster Republic' with relatively little bloodshed.

Once more the Dublin Guards acted as the shock troops, and 450 of them, led by Daly and supported by the ubiquitous armoured car and field gun, landed from the SS *Lady Wicklow* at Fenit, Co. Kerry on 2 August. By 6.30 p.m. they had driven Republican elements of No. 1 Kerry Brigade IRA out of Tralee for the loss of nine dead and 35 wounded. The next day Col Comdt Michael Hogan left Co. Clare and crossed the Shannon with 250 men at Kilsrush in fishing boats to reinforce Daly's position. The landing was one of the nails in the coffin of Deasy's defence of Kilmallock.

The real blow fell some six days later when Dalton embarked 800 men, two field guns, three armoured cars and several Lancia armoured personnel carriers on the SS *Arvonia*, SS *Lady Wicklow* and SS *Alexandra*, which were commandeered in Dublin

NA troops boarding the SS *Arvonia* in Dublin on Monday 7 August 1922. A Peerless armoured car and a Lancia APC are being loaded onto the deck and sandbags have been stacked along the waist in anticipation of resistance in Cork. (George Morrison)

on Monday 7 August for the purpose of invading Co. Cork. The Welsh crew of the *Arvonia* were extremely unhappy with the situation and its captain was convinced that mines would sink his ship before it reached Cork.

Collins had initially asked the British to hand over the naval base at Queenstown as a springboard for an attack on Cork but they had refused. Instead Vice-Adm Somerville, the Royal Navy officer in command of the Southern Irish coastguard, supplied the Provisional Government with details of defensive minefields in the approaches to Cork. Somerville was later killed by the IRA on 24 March 1936 while living in retirement in his native Co. Cork.

Thus, even without proper charts Dalton's expedition was not as unprepared as the captain of the *Arvonia* believed. Thanks to aerial reconnaissance missions flown by Col C. F. Russell of the Irish Air Corps and information from covert intelligence officers in Cork, Dalton also had a fair idea of where the enemy had deployed its forces.

Although the Treaty barred the *Saorstát* from possessing a navy, as coastal defence remained a British responsibility, the British had handed over several gunboats to the Provisional Government to act as 'revenue cutters'. Among them was the *Helga*, the vessel that had shelled Liberty Hall, the HQ of the ICA, and other central Dublin locations in 1916. The *Helga* accompanied Dalton's expedition, probably making it one of the first operations to be carried out by the Irish Navy. In 1923 *Helga* was renamed *Muirchú*, which means sea-hound in Irish.

According to Coogan the Royal Navy intercepted Dalton's task force and he persuaded them not to compromise him. Considering Somerville's involvement it is more likely that they were dispatched to ensure that Dalton reached the approaches to Cork safely. By 10 p.m. the *Arvonia* was off Roche Point at the mouth to Passage West outside Cork.

It was at this point that *Helga*, with 200 men, a field gun and two Lancia armoured personnel carriers, sailed for Youghal, where they landed without incident. A further 180 men on the *Alexandra* landed at Union Hall, Glandore, in the face of small-arms fire from Republicans in fishing boats. By the time they had managed to unload their armoured car and three armoured personnel carriers, the IRA had melted away and the town was secured.

General John Prout outside his HQ in Carrick-on-Suir, 4 August 1922. Prout had served in the US Army during the Great War. (George Morrison)

Dublin Guards disembark from SS *Lady Wicklow* at Fenit, Co. Kerry on 2 August 1922. (George Morrison)

The troops used at Youghal and Union Hall were for the most part raw recruits, as Dalton kept hold of 456 men drawn from 1st Battalion, Dublin Brigade on the *Arvonia*. He also hoped that the two diversionary landings would distract the Republicans' attention from his main assault on Cork itself. His deception was so successful that when the captain of the *Arvonia* requested a pilot to assist in navigating Passage West one was dispatched without any hint of suspicion of the vessel's true intent. When the pilot became reluctant to help, Dalton's threat to shoot him rapidly overcame his misgivings.

Dalton had originally planned to land at Ford's Wharf but the way was barred by a blockship. This meant that the only other unmined deep-water berth available was the Cork Shipbuilding Company's dock at Passage West, which he reached in the early hours of Tuesday 8 August. At 2 a.m. Capt Frank Friel and 20 men rowed ashore and discovered that the Republicans had abandoned their posts when they had sighted the *Arvonia* and *Lady Wicklow* entering the harbour.

At dawn Dalton landed 150 men, an armoured car and a gun to establish a defensive cordon about half a mile inland from the berth. Once the area had been secured he offloaded the rest of his force. IRA Irregular Frank O'Connor observed that 'Technically, a landing from the sea is supposed to be one of the most difficult military operations, but as we handled the defence it was a walkover'.

Because the Republicans had not anticipated an amphibious attack their troops in the area were, according to IRA Irregular Mick Leahy, the 'poorest type of men'; in the view of Tom Crofts they had 'been in the line fighting for weeks and they had been brought back there without sleep'. Consequently few were in a position to put up a fight when Dalton landed.

Once the initial shock wore off the Republicans swiftly attempted to block Dalton's advance at Rochestown on the road to Cork, where they demolished the bridge leading into the town and fortified several buildings. Exhausted IRA reinforcements were brought in by train from Kilmallock to bolster the defence but, as Crofts had pointed out, these men were already spent.

By the evening of 8 August the IRA had been shoved out of Rochestown and driven back to Old Court Woods to the west. An attempt to turn their flank on 9 August foundered in the face of massed machine-gun and rifle fire from 200 defenders. In the end Capt Friel and Capt Peter Conlon with 12 men secured a *Saorstát* victory by assaulting Cronin's Cottage on Belmonte Hill and both earned instant promotion to commandant.

Although the British only supplied the NA with nine field guns, artillery support featured in every major operation. Here one of Gen Murphy's 18-pdrs is towed over a ruined bridge across the river Maigue, Co. Limerick during the Kilmallock campaign, August 1922. (George Morrison)

Considering the small numbers involved in the battle, casualties were relatively high and seven out of 200 IRA and nine out of 456 NA soldiers were killed. According to Walsh there were also a considerable number of wounded to contend with. Among the IRA dead was a Scot named Ian MacKenzie Kennedy, whom Dalton singled out for his bravery.

Dalton pressed his attack on Thursday 10 August against Douglas on the outskirts of Cork. The battle for Douglas was a confused close-quarter affair involving armoured cars and automatic weapons. Once more Conlon found himself at the point of the spear leading the NA assault and narrowly escaped an IRA ambush when a local woman tipped him off. Supported by eight men he attacked his would-be ambushers, capturing 32 of them. After three days in contact with the enemy Dalton feared that his men would run out of steam and so intended to pause overnight in Douglas. Much to his surprise his officers pressed for him to push on into the city. True to form the Republicans burned their barracks and abandoned Cork. By the evening of 10 August the last Irish city in Republican hands had fallen and the Munster Republic had been overthrown.

While the NA onslaught was underway in Co. Limerick and Co. Cork, Republicans Dinney Lacey and Dan Breen attacked Prout's forces at Redmondstown in south Tipperary on 9 August. Outgunned and subjected to artillery fire, they retreated towards the Nire Valley. On 11 August Lynch abandoned Fermoy, the last Republican stronghold in Co. Cork, to the NA while 200 Government troops under the tactical command of Comdt Tom O'Connor landed at Kenmare.

So sudden was the collapse of Republican resistance that the *Irish Times* reported rather optimistically on 16 August that 'the advance is becoming swift but the retreat, or, as I should prefer to call it, the disappearance is swifter'. Predictions of a Republican collapse proved to be premature and the war would drag on for another eight months or so before it fizzled out.

Despite the fact that the NA had driven the IRA out of every major town in the country O'Duffy reported on 22 August that '… the Irregulars in Cork and Kerry are still intact. Our forces have captured towns, but they have not captured Irregulars and arms on anything like a large scale, and, until that is done, the Irregulars will be capable of guerrilla warfare … Our present position leaves us particularly disposed to guerrilla warfare.'

Almost in recognition of their defeat in open warfare the IRA Adjutant General, Con Moloney, issued an order on 19 August for the IRA to abandon conventional operations and form ASUs not exceeding 35 men to conduct guerrilla attacks. In addition the IRA authorized its men to commandeer Unionist property for the war effort. The final phase of the war had begun.

The guerrilla war, 19 August 1922–24 May 1923

The guerrilla phase was the longest and in many respects the bitterest stage of the Civil War. In all it would last nine months and see an Irish government's frustration manifest itself in a willingness to act ruthlessly.

Although the fall of Cork did much to undermine the Republican cause the Provisional Government suffered a double blow when Griffith died of a brain haemorrhage on 12 August and Collins was killed in an IRA ambush on 22 August at Béal na mBláth, Co. Cork. No one really knows who fired the fatal shot but the most likely candidate is an ex-British soldier, Denis 'Sonny' O'Neill, who was one of the IRA ambushers.

Mulcahy replaced Collins as Commander-in-Chief, while Cosgrave and Kevin O'Higgins provided the civilian leadership of the Provisional Government. All three men envisaged a democratic Ireland with an apolitical army and police serving the Irish people. Consequently all three viewed the Republicans as traitors who sought to destroy their fledgling democracy.

O'Higgins believed that 'soldiers make bad policemen' but had to accept that until the Civic Guard established themselves the state had no alternative but to use the Army to maintain law and order. Ironically, according to Dalton, the Republican guerrillas placed the NA 'in the same position as the British were a little over a year ago'.

Much as the British had before them, the Provisional Government also resorted to harsh legislation to justify their activities against the IRA. The Provisional Government ceased to be 'Provisional' in September 1922 when it oversaw the merger of the Southern Irish Parliament and the Dáil, which became its lower chamber, and approved the *Saorstát* Constitution.

The Senate created by the Government of Ireland Act also continued to act as the upper chamber, providing a forum for Southern Unionists to participate in government. One of its first acts was to pass the Public Safety Act (PSA) giving emergency powers to the NA. By December the *Saorstát* had been formally established in British and Irish law and Tim Healy was appointed Governor-General.

Unlike the British administration the new Dublin Government enjoyed the popular support of the Irish public, so when its forces carried out reprisals in response to IRA attacks they tended to be against individuals rather than property. The emergency powers granted to the NA under the PSA and, ironically, the still-extant Restoration of Order in Ireland Act allowed them to court-martial and execute anyone caught illegally carrying weapons.

The first executions took place on 17 November when four Irregulars – Peter Cassidy, James Fisher, John Gaffney and Richard Twohig – were shot in Kilmainham Gaol, Dublin. The policy was controversial from the start and Labour TD Tom

Johnson protested, but was told by Mulcahy that stern measures were necessary against those 'assassins and wreckers who would destroy the country'. On 24 November Childers was shot under the provisions of the PSA. Dalton was uncomfortable with this policy and asked Mulcahy if he was expected to execute the 1,800 Irregulars he had incarcerated in Cork Prison. Although he was reassured that such an act was not necessary Dalton felt compelled to resign his commission and played no further part in the war. This gesture did nothing to end the shootings and barely a month went by without a firing squad being convened.

Lynch's response as IRA Chief of Staff was to order the assassination of all TDs who had voted for the PSA as well as high court judges and hostile newspaper editors. When the IRA assassinated pro-Treaty TD Maj Gen Seán Hales outside Leinster House on 7 December the Republicans once again totally failed to anticipate the Government's response – the executions of Rory O'Connor, Liam Mellows, Joe McKelvey and Dick Barrett without even the pretence of a trial.

In one respect the reprisals worked, as attacks on TDs ceased. Instead the IRA targeted the property of pro-Treaty politicians, burning 37 of their houses in the first two months of 1923, as well as destroying railway stations and lines. The attacks on the railways especially did nothing to endear the IRA to the public and they failed to exploit fully the propaganda value of the Government's executions policy. More significantly the rules of engagement were changing. Not only were IRA prisoners being court-martialled and executed in accordance with the PSA but, in disturbing echoes of the Anglo-Irish War when death squads on both sides had murdered suspected enemies, NA troops began to carry out 'unofficial' reprisals. Historian Peter Hart notes that Irish officers quickly adopted attitudes towards the IRA that were remarkably similar to those of their former British adversaries.

The guerrilla struggle in Co. Kerry was particularly bitter and saw some of the worst atrocities of the war. At Ballyseedy Cross nine IRA prisoners were tied to a landmine and blown up, with eight of them killed. Four more were murdered at Countess Bridge, Killarney, and five others tied to a mine and killed at Caherciveen.

Daly's Dublin Guards earned a fearsome reputation for brutality in Co. Kerry, as did Col David Neligan. Neligan had been one of Collins' key intelligence officers during the Anglo-Irish War and as the head of NA intelligence in Co. Kerry was accused of torturing and executing Republican prisoners.

Sadly both sides violated the rules of war and the IRA was not above shooting unarmed civilians, using the excuse that supporters of the Treaty were effectively 'combatants'. In November an unarmed NA medical orderly, John Lydon, was shot outside Tralee, Co. Kerry and in March 1923 four NA prisoners were executed in Wexford on the orders of Bob Lambert, the local IRA commander.

The Government was astute enough to realize that coercion alone would not work and in October 1922 offered to grant an amnesty to any Irregular who signed an undertaking to abandon the struggle. While some took advantage of the offer many Republicans remained in arms. *Saorstát* supporters viewed these people as traitors, which probably explains why NA soldiers were willing to treat them so ruthlessly.

The Republican cause was dealt a further blow when the Catholic Church recognized the pro-Treaty administration in Dublin and condemned the Republican cause. While Lynch was contemptuous of politicians, writing that 'at present it is a waste of time to be thinking too much about policy', de Valera knew that some form of Republican 'Government' was essential.

De Valera argued that, as the pre-Treaty 2nd Dáil was still the legitimate government of Ireland, those of its members in arms against the *Saorstát* were in effect the *de jure* Irish government. Once more de Valera styled himself 'President of the Irish Republic' and appointed a 12-man Council of State consisting of Austin Stack, Robert Barton, Count Plunkett, J. J. O'Kelly, Mrs O'Callaghan, Mary MacSwiney, P. J. Ruttledge, Seán Moylan, M. P. Colivet and Seán Mahoney.

The Republican Government was virtually penniless and its members ignored by the IRA command. Consequently de Valera never really expected it to function properly but rather to provide continuity between the 2nd Dáil and what would follow a Republican victory. The Republicans' lack of financial resources meant that looting and commandeering became a necessary means for the Republican forces to survive. According to Hart the IRA carried out more than 141 armed robberies and 111 raids on the mail, and attacks on grocery and bread vans along with the destruction of bridges and railway lines did little to gain public support.

Although the *Saorstát's* August offensive had put the IRA on the back foot it was not beaten. Again adopting British tactics the NA conducted large cordon-and-search operations that resulted in the capture of several Republican leaders including O'Malley, Deasy and Moloney. It was during such an operation that Lt Larry 'Scorecard' Clancey fatally wounded Lynch in the Knockmealdown Mountains, Co. Waterford on 11 April 1923.

Command passed to Aiken, who had declared for the Republican cause in August 1922. IRA activity was highest in the remote areas of the south and west; they did carry out some successful attacks on NA garrisons but rarely held onto captured towns. Instead they resorted to ambushes, although few were executed with the determination of the earlier conflict.

When Deasy called from his prison cell for an 'immediate and unconditional surrender of arms', and Republican prisoners held in Limerick, Cork and Clonmel gaols also publicly appealed for an end to the war, it was obvious that the IRA was losing heart. Despite hardliners on both sides rejecting calls for a truce Aiken, Barry, Collins, Dalton, Deasy, Mulcahy and de Valera had all made tentative approaches to the other side to discuss peace. In fact this may have been one of the reasons why Collins made his ill-fated trip to Co. Cork in August 1922.

After Lynch's death in April 1923 it became increasingly obvious to the majority of Republicans that the war was unwinnable. More than 12,000 IRA were in prison along with many of their leaders. The Government's use of executions and amnesties had also taken its toll, leaving a small hardcore of guerrillas in the field. Republican Tom Crofts was convinced that 'if five men are arrested in each area we are finished'.

Despite his solid Republican credentials Aiken had never been enthusiastic about the 'armed struggle' against his former comrades-in-arms in the NA, and one of his first acts as IRA Chief of Staff was to sound out his commanders' attitudes to a ceasefire. By 14 May 1923 both the Republican Government and the IRA Executive endorsed this policy and ten days later he ordered his troops to dump arms and go home.

De Valera issued a statement claiming that 'further sacrifice on your part would now be in vain and the continuance of the struggle in arms unwise in the national interest. Military victory must be allowed to rest for the moment with those who have destroyed the Republic.' To all intents and purposes the Civil War was over.

Portrait of a soldier: Maj Gen Emmet Dalton MC

Considering that Emmet Dalton was a Secretary to the Senate, played such a prominent role in the IRA during the Anglo-Irish War, commanded the artillery that attacked the Four Courts, broke the back of the 'Munster Republic' and was with Collins when he was killed at Béal na mBláth it is astonishing that so little information about his life seems to have survived.

His name crops up again and again in accounts of Ireland's revolution yet a casual search of the Internet turns up very little. He left no published memoirs and except for a series of interviews for RTE no biography of Emmet Dalton has yet been written.

Born in the United States on Friday 4 March 1898, James Emmet Dalton grew up at 8 Upper St Columbus Road, Drumcondra, a solidly middle-class Catholic suburb of Dublin, and was educated by the Christian Brothers at their school in North Richmond Street. Dalton's father was a third-generation Irish-American Republican who had returned to Ireland in 1900 and his family's political activism probably explains why he joined the Dublin Volunteers at their inaugural meeting in 1913 at the age of 15, and was actively involved in smuggling arms by the time he was 16. His younger brother Charlie also joined and went on to become a member of Collins' inner circle.

Much to his father's chagrin the 17-year-old Dalton answered Redmond's call to arms in 1915 and became a British Army temporary 2nd Lieutenant in the 7th (Service) (Dublin Pals) Battalion, Royal Dublin Fusiliers. When the Easter Rising took place Dalton was serving with 9 RDF, 48th Infantry Brigade, 16th (Irish) Division under Maj Gen W. B. Hickie. The Division was firmly Redmondite in its sympathies and Dalton, like the rest of his fellow officers, was horrified by the news of events in Dublin.

Maj Gen Emmet Dalton MC, Director of Operations of the National Army and architect of the Free State victory in the southwest. He was with Collins when he died. (Corbis)

It was while serving with the 9th 'Dubs' that Dalton befriended an old acquaintance of his father, Lt Tom Kettle MP, the alcoholic 36-year-old Nationalist MP for East Tyrone and Professor of Economics at University College Dublin. It was Kettle who had famously declared that Irishmen should fight 'not for England, but for small nations', a sentiment that Dalton seemed to fully endorse. Kettle hoped that, 'with the wisdom which is sown in tears and blood, this tragedy of Europe [World War I] may be and must be the prologue to the two reconciliations of which all statesmen have dreamed, the reconciliation of Protestant Ulster with Ireland, and the reconciliation of Ireland with Great Britain'.

By the summer of 1916 the 16th (Irish) Division were fully embroiled in the bloody battle of the Somme. On 9 September 9 RDF attacked the Germans near the village of Ginchy and Kettle, then acting as OC B Company, was shot and killed within sight of Dalton. The fighting around Ginchy was bloody and along with Kettle more than 4,314 Irishmen became casualties; 1,167 of them were never to see Ireland again. It was also a battle where heroism went hand in hand with sacrifice. Dalton was among those recognized for their courage and was awarded the Military Cross, while Lt John Holland of the Leinsters won a Victoria Cross.

For the rest of his life Dalton was known as 'Ginchy' and according to his Military Cross citation he 'led forward to their final objective companies which had lost their officers. Later while consolidating his position, he found himself with one sergeant, confronted by

21 of the enemy, including an officer, who surrendered when he attacked them.' He was presented with his medal by King George V at Buckingham Palace and he was fêted by Irish MPs while he stayed in London. In many respects it was typical of the courage he demonstrated throughout this military career, and such was his pride in the award that on occasion he even wore the ribbon on his NA uniform.

By 1917 Dalton had returned to his old battalion – 7 RDF, 30 Brigade, 10th (Irish) Division – which was now in Palestine, where he first commanded a rifle company and then became OC of a sniping school. By 1918 what was left of 7 RDF along with A/Maj Emmet Dalton MC redeployed to the Western Front. Speculation that he once served on the staff of Sir Henry Wilson is unfounded, as is the unsubstantiated innuendo that he was a British spy and shot Collins. Like thousands of other Irish soldiers he returned to Ireland after the war.

While Dalton was 'away at the wars' his brother Charlie was an active Volunteer who became a member of Collins' Squad, his hand-picked team of assassins, and was

On board the SS *Arvonia*, Maj Gen Dalton (second from left) discusses his plans with his second-in-command, Tom Ennis, August 1922. (George Morrison)

one of the participants in the Bloody Sunday killings of 21 November 1920. It is unclear whether he used the German pistol his brother had given him as a souvenir.

It was probably inevitable, given Charlie's connections and his military experience, that Dalton rejoined the Volunteers on leaving the Army. As a disillusioned Redmondite he probably felt that after the 1918 General Election the Dáil and the IRA best represented the will of the Irish people. He had fought for Ireland during World War I and once said that he had no difficulty fighting for Ireland with the British, or fighting for Ireland against the British.

Regardless of his personal beliefs Dalton developed a close friendship with Collins and in an interview screened by RTE on the day he died in 1978 said, 'I loved him. I use no other word. I loved him as a man loves another man, with pure love.'

When Seán MacÉoin was captured in March 1921 it was Dalton who led the attempt to rescue him from Mountjoy Gaol. Dressed in his old uniform and leading members of Collins' Squad, he had devised a plan that was typically daring and involved a stolen armoured car, British Army uniforms and a lot of luck. Dalton and Joe Leonard,

Generals Tom Ennis, Eoin O'Duffy and Emmet Dalton take the salute as National Army troops take control of Portobello Barracks, Dublin (now Cathal Brugha Barracks) in February 1922. (Hulton-Getty Library)

dressed as British officers, managed to bluff their way into the Governor's office on the pretence of moving MacÉoin to another prison before they were rumbled and shooting broke out near the prison gate. Although the rescue attempt failed Dalton managed to extract his raiding party intact.

His raw courage as well as his wealth of military experience won him the admiration and trust of both Collins and Mulcahy. It is unclear whether Dalton was a member of the IRB; however, it would have been unusual for a member of Collins' inner circle not to have been so. His loyalty to Collins was purely personal rather than doctrinal and despite his pedigree as an ex-British officer he rose rapidly through the IRA's ranks to command the ASU during the failed attack on the Customs House in May 1921. In addition he became the first Director of Munitions and, by the time the Truce was agreed in July 1921, the IRA's Director of Training.

When Collins was nominated to go to London as part of the Irish peace delegation Dalton was dismayed that the 'Big Fella' would be negotiating with the British but accompanied him nonetheless as his military adviser and head of security. He felt that the Treaty was the best deal that Ireland could get and true to his loyalty to Collins he came out in support of it.

In January 1922 Dalton became a brigadier in the new NA when his unit was absorbed into the Dublin Guards. Dalton was one of the few senior officers in the NA with formal military training. When Dalton's troops began shelling the Four Courts on 28 June 1922 he even helped aim and fire the borrowed British guns for their inexperienced crews.

Dalton's real *coup de main*, however, was his amphibious attack on Cork on 8 August 1922. Michael Hayes told Mulcahy that the attack broke 'all the rules of common sense and navigation and military science'. Without charts and at one point holding a gun to the head of the captain of his ship, the *Arvonia*, Dalton put ashore 456 men, an armoured car and an 18-pdr gun outside Cork. According to Tom Crofts 'there was panic' and, after fighting at Rochestown and Douglas, Cork fell to Dalton on the 9th, making a *Saorstát* victory almost inevitable. In fact Dalton complained bitterly that the war could have been brought to a close in September 1922 if troops had also attacked overland from Dublin at the same time.

On 12 August the now Maj Gen Dalton was appointed General Officer Commanding (GOC) Southern Command and he announced that it was his avowed aim to restore normality to Cork City and helped establish a temporary police force until the Civic Guard arrived on 16 September. In late August Collins was in Co. Cork, ostensibly on an inspection tour but also attempting to make contact with leading Republicans to end the war; according to Coogan's biography of Collins, Dalton had been central to this 'peace' process and acted as an intermediary.

When Collins was warned that it was not safe for him to drive around the county he told local NA commander Joe Sweeney that 'whatever happens, my fellow countrymen won't kill me'. When the IRA ambushed Collins' convoy on 22 August Dalton had shouted, 'Drive like hell' but Collins overruled him. Dalton attributed Collins' death to his lack of combat experience: '… if Mick had ever been in a scrap he would have learned to stay down'.

To this day no one really knows what happened at Béal na mBláth but it was obvious that Collins' death affected Dalton. When he returned from his honeymoon in September 1922 his heart was no longer in the fight. He objected to the executions of captured Irregulars and resigned his commission in December to work briefly as the Secretary to the Senate. In a military career that had spanned eight years he had become a retired major general at 24 on a pension of £117 per annum.

Despite being an accomplished soldier Dalton had always been interested in the cinema and by the late 1920s was working as a film producer who gained some transatlantic success. In the late 1950s he helped establish the Irish Ardmore Studios where the films *The Blue Max*, *The Spy Who Came in from the Cold* and *The Lion in Winter* were filmed in the 1960s.

After 1922 Dalton never held a military appointment again, even though Lord Mountbatten offered him the command of an Irish special operations unit in World War II. Dalton declined, preferring to follow horse racing and produce his movies. On his 80th birthday, 4 March 1978, Emmet Dalton died in Dublin, barely commemorated by the state he did so much to create.

IMPACT OF THE IRISH CIVIL WAR

Northern Ireland

Even though the bulk of military activity during the Anglo-Irish War had taken place in south-west Ireland it was events in the north-east that precipitated the cycle of violence that led to the Truce in 1921.

Ulster was unlike the rest of the country in that it was where the bulk of the Protestant population was concentrated and where the majority supported Unionism. Unionists considered the creation of Northern Ireland as the end of the Home Rule issue and consequently felt that the Anglo-Irish Treaty was nothing to do with them. It was in essence an agreement between the Catholic, Nationalist South and the United Kingdom and as such the Unionist leader, Sir James Craig, refused to have any part in it.

This, of course, was a source of great irritation to Republicans, who viewed all of Ireland as an indivisible unit and partition as yet another example of British divide and rule. In truth the British would have quite happily included Ulster in the deal and Lloyd George did try to persuade Craig to participate.

Craig's price for participation was recognition of Northern Ireland as a separate entity by the Dáil. Although the reality was that Ireland was already divided, few Nationalists were willing to accept this. It was certainly a price that de Valera, as President, was unwilling to pay, which guaranteed that the Northern political establishment played no active role in the Treaty negotiations.

Consequently tensions increased rather than decreased in Ulster after the Truce and attacks on British forces in the North continued apace, leaving 19 members of the British security forces dead and 46 wounded at a cost of three dead IRA. However, after fighting broke out in the South in June 1922 IRA attacks on the security forces virtually ceased. Tactically the IRA faced a very different situation in most of Ulster

British troops occupying Belleek, Co. Fermanagh after the town was recaptured from the IRA on 4 June 1922 in order to form a buffer between Republican and Loyalist forces on the Fermanagh–Donegal border. (Corbis)

than they did in the rest of the country. Here the enemy was not just the British security forces but also a significant portion of the population.

It was because of this that Ernest Blythe TD believed that attempts to coerce the North would be counterproductive. Although Blythe was a member of the IRB and the Dáil and a Provisional Government minister he was also an Ulster Protestant, which gave him a unique insight into the Ulster Unionist mind. He also believed that as long as the South teetered on the brink of civil war, Ulster Unionists would see no merit in reunification.

That is not to say that all Ulster Unionists were content with partition. Many would have preferred to remain *Irish* Unionists within the United Kingdom, but this was not a realistic option after 1921. Only the Ulster Unionists viewed the division as permanent, as both the Nationalists and the British hoped that reunification was possible; where they differed was in how it could be achieved.

While both the British and Provisional Governments had publicly rejected coercing the North into a unified Irish State, behind closed doors Collins was in contact with anti-Treaty IRA leaders to plan an offensive against Northern Ireland. This offensive, in combination with the 'Belfast Boycott', would destabilize Northern Ireland, leaving it with little alternative but to join a united Ireland.

The Northern Offensive was part of the attempt to maintain IRA unity but when it finally came it was a dismal failure. Despite being on opposite sides in the South both Collins and Lynch cooperated in planning the offensive and supplying arms to Northern IRA units. Collins had privately reassured officers of Comdt Gen Charles Daly's anti-Treaty 2nd Northern Division IRA that partition would never be recognized even if it meant 'the smashing of the Treaty'.

Collins was desperate to avoid implicating the Provisional Government in IRA activity in Ulster and made sure that none of the weapons supplied could be traced back to NA sources. Unfortunately the British were well aware of Collins' involvement because Lynch had publicly complained about shortfalls in the supply of laundered weapons, which only helped to fuel the growing mistrust between pro- and anti-Treaty IRA.

Operational security was lax and it was claimed that the offensive's start date, 19 May, was common knowledge in Dundalk pubs. A pre-emptive attack on Musgrave Street Barracks, Belfast, went wrong on 17 May, resulting in talk of aborting the offensive. Once more contradictory orders and confusion plagued IRA activity and Roger McCorley, a Belfast IRA officer, complained that 1st and 4th Northern Divisions failed to act. Another IRA officer, Tom MacAnally, accused the 2nd Northern Division of not 'doing a damned thing'. Only the 3rd Northern Division carried out any attacks.

Any pretence that the offensive was the work of the anti-Treaty IRA was exposed when fighting broke out between the USC and pro-Treaty troops under the command of Comdt Gen Joe Sweeney in Belleek on 28 May, resulting in the death of Special Constable Albert Rickerby. Sweeney's men were also engaged with the USC in Pettigo further along the Donegal–Fermanagh border.

The situation was doubly sensitive, not only because both Belleek and Pettigo straddle the border but also because Sweeney had been conducting unauthorized cross-border raids into Northern Ireland to confiscate arms. On 21 March 1922 *The Times* had already referred to a 'state of guerrilla war on the border' that the Belleek–Pettigo incident did little to dispel.

To make matters worse the British Army was drawn into the fighting and on 4 June, after a brief bombardment that killed seven IRA and wounded six others, they occupied Pettigo, taking four IRA prisoners. For the next couple of months the British Army occupied the Belleek–Pettigo area, in effect creating a buffer zone between the IRA and the USC.

While it was humiliating that the British had occupied territory on their side of the border the Provisional Government felt powerless to do much about it. The offensive was dealt a further blow when over 350 Northern IRA and Sinn Féin members were rounded up and imprisoned after William Twaddell, a Belfast Unionist MP, was assassinated on 22 May. In addition all Republican organizations were proclaimed illegal.

Gen Macready reported that 'the disorganisation caused by the action of the police since 22 May has been greater than was supposed'. IRA reports talked of demoralization and disintegration. It was a blow that would ensure that IRA activity within the 'occupied six counties' had virtually ceased to exist by the time the Civil War broke out in the South.

The outbreak of Civil War made the lot of the Northern IRA even more miserable, as despite their opposition to the Treaty many attempted to remain neutral. In the end Aiken reluctantly threw in his lot with the Republicans because he had been arrested by Provisional Government troops in Dundalk and when he became IRA COS after Lynch's death he did his utmost to end hostilities.

As indicated by *The Times*, the border was a major bone of contention in Anglo-Irish affairs. The Treaty had provided for a Border Commission but the Ulster Unionists simply abstained from participation. Having already lost the three Catholic-dominated Ulster counties of Cavan, Donegal and Monaghan, Unionists were unwilling to surrender any of the remaining six. In fact Craig had famously stated that 'what we have now we hold, and we will hold against all combinations'.

To make matters worse the Provisional Government's Home Affairs Minister, Kevin O'Higgins TD, doubted whether anyone in Northern or Southern Ireland or Britain had any faith in the Commission. In the end its findings were never published and the *de facto* border was only formally recognized as part of the 1998 Good Friday Agreement.

Of course the Belleek–Pettigo crisis was not the first major incident involving the border. In January the Monaghan Gaelic football team, which included IRA Maj Gen Dan Hogan, had been arrested en masse on their way to play in the final of the Ulster championships in Londonderry. In February the IRA crossed the border and kidnapped 42 prominent Loyalists as hostages to gain the release of the footballers. To make matters worse a trainload of USC clashed with the IRA at Clones Station, in the South, and Craig advocated sending 5,000 men over the border to rescue the captive Loyalists. The British suspended troop evacuations and feared that open conflict was about to break out between the two Irish states. Ultimately Hogan and the others were released and the crisis passed.

Even though Collins claimed in the *Daily Mail* that his policy towards Ulster was 'not understood' he was optimistic that, despite the friction between North and South, mutual interests and economic persuasion would bring about reunification. For Collins the IRA campaign was only one element of a broader strategy.

Economic persuasion took the form of the 'Belfast Boycott', which targeted Northern Irish goods and services. As Protestants owned the majority of Northern businesses the boycott did nothing to endear the Southern State to Northern Unionists and one IRA report claimed that military action was not only 'futile and foolish' but also increased the risk of exposing the Catholic minority to sectarian violence.

Sadly sectarian violence in Ulster was rife and historian Peter Hart points out that while the Catholics made up only 23 per cent of the Northern Ireland population they amounted to 44 per cent of the casualties and 20 per cent of refugees from the six counties. Between 1920 and 1922 more than 259 Catholics and 164 Protestants died as a result of sectarian attacks. In addition more than 1,000 Protestants were driven from their homes in Nationalist areas and as many again lost their jobs in the Belfast shipyards alongside Catholic colleagues for being too Socialist or insufficiently Loyalist.

As a consequence of sectarian violence in the north-east, Southern Protestants became extremely vulnerable to revenge attacks. Unlike their Northern co-religionists Southern Protestants had played almost no part in the Anglo-Irish War; they had no political party or paramilitaries to 'defend' their interests. By Ulster standards, sectarian violence in the South was on a small scale with the worst incident being the killing of 13 West Cork Protestants by anti-Treaty IRA on 26–28 April 1922.

Although both the Provisional Government and the IRA condemned these attacks the general breakdown of law and order in rural areas ensured that both were powerless to prevent them. The net result was that the Protestant population of Southern Ireland declined, causing a minor refugee crisis in Britain during 1922, and 34 per cent had emigrated by 1926.

Soldiers of 1st Bn, The Lincolnshire Regiment occupy a fort on the Northern Ireland–Irish Free State border during the operations to end fighting between the IRA and USC near Belleek, Co. Fermanagh. (© Bettmann/Corbis)

It would be wrong to imply that because of their fundamental differences politicians from North and South did not talk directly with each other; they did. In January Craig and Collins agreed the first of two pacts aimed at reconciling their differences. The pact promised to end sectarian violence and the Belfast Boycott and peacefully resolve the border issue. Unsurprisingly it failed to deliver because of Southern unwillingness to recognize Northern Ireland and Unionist intransigence over the border. The hope had been that the two Irelands could solve their problems bilaterally without recourse to the British. Unfortunately the collapse of the pact created a situation that many felt could only be resolved by British intervention.

In March Churchill brokered a second 'Collins–Craig Pact'. Collins agreed to use his authority to end IRA activity in the North while Craig undertook to release political prisoners and seek the restitution of sacked Catholic dockyard workers. Although the pact boldly proclaimed that peace was declared and it was welcomed by the media in both Northern and Southern Ireland, it triggered a wave of sectarian violence in Belfast. Thus, after several weeks of bitter debate, acrimonious correspondence and double dealing by both Collins and Craig, the second pact went the way of the first. It would

The St John Ambulance Brigade provided medical support to casualties on both sides during both the Easter Rising and the fighting in Dublin during the civil war. Here a wounded National Army soldier receives first aid, July 1922. (Hulton-Getty Library)

be another 50 or so years before any attempt would be made to gain a North–South consensus on the governance of Northern Ireland.

Both pro- and anti-Treatyites opposed partition and Mulcahy had argued that carrying out all the Treaty's terms would 'ultimately unify the country and destroy the Northern Parliament'. By attacking the North the Republicans had merely fuelled Unionist intransigence and exposed the Catholic minority to further attack. The result, Hart argues, was that the gunmen on both sides became more proficient at killing unarmed civilians than each other.

Unfortunately, distracted by internal conflict, the Provisional Government was unable to influence events north of the border or offer much succour to Northern Catholics. In addition, with the Northern IRA effectively neutralized and the Southern IRA at war with itself, the Unionists were able to stabilize their position.

Thus, ironically, the internecine struggle in the South guaranteed the continued partition of Ireland, allowing Northern Ireland formally to vote to remain apart from Southern Ireland. Dominated by a Protestant population that distrusted both its southern neighbour and the British government, Northern Ireland was deeply divided, which merely stored up problems for future generations to solve.

Great Britain

There can be little doubt that the British would have preferred that the Home Rule Bill had not been passed and that the Troubles that followed had not taken place. Conservative Party sympathy for the Ulster Unionists ensured that Britain failed to deal effectively with the threat of Unionist violence manifested in the UVF and arguably the crisis was only averted by the advent of World War I.

Although not defeated by the IRA the British were painfully aware that they were not winning the Anglo-Irish War either. When a truce was finally agreed in July 1921 the British were determined to salvage what they could from the situation and protect their strategic interests. To that end the key issue for the British was Ireland's relationship with the Empire and the Crown and the 1920 Government of Ireland Act had reluctantly envisaged a 'two Irelands' solution to the Home Rule question. The Protestant north-east would become Northern Ireland, with its Parliament in Stormont Castle, outside Belfast, while the rest of the country would become Southern Ireland with a Parliament in Dublin. It was hoped that these parliaments would eventually merge to create a united self-governing region within the UK.

British hopes for the Government of Ireland Act as a solution to the Troubles failed to materialize; however, during the Treaty negotiations it was obvious that Lloyd George outclassed the Irish plenipotentiaries led by Collins. By continually threatening

to renew hostilities Lloyd George was able to browbeat the Irish representatives into agreeing to a settlement that was to split the Republican movement.

The Treaty went further than the 1914 Home Rule Act in that it gave Ireland limited independence and its own armed forces but fell far short of the independent Irish Republic originally envisaged by the Dáil and the IRA. What emerged was a British Dominion within the Empire that continued to recognize George V as its king. It also left Britain in control of key naval facilities, strategic defence and telegraph communications.

From a British perspective it would have been impossible to allow what had, rightly or wrongly, been an integral part of the UK to become an independent republic on Britain's western flank, and in 1921 Dominion status was as far as they were prepared to go. Even de Valera recognized that Britain's strategic interests could not be ignored but he preferred the rather vague concept of external association with the Commonwealth as a way of satisfying them. Because the British could not countenance an Irish Republic on their doorstep they were willing to do almost anything to ensure that the Treaty and the *Saorstát* survived, which is why they supplied it with arms and maintained a military presence in Dublin.

The British also maintained a garrison in Northern Ireland and in theory they controlled the RUC and USC, although in reality they answered to the Stormont Government rather than Westminster. When the IRA and USC clashed in the vicinity of Belleek–Pettigo it was the British Army who intervened to keep the two sides apart. The British condemned any attempt to subvert the Treaty, such as de Valera's attempts to amend it in the Dáil, the de Valera–Collins election pact and prevarication about the contents of the *Saorstát* constitution. To apply pressure they suspended troop withdrawals, or, in the case of the Four Courts occupation, threatened to use force themselves.

When Comdt Reginald Dunne, OC London IRA, and Joseph O'Sullivan assassinated Sir Henry Wilson in London on 22 June 1922, possibly on Collins' orders, the British chose to blame the anti-Treaty Republicans. They also chose to overlook Collins' involvement in planning IRA activity in Northern Ireland.

Both his killers, O'Sullivan and Dunne, the second-in-command of the London IRA, were ex-soldiers. O'Sullivan had lost his leg at Ypres while serving with the Royal Munster Fusiliers, which is why he was unable to run away after the shooting and Dunne, an ex-Irish Guardsman, refused to abandon his comrade. They were both hanged on Thursday 10 August 1922 at Wandsworth Gaol.

When open warfare finally broke out between the rival factions within the IRA the British openly supplied the Provisional Government with arms to equip its embryonic army. By September 1921 the British had supplied more than 27,400 rifles, 6,606 revolvers,

The state funeral procession of Sir Henry Wilson, shot dead by IRA assassins on the steps of his home in London. Full military honours were accorded to the late Field Marshal, while thousands lined the streets to pay homage. Sir Henry's white horse can be seen following the funeral cortège.
(© Bettmann/Corbis)

246 Lewis guns, five Vickers heavy machine guns and field artillery as well as several warplanes and gunboats. Even though the Treaty provided for the withdrawal of British forces from Southern Ireland British intelligence officers continued to operate there, and British intelligence also worked closely with their Irish G2 counterparts in the UK

While the British IRA had been very active during the Anglo-Irish War their effectiveness was greatly undermined during the Civil War by Anglo-Irish cooperation and the British police and Special Branch developed significant expertise in countering their activities. Such was the degree of cooperation between British and Irish intelligence that Liam Lynch commented that a 'large quantity of supplies are available in England; the trouble is getting them across'. The fact that the British retained control of issuing passports to *Saorstát* citizens also allowed them a high degree of control over the movements of Irishmen abroad.

Of course, the British IRA was as divided over the Treaty as the rest of the organization. In fact Dunne's attack on Wilson may well have been a last-ditch attempt to maintain unity. According to Hopkinson the Treaty also effectively destroyed the Irish Self-Determination League and Sinn Féin in Britain. Overall the majority of the diaspora in Britain and the Empire appear to have accepted the Treaty or desired to remain neutral in the ensuing split.

Lynch did attempt to reorganize his supporters and appointed Pa Murray from Cork as 'OC Britain' with the vague brief to 'take charge of London'. His efforts proved fruitless and by April 1923 Moss Twomey reported that 'the chances of operations in Britain are now negligible if not all together impossible'. In March 1923 over 110 Republican sympathizers were arrested on the orders of the British Home Secretary, Winston Churchill, under Article 14b of the Emergency Powers Act 1920. They were bundled onto British warships and deported to Ireland, where they were immediately detained by the Irish security forces under the PSA and, ironically, the still-extant Restoration of Order in Ireland Act.

These Acts had been intended for use during states of emergency and the House of Lords, the highest law court in the British Empire, ruled the deportations illegal. Consequently the British were forced to ask for their return, and although the Irish complied in the majority of cases the Civil War was virtually over and the damage had already been done. It was to prove to be the first of many Anglo-Irish extradition controversies.

Suitably distracted by events in Southern Ireland the British Government rapidly lost interest in Northern Ireland, whose internal governance passed from Westminster to Stormont. Inequalities in the 'Province' passed unnoticed in Westminster until the British Government was forced to impose direct rule on 30 March 1972 as a result of the Troubles that broke out in 1969.

The United States of America

The relationship between the United States of America and Ireland has always been perceived as close. The United States was the birthplace of the Fenian Brotherhood and Irish-American émigrés were and remain a significant source of support to the Republican movement.

During the Anglo-Irish War, de Valera had spent a year in the land of his birth trying to win support for the Republic from the US Government. Reluctant to turn on their wartime ally, the President refused to meet him and the US Congress never went further than passing resolutions sympathizing with the Nationalist cause.

The problem that de Valera faced was that 'the Cause' in the United States was already in decline long before the Treaty. Although the Irish-American diaspora was large, only a small number were politically active. The claim by the American Association for the Recognition of the Irish Republic (AARIR) that it had more than 750,000 members was probably an exaggeration.

Donal O'Callaghan TD commented that 'it was all a myth talking about 20 millions of their people in America. There have never been more than half a million in the Irish movement in America.' In addition it would be an exaggeration to claim that Irish-America was a united entity. During his year-long stay in the USA, de Valera managed to clash with the leaders of two major Irish-American organizations, John Devoy of *Clan na Gael* and Daniel F. Cohalan of the 'Friends of Irish Freedom'. None of these differences helped the Republican cause in Ireland.

When the Treaty was finally agreed, the majority of US newspapers and Irish-Americans welcomed it. James J. Phelan, a wealthy Boston-Irish banker, telegrammed the Lord Mayor of Dublin thanking God for peace and stating that he believed he expressed the 'feeling of all true friends of Ireland and England the World over'.

The fact that the mainstream Irish-American community appeared to be prepared to accept the outcome of the Dáil Treaty debates also placed those organizations with links to the anti-Treaty Republican movement in an awkward position. To defy mainstream opinion would inevitably undermine their credibility and support, as the demand for Irish self-determination appeared to have been satisfied.

Although Mulcahy had been disappointed by the Irish-American contribution to the war effort against the British he did not underestimate its potential. When the Civil War broke out the Provisional Government requested and was granted a temporary injunction by the US Supreme Court effectively freezing Republican assets in the United States, which according to a report in *The Times* on 23 August 1922 'struck at the most sensitive part of their organization'.

The Catholic Church, always a key player in the Irish-American community, was less than impressed with the divisions over the Treaty. Archbishop Curley of Baltimore believed that Ireland's American supporters 'have been humiliated by the present state of things' and worse still that Ireland was 'becoming a laughing stock'. According to Hopkinson the deaths of Collins and Boland also helped depress Ireland's stock even further in America. In July 1922 the President of the AARIR, James Murray, even publicly announced that 'if the people of Ireland are bound to destroy each other and ruin their chances of freedom, it is their funeral not ours'.

Reluctantly de Valera was forced to accept that Irish issues were of little importance in US national politics and only mattered in cities like Boston or New York, where significant Irish communities were concentrated. Even among these communities the anti-Treatyites had made little attempt to win over public opinion until well into the Civil War.

When the Republicans finally set out to woo Irish-America their efforts were marred by squabbling. Seán Moylan and Mick Leahy, veterans of the Cork IRA, were dispatched as military liaison officers while J. J. O'Kelly and Joseph O'Doherty represented Sinn Féin. In addition Austin Stack, Mrs Muriel MacSwiney, Fr Michael O'Flanagan and Countess Markievicz also visited to fly the tricolour in the USA.

Moylan described Laurence Ginnell, the Republican representative in Washington, DC, as a 'damn nuisance' and de Valera wrote to O'Kelly despairing that 'there are five or six of you over there, and America is a big place. Surely it should have been possible to secure harmonious working.' In the end the divisions were so bad that O'Kelly and Fr O'Flanagan left for Australia to raise funds there.

Irish-American contributions to the Republican war chest were disappointing compared to during the Anglo-Irish War and Moylan felt that a target of just $100,000 was realistic. He had little faith in the AARIR, which was, according to the Irish-American journalist J. C. Walsh, virtually non-existent as a result of the split in the Dáil. *Clan na Gael*'s leader Devoy was placed in an impossible position and inevitably the organization split into two factions. Devoy's faction, based in New York, had a degree of sympathy for the pro-Treatyites but the Provisional Government's prosecution of the war made it impossible for him to support it.

On the other hand Philadelphia-based veteran Republican Joe McGarrity and his supporters in *Clan na Gael* came out against the Treaty. The split came with the blessing of Boland, who always emphasized the importance of US funding, but was deeply regretted by Collins. The confusion over which *Clan na Gael* faction was recognized by the IRB further degraded the Irish cause in the US.

Both sides saw the USA as a key battleground in legitimizing their cause and did what they could to court Irish-American opinion. Although Irish-Americans have proved to be a constant source of support for their kin across the water, the Republicans never received official recognition from the US administration during either the Anglo-Irish War or the Civil War.

When the US government finally met an Irish Government official, it was Professor Timothy Smiddy, the Provisional Government's envoy to the United States. Ultimately it was the pro-Treatyites with their electoral mandate and their democratic successors rather than Republican revolutionaries who won the battle for the hearts and minds of the US diaspora.

Portrait of a civilian: Robert Erskine Childers DSO TD

Erskine Childers was many things, soldier, author, British civil servant, gunrunner and member of the Dáil for Co. Wicklow, yet he was never really accepted by his fellow Republicans, who never forgave his Anglo-Irish origins. He dedicated much of his life to the cause of Irish independence and much to the chagrin of his contemporaries became a close confidant of de Valera.

Despite his holding no military appointment during the Civil War both the British and Irish governments vilified Childers and claimed he was the evil genius behind the rebel war effort. Nothing could have been further from the truth, yet such was the loathing for Childers in *Saorstát* circles that he was executed under the provisions of the PSA.

Of Anglo-Irish Protestant stock, Childers' family was from Glendalough, Co. Wicklow, although he was born in London on 25 June 1870. His mother was Irish but his father was a distinguished English academic, Professor Robert Childers. Despite being orphaned as a child and placed in the care of an uncle in Co. Wicklow, Childers was educated in England at Haileybury College and Trinity College, Cambridge, which is why he sounded like an upper-class Englishman rather than an Irishman.

In 1895 he took a job as a clerk in the House of Commons and was an enthusiastic supporter of Empire. His cousin, Hugh Childers, had been Gladstone's Chancellor of the Exchequer from 1882 to 1885 and was a supporter of Irish Home Rule, and it is likely that he influenced Childers' own conversion to the Nationalist cause. When the Second Boer War

Erskine Childers, the Anglo-Irish Republican TD for Co. Wicklow who was executed by the Provisional Government on 24 November 1922 for being in possession of a pistol that, ironically, was a gift from Michael Collins. (Hulton-Getty Library)

broke out in 1899 Childers joined the City Imperial Volunteers to fight in South Africa and was wounded in 1900. He was invalided out of the army and once back in Britain resumed his career as a clerk in the Commons.

On his return from the Boer War Childers discovered a taste for writing and in 1903 wrote the novel *The Riddle of the Sands*, which predicted war with Germany. The book was a bestseller and according to Churchill it played a key part in getting the Admiralty to open bases at Invergordon and Scapa Flow, although in one of his more acerbic moments Arthur Griffith credited it with causing World War I.

Childers' literary talents went beyond that of a novelist and included factual studies of military operations. In 1907 *The Times* commissioned him to write Volume V of its *History of the War in South Africa*. His analysis of the war criticized the British and showered praise on the Boer commandos. In 1910 he wrote a treatise on mounted warfare, *War and the Arme Blanche*, and in 1911 he published *The German Influence on*

Erskine Childers as a volunteer in the Honourable Artillery Company, a regiment of the British Army, photographed c. 1900. (Photo by Hulton Archive/Getty Images)

the British Cavalry. The future of mounted operations was one of the hot topics in military circles before World War I and he was critical of British methods.

Childers was not only an accomplished writer but also an enthusiastic and expert yachtsman. When he visited the USA in 1903 he met and fell in love with fellow sailing enthusiast Molly Osgood. They were married within a year and by 1905 had a son, also named Erskine. De Valera once quipped that Childers was an 'inflexible idealist' and when he became a convert to Irish Nationalism he became one of its strongest advocates. In the finest traditions of the Anglo-Irish Childers became *Hiberiores hibernis ipsos* – more Irish than the Irish.

In 1910 he resigned from his job in the Commons and in 1912 wrote *The Form and Purpose of Home Rule.* But Childers was not just an intellectual Nationalist and on 26 July 1914 he sailed his yacht, *Asgard,* into Howth, Co. Dublin, carrying 900 rifles and 26,000 rounds for the IVF. But despite his gunrunning Childers had not fully abandoned the British Empire in 1914 and when war came he joined the Royal Naval Air Service as an intelligence officer. He saw action in the North Sea and the Dardanelles and was awarded the DSO for his efforts. By 1916 he was a lieutenant commander, when his anger at the violent suppression of the Easter Rising nudged him further down the road to Republicanism. In 1917–18 he was on the Secretariat of the Irish Convention.

By 1919, Childers was a major in the newly formed RAF and as soon as he was demobbed he made his way back to Ireland and joined Sinn Féin. He was soon appointed Director of Publicity for the first Dáil and became a close friend of both Collins and de Valera. An articulate advocate of Irish independence he represented the Irish Nationalists at the Versailles Peace Conference and in 1920 put pen to paper once more to attack British policy in *Military Rule in Ireland.* By 1921 his zeal for the cause earned him a place in the Dáil as the member for Wicklow.

His pamphleteering continued with 'Is Ireland a Danger to England?' in which he launched a strong attack against the British Prime Minister Lloyd George and his government's policies in Ireland. Both Collins and de Valera recognized his value as a propagandist and he was made editor of the *Irish Bulletin.*

Both Childers and his cousin Robert Barton accompanied the Irish delegation to London in the winter of 1921 to negotiate a treaty. Collins was convinced that de Valera had ensured that Childers was appointed secretary to the delegation so that he could act as de Valera's eyes and ears, and made sure that he was excluded from much of the negotiations. Childers was horrified that the Treaty finally signed by the Irish delegates in December 1921 bound Ireland to the British Empire and spoke out against it in the Dáil. He felt that the retention of the monarchy, the acceptance of partition and Dominion status were all fundamental betrayals of 'the Republic'.

Childers and his wife aboard his yacht, the *Asgard, c.* 1910. Childers used *Asgard* to run guns for the Irish Volunteers, bringing in a cargo of rifles and ammunition prior to the Easter Rising. (Hulton Archive/Getty Images)

His exchanges with Arthur Griffith were particularly bitter and on one occasion Griffith even exclaimed, 'I will not reply to any damned Englishman in this assembly', such was his loathing for the 'disgruntled Englishman'.

Despite being as Irish as de Valera or even Patrick Pearse, Childers never shook off the perception that he was really an Englishman. Even the British saw him as a traitor to the land of his birth and vilified him for it. When civil war came Childers sided with the Republicans, which earned him the hatred of the *Saorstát* Government. In effect Childers became the bogeyman behind every outrage and on 6 September 1921 the *Irish Times* reported that 'There is no doubt that Mr Childers is the chief military brain amongst the Irregulars'.

In reality Childers was the Director of Propaganda and Publicity for the Republican 'Government' and had no military status. Like de Valera he was more or less ostracized by the Republican military leaders who did not trust the 'Englishman' any more than the Free Staters did.

He was temporarily an assistant editor of the *Cork Examiner* until Dalton overran Cork. After that he was effectively on the run with his monocled associate David Robinson, another ex-British Army officer turned Republican, who claimed that Childers was liked by everyone who met them on their travels.

According to Hopkinson in his book *Green against Green* Childers and Robinson resembled a couple of characters from a P. G. Wodehouse novel as they drifted around south-west Ireland in a horse and cart. Isolated from Dublin and ignored by the Republican military leadership, Childers began to despair of his situation. A plan to smuggle him to the Continent came to nothing and *Saorstát* propaganda continued to demonize this rather effete revolutionary. Childers was well aware of British and *Saorstát* efforts to blacken his name but what hurt him most were the insinuations that he was actually a British spy all along.

Interestingly Michael Foy suggests in *Michael Collins's Intelligence War* that Childers' wife Molly, who had been awarded a CBE by the King for her work with Belgian refugees during World War I, was in fact a British spy and supplied the British with high-grade intelligence from within the upper echelons of Sinn Féin and the Dáil.

Eventually de Valera summoned Childers back to Dublin to take up an appointment as the secretary to the underground Republican Government. En route he stopped off to visit his cousin Robert Barton at his childhood home, Glendalough House, Co. Wicklow, where he was arrested by NA troops. Although Childers was armed with an automatic pistol that had been a present from Collins he declined to use it for fear of injuring the ladies present in the house.

Childers was taken to Dublin and tried by a military court under the provisions of the PSA on 16 November 1922. He was charged with the illegal possession of a pistol, the very weapon that had been a gift from his friend Michael Collins. The weapon, a Spanish .32cal automatic No. 10169, was eventually returned to Childers' family on 4 November 1939 by Cahir Davitt. But such was the animosity that he generated in Griffith and O'Higgins that the only possible outcome of his trial was a guilty verdict and a death sentence, and on the morning of 24 November 1922 Childers was led out of his cell in Beggars Bush Barracks, Dublin, to face his executioners.

Unfortunately it was too dark at the appointed hour and tragically Childers was forced to wait until the light improved. To kill the time he chatted with the firing party and smoked. Whatever else may be said about Childers, he was a brave man who faced death with remarkable courage. He told the firing squad that he bore them no ill will and even joked that his executioners should 'take a step or two forward, lads. It will be easier that way.'

When Churchill heard of Childers' arrest he commented that 'no man has done more harm or done more genuine malice or endeavoured to bring a greater curse upon the common people of Ireland than this strange being, actuated by a deadly and malignant hatred for the land of his birth.' Childers did not see his actions in this light and in a letter to his wife written before his execution wrote, 'I hope one day my good name will be cleared in England ... I die loving England and passionately praying that she may change completely and finally towards Ireland.'

To a degree Childers got his wish during the long years of de Valera's domination of Irish politics in the middle years of the twentieth century, when his British-born son Erskine Hamilton Childers became a naturalized Irish citizen and served as a *Fianna Fáil* TD from 1938–73, rising to be Deputy Prime Minister in 1969. His career as a TD came to an end in 1973 when he was elected as the fourth President of the Republic of Ireland.

THE CLOSE OF THE WAR: TENTATIVE DE-ESCALATION

There were parallels between the end of the Civil War and the Anglo-Irish War in that no one could be sure that it was really over. Unlike the Anglo-Irish War, however, there was no truce, no negotiations no settlement; the Republicans conceded nothing, not even defeat, and Ireland remained on a war footing. The IRA's guerrillas simply dumped their weapons and went home to await the next time.

The fact that the IRA had not been defeated would come back to haunt the Irish Government for decades after the Civil War. Although the NA had wrested control of Ireland's towns from the IRA in the opening weeks of the war, Republican forces were still operating with impunity in many rural areas.

Almost 1,000 IRA guerrillas were still at large in the mountainous areas near Macroom and Bantry in Co. Cork, although by May 1923 they had little stomach for the fight. Ever since Dalton had overrun the county the NA occupation had been fairly benign and IRA leader Tom Crofts even described their commander, Maj Gen David Reynolds, as 'decent for he did not want executions'.

The same was not true of the war in Kerry, where some of the worst atrocities of the war had taken place. In the end approximately 400 well-armed IRA guerrillas were engaged in a bitter game of cat and mouse with 2,000 or so Government soldiers. IRA guerrillas were also active in north and west Mayo as well as along the border with Sligo and Leitrim.

While none of these forces had been beaten in the field the constant pressure of being on the run steadily wore them down. Conventional military operations became less and less common as attacks on Unionist and *Saorstát* sympathizers and their property increased along with looting, road trenching and destruction of railway infrastructure and engines.

Early defeats had also left the IRA in counties Limerick and Tipperary demoralized and relatively ineffective. Despite establishing both an army HQ and an underground Government in Dublin there was little IRA activity of any note in the city or the county after the fighting in the summer of 1922.

In fact Co. Wexford was probably the only area in eastern Ireland where IRA activity increased rather than declined as the war progressed. When Aiken ordered his men to go home some areas of rural Wexford were firmly under IRA control. A *Times* report speculated that this was because a 'large portion of it [the NA], variously estimated, sympathized with the Republican cause'.

According to O'Halpin the IRA campaign was increasingly seen as illegitimate, lawless, undisciplined and ruthless. It is difficult to see the military logic of an IRA attack in Ballina, Co. Mayo where they 'demolished the park enclosure and released the hares'. O'Higgins was quite explicit that 'we are not engaged in a war properly so called, we are combating organized sabotage and a kind of disintegration of the social fabric'.

The Government undoubtedly exaggerated the extent to which social disorder in some areas was linked to Republicanism, except in the context that the rule of law had been steadily undermined since the start of the IRA offensive against the British in 1919. In attempting to restore order the Irish Government faced similar difficulties to the British but unlike them they were willing to openly go beyond their legal powers to suppress the insurrection.

O'Higgins was no fan of the NA but accepted that it had to 'perform many duties which, strictly and technically, might be said to be those of armed peace rather than military'. He firmly advocated that 'there should be executions in every county. The psychological effect of an execution in Dublin is very slight in Wexford, Galway or Waterford … local executions would tend considerably to shorten the struggle.'

The *Saorstát* Minister for Agriculture, Patrick J. Hogan TD, also believed that 'the people are thirsty for peace, and thirsty for strong ruthless measures … an unusually steady, disciplined Army acting with the utmost efficiency and ruthlessness'. Even Mulcahy had told Dalton that he could not afford to be broad-minded when dealing with the IRA.

What was remarkable about the executions and illegal killings carried out by *Saorstát* forces was that the Irish public seemed to accept them without much complaint. This was in stark contrast to the attitude of the public, in both Britain and Ireland, towards the executions carried out under the auspices of the previous administration in Dublin – probably because the *Saorstát* Executive Committee constantly emphasized that they were defending the rule of law and democratic institutions against Republican disorder. Even de Valera despaired at times of the IRA's lack of democratic legitimacy. Claiming a mandate from the first Dáil was all well and good but the Irish electorate had already moved on.

Even as the Civil War was drawing to a close the IRA failed to grasp the significance of the Clausewitzian maxim that war is the continuation of politics by other means, issuing a statement that 'suggestions as to methods of ending the present struggle will be effectively dealt with by Government. Such questions do not concern the Army, whose duty is to prosecute the war with redoubled vigour.'

From the start they focused on waging war rather than developing a coherent strategy that went beyond destroying the *Saorstát*. The IRA Executive had always been lukewarm about the prospects of a negotiated peace, especially on anything other than their own terms. Throughout the conflict attempts had been made to bring both sides to the negotiating table with little success.

On 3 May 1923 *Saorstát* Senators Andrew Jameson and James Douglas met with de Valera to discuss the possibility of peace talks but they foundered when he refused to sign a statement recognizing the *Saorstát* Government. De Valera claimed that he wanted 'a peace which would enable his followers to return to constitutional action,' but he 'doubted whether his followers would be willing to publicly hand over arms'.

When Mary MacSwiney criticized de Valera for opening dialogue he scolded her for speaking 'as if we were dictating terms and talk … of a military situation. There is no military situation. The situation now is that we have to shepherd the remnant of our forces out of this fight so as not to destroy whatever hope remains in the future by allowing the fight to peter out ignominiously.'

De Valera was not alone among leading Republicans in wanting to end the war, and salvage what he could. Tom Barry was actively seeking to bring about an end to the conflict and Aiken believed that the best hope for furthering the Republican cause lay with the Sinn Féin clubs through political rather than military action. Unfortunately for the Republicans the *Saorstát* Government was unwilling to renege on the Treaty, which made a negotiated solution unlikely. With thousands of IRA guerrillas in custody and most of the country in Government hands Cosgrave, O'Higgins and Mulcahy showed no sign of letting up pressure on the IRA despite Aiken's orders to cease offensive operations.

The last executions of the Civil War took place on 30 May in Tuam, Co. Galway, when Michael Murphy and Joseph O'Rourke were shot for their part in a failed armed robbery. De Valera was arrested on 15 August in Ennis, Co. Clare, during a political rally and between 13 October and 23 November 1923 possibly as many as 8,000 of the 12,000 Republican prisoners went on hunger strike.

Fortunately for the Government only two prisoners died during the strike and the Republicans failed to fully exploit its propaganda value. More alarmingly the strike showed that despite their captivity many IRA prisoners were far from demoralized. When the strike was finally abandoned not everyone was pleased with the order and one prisoner was heard to comment that 'I would rather have faced the firing squad than call it off, but there was Divisional Officers ordering their men off.'

With over £30m (over £4 billion in current terms) worth of damage done, £2m of uncollected rates in Co. Clare alone and £17m spent on the war effort, Cosgrave was far from happy with the situation he faced in June 1923. Although the Republicans had lost, the *Saorstát*'s victory was far from clear and it would be several years before the Government felt confident enough to consider the Civil War over.

CONCLUSIONS AND CONSEQUENCES

The most obvious consequence of the political violence between 1913 and 1923 was the creation of a relatively autonomous Irish state free from British control. However, it was not an end to what could be called British influence. The *Saorstát* that was created by the Treaty was to all intents and purposes still a satellite of the UK and a member of the Commonwealth, with the King as the head of state. It also left the UK with naval bases at Berehaven, Queenstown (Cobh), Belfast Lough (in Northern Ireland) and Lough Swilly. Partition was a pragmatic solution and its supporters knew it.

The Ulster Unionists never ceased to suspect that Britain would shed itself of all responsibility for Ulster at the first opportunity, and so the years that followed were dedicated to strengthening the viability of Northern Ireland. In 1914 the Unionist leader Sir Edward Carson had seen himself as an Irishman who was British; by 2004 few Ulstermen would feel comfortable with the epithet 'Irish', preferring to call themselves 'Northern Irish' or simply British.

A STATE DIVIDED

Because the IRA had more or less ceased operations without actually admitting defeat, Cosgrave's government spent the best part of a decade trying to contain the remnants of what would now be termed 'physical force' Republicanism – exemplified by the modern IRA splinter groups. Most commentators agree that the 1920s were unhappy times for Ireland, and when the IRA shot O'Higgins in 1927 many feared a second civil war.

Fortunately the shooting did not herald renewed violence but clearly illustrated the Republican movement's willingness to exact revenge on its enemies. The killing not only confirmed the Government's worst fears about the IRA threat to the Irish state but also acted as the catalyst for de Valera's re-engagement with constitutional politics.

The Blessing of the Colours by Sir John Lavery, 1922 – a tribute to the honour of the new state and its army. The Catholic Church threw its considerable weight behind the *Saorstát*'s cause. (Dublin City Gallery, The Hugh Lane)

Gen Michael Collins at the height of his power as C.-in-C. of the National Army and effectively head of the Provisional Government. Six days after this picture was taken Collins was killed in an IRA ambush in Co. Cork. (National Library of Ireland)

The 1918 Irish General Election had given Sinn Féin enough parliamentary seats for them to credibly argue that Dáil was morally and legally the real seat of Irish Government, rather than the Westminster Parliament. Unfortunately attempts to deal with the *Saorstát Dáil* in a similar fashion failed miserably and despite winning

44 seats in 1923 they were unable to drive a wedge between the Irish electorate and the pro-Treaty Government.

The 1922 and 1923 General Elections ably demonstrated that the Treaty's supporters had a stronger and more recent mandate than the Republicans. De Valera realized that Sinn Féin's policy of abstaining from the Dáil was counter-productive, merely enabling Cosgrave to entrench pro-Treaty attitudes. O'Higgins' death was the final straw that led him to leave it. What resulted was a new party – *Fianna Fáil* (Soldiers of Destiny) – and as its leader de Valera went on to dominate Irish politics until his death in 1975.

De Valera was not alone in seeking an alternative force to a waning Sinn Féin. The Civil War had stymied de Valera's earlier attempts to create a new Republican Party, *Cumann Poblachta*, but it was the creation of the pro-Treaty *Cumann na nGaedhael* (Society of Gaels) in March 1923 that proved that Nationalist unity was finished.

By 1933 *Cumann na nGaedhael* had merged with the Centre Party and the Army Comrades Association (ACA) to become *Fine Gael* (the United Irish Party), modern Ireland's principal centre-right party.

Thus, the two political parties that dominate modern Irish politics, *Fianna Fáil* and *Fine Gael*, have their roots in the disintegration of Sinn Féin and the Civil War. Consequently from the late 1920s former enemies faced each other across the floor of the Dáil ensuring that bitterness and confrontation rather than cooperation dominated Irish politics for decades after the fighting had ended.

Worse still these animosities, as highlighted by Ryle Dwyer and Kingsmill Moore, who said in 1948 that 'even now Irish politics is largely dominated by the bitterness of the hunters and the hunted of 1922', were passed down to their children, who often followed them into the Dáil, and these have only just begun to dissipate.

Mainly because there had been no outright victory Cosgrave's Government dedicated much of its time and effort to restoring law and order in a deeply divided country. The absence of an effective police presence in many areas led to a degree of lawlessness that could only be controlled by the military and the continuation of emergency legislation, and until the *Garda* was able to establish itself fully the NA remained responsible for policing as well as customs and excise duties.

O'Higgins was never happy with this state of affairs and along with Cosgrave was determined to reduce the NA, curb its power and re-establish civil governance. After a poor start the new Irish police, the Civic Guards, were disarmed and reorganized in 1923 into *An Garda Síochána*. Despite a handful of fatalities in 1923–24 the *Garda's* lack of involvement in the war worked in its favour and allowed it to gain acceptance even in strongly Republican areas.

The war had cost the Irish economy money it could ill afford and Cosgrave's government spent much of the 1920s attempting to balance the books and restore its sources of income. His pro-British, Free Trade policies were unpopular with many but they brought a degree of stability to the country, creating institutions that in essence became the foundations of the modern Republic of Ireland.

Although Cosgrave's government became associated with both steady and reliable leadership as well as repressive internal security policies, his ally O'Higgins, when he became Minister of External Affairs, was able to increase Ireland's autonomy within the Commonwealth. When de Valera finally became President of the Executive Council in 1932 he too realized how much leeway the Treaty actually gave Ireland to govern itself.

In 1927 the Royal and Parliamentary Titles Act changed the title of George V from that of King of the United Kingdom of Great Britain and Ireland to that of King of the United Kingdom of Great Britain and Northern Ireland, and separately King of Ireland. This altered the constitutional position of the King and effectively removed the British Government's right to appoint the Governor-General and offer advice on Irish issues. After 1927 only the Irish Government could appoint the Governor-General and advise the King on Irish affairs.

A similar situation was also created in the other self-governing Dominions of Australia, Canada, New Foundland, New Zealand and South Africa, with Britain

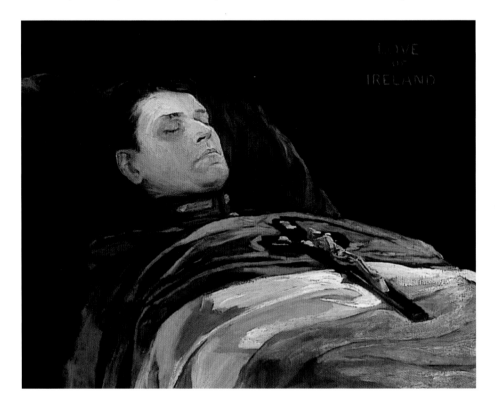

Love of Ireland by Sir John Lavery, 1922, picturing Michael Collins on his deathbed. The killing of Collins, a hero to many and the most powerful figure in the Provisional Government, shocked both the population of Ireland and the diaspora. (Dublin City Gallery, The Hugh Lane)

increasingly leaving them to their own devices. Unlike the rest of the Commonwealth, however, Ireland was also granted its own Great Seal, re-emphasizing its secession from the UK.

Britain's hold over its Empire was further weakened by the 1931 Statute of Westminster, which granted the parliaments of self-governing dominions equal status to the Westminster parliament. In essence the statute removed British interference from the dominions' internal affairs and established the principle that the UK would not block appointments or legislation passed in the dominions even if they were 'repugnant to the law of England'.

The 1936 abdication of Edward VIII gave de Valera, then Irish Prime Minister, the opportunity to remove all reference to the monarchy from the Irish constitution. Irish voters approved a new constitution, *Bunreacht na hÉireann*, in 1937, renaming the country Éire or simply Ireland. The new constitution not only explicitly laid claim to Northern Ireland but also made Ireland a republic in all but name. Despite this sleight of hand Ireland remained a monarchy and Commonwealth member until 1949 when the Republic of Ireland Act came into force, finally making the Republic a reality once more. Significantly the British did nothing to prevent it happening, so much had Britain's relationship with its Empire changed in the aftermath of World War II.

When war broke out in 1939 Ireland was the only Commonwealth country not to declare war on Germany, and it remained neutral throughout what the Irish euphemistically called 'the Emergency'. Neutrality was a central tenet of de Valera's foreign policy and, to the astonishment of many at home and abroad, he even offered his condolence to the German ambassador when he received news of Hitler's suicide.

The return of the Treaty Ports in 1938 had indicated Britain's belief that even under de Valera Ireland would help out in any future war. Consequently, the British were far from happy with Irish neutrality, although in reality the Irish Government discreetly aided the Allies. Ireland was as dependent on the North Atlantic convoys for its survival as the United Kingdom was, and more than 100,000 Irish citizens fought in the war. At least 3,000 even deserted from the Irish military to do so.

Despite Ireland being economically and strategically linked with the UK, Irish neutrality continued after the war and created problems for its armed forces, whose preoccupation was internal security, until 1958 when Ireland began to contribute to the United Nations and, more recently, to other international peacekeeping operations. Mulcahy had wanted to create a professional, politically neutral military that would in his own words serve 'even a de Valera Government' and in that he was largely successful.

The army that emerged 'victorious' from the Civil War was, however, far from politically neutral and was deeply divided. Personal loyalties – especially to Collins – rather than a belief in the Treaty had brought many into the NA. The members of

People line the streets of Dublin to watch Collins' funeral procession on its way to City Hall to lie in state. (Corbis)

The Squad were particularly problematical. They had carried out some of the least savoury operations for Collins and later as members of 'Oriel House' were probably responsible for dozens of illegal killings during the conflict.

Gen Liam Tobin eventually became their spokesman and in January 1923 formed the 'Old IRA' to safeguard the interests of IRA veterans serving in the NA. Many of them felt that they deserved better treatment than they received, but with a Government deficit of over £4m huge defence cuts were inevitable and thousands of soldiers had to be discharged.

The 'Tobinites' believed that Mulcahy favoured retaining ex-British officers and by March 1924 tensions within the Army were such that the Old IRA issued an ultimatum, warning that unless Mulcahy was dismissed and there was an end to demobilization, they would 'take such action that will make clear to the Irish people that we can no longer be party to the treachery that threatens to destroy the aspirations of the nation'.

As a result 50 officers resigned their commissions and some absconded with their weapons, again leading to Government fears that they were in cahoots with the Republicans. Cosgrave's ill health gave O'Higgins the opportunity to exploit the situation and dismiss Mulcahy along with his Chief of Staff MacMahon, the adjutant general Lt Gen Gearóid O'Sullivan and the quartermaster-general Lt Gen Seán O'Muirthile. Although Mulcahy's removal had been one of the mutineers' aims the Government refused to give in to the rest of their demands and the mutiny collapsed.

The 1924 Defence Forces Act finally put the Permanent Defence Force (PDF) – a new name for the NA – on a stable footing and banned its members from belonging to oath-bound organizations such as the IRB, IRA or Freemasons. Consequently when *Fianna Fáil* formed a government in 1932 its fears about the Army proved unfounded and de Valera was pleasantly surprised how apolitical the PDF had become. In the years that followed the mutiny the PDF was often starved of funds and neglected by

Irish revolutionary leader Èamon de Valera, reading from notes, addresses a huge crowd of Dubliners during his years as Prime Minister of Ireland. De Valera was among the most influential of Irish Republican leaders of the 20th century; he played a large role in creating the Irish Free State in 1922, and then in 1937 led the initiative to sever Ireland's ties to the British Commonwealth and become a sovereign state. (Corbis)

successive Irish Governments. Despite this it has evolved into an extremely efficient and professional force whose loyalty, quite rightly, is to the democratically elected Government of Ireland, regardless of that government's politics.

Although the Tobinites had failed to restore their fortunes within the NA the collapse of the mutiny did not end their intrigues. By the end of 1925 there was significant evidence to indicate that they were involved in negotiations with the Republicans to 'act together to overthrow the government'. In the end the talks came to nothing but according to O'Halpin they afforded a rapprochement between the Tobinites and Republicans. Such intriguing ensured that the Irish security forces expended much effort in monitoring clandestine organizations such as the IRA who posed a threat to the state.

It is easy to forget that the IRA never recognized the legitimacy of the Irish State and considers its 'Army Council' as the successor to the pre-Civil War Dáil and thus effectively the Provisional Government in exile of the Irish Republic. Even when de Valera came to power he did what he could to curb IRA activities in Southern Ireland.

By the 1950s 'physical force' Republicanism had become a spent force in the politics of Ireland even if the same was not true of Northern Ireland. Although partition had been one of the catalysts of the Civil War it was not the central one and successive Irish governments did little to end it. The failed IRA campaign from 1956 to 1962 did nothing to improve the lot of Nationalists in Northern Ireland or weaken the resolve of Unionists to keep their province out of a united Ireland.

The RUC had more or less neutralized the Northern IRA at the start of the Civil War and kept a close eye on Republican activity within its borders. Unionists feared that the IRA was being sustained by Dublin and the presence of men like de Valera, Aiken and O'Malley in the Irish government did little to persuade them otherwise. In reality the Irish Army and *Garda* deployed significant resources to interdict IRA incursions from the Republic.

When the Northern 'Troubles' broke out in 1968 the Irish government did contemplate using its army to secure areas along the border to create 'safe havens' for Catholics displaced by sectarian violence. In the end such action became unnecessary when British troops were deployed, much to the horror of the IRA, to defend Catholic enclaves from Loyalist attacks.

The IRA response was slow in coming and resulted in yet another schism in the organization when – true to the quip attributed to Irish playwright (and IRA member) Brendan Behan that 'the Split' was the first thing on the agenda of any IRA meeting – it divided into the 'Official' and the predominantly Northern 'Provisional' IRA in the early 1970s. When the Provisional IRA declared a ceasefire in 1997 two splinter groups, the 'Continuity' and 'Real' IRA, emerged briefly and spasmodically to continue the 'armed struggle'. In 1972 the British suspended Northern Ireland's Parliament for failing to deal effectively with the Troubles and spent the next 30 years trying to end the conflict. Of course, to Republicans Britain was as much a part of the problem as the Unionists and it was not until the 1998 Good Friday Agreement (GFA) between Unionists and Nationalists as well as the British and Irish governments that a solution seemed possible.

One consequence of the GFA is that the Republic renounced its territorial claim over Northern Ireland although its residents retain the right to Irish citizenship, thus ending one of the major stumbling blocks in Anglo-Irish relations. Despite the continuation of low-level paramilitary violence the declaration in 2006 by the Provisional IRA that its campaign was over was also another significant milestone. Although the issue of partition remains as yet unresolved it appears that paramilitary violence is passing out of Northern Ireland's politics as it has done in the Republic. Even if the scars of the Civil War are still sore in some parts of Ireland they have at least begun to heal. Since the 1970s the conflict's protagonists have slipped from the stage, leaving politicians with no personal experience of the war to govern.

Memorial to the O'Rahilly in Sackville Lane, the only senior Volunteer officer to be killed in action during the Rising, takes the form of his final letter to his wife, written as he lay mortally wounded following an attempt to storm a British barricade at the junction of Moore Street and Henry Street. (Michael McNally)

Bitter though the Civil War undoubtedly was and despite the many difficulties experienced since, Ireland has developed into a less introspective, more stable and prosperous liberal democracy playing a full and valued part in both the European Union and the United Nations. Ultimately, perhaps Collins was right all along when he claimed that the Treaty had given Ireland the 'freedom to achieve freedom'.

COMING TO TERMS WITH THE PAST

In the words of historian Oliver Knox, 'There is no such thing as Irish history at all – the past, the present and the future being the same thing, one and indistinguishable.' and in some respects this perspective is true of the impact of the Irish revolution of 1913–23 on both sides of the Irish Sea.

While the cycle of violence that began in Easter 1916 and ended with the IRA dumping arms in the summer of 1923 have been neatly packaged by Nationalists into phases remembered respectively as the Anglo-Irish War and the Irish Civil War, Unionists see the entire period as a civil war that ended in the creation of two Irish successor states, one of which remains within the UK.

While the Nationalist narrative emphasizes the Anglo-Irish War as a struggle between a colonial people and an oppressive colonial master, it fails to address the fact that even in the South thousands of Irishmen supported the Crown. True, in the South they may not have been the majority; however, many of these Loyalists were constitutional Nationalists rather than militant Republicans, and yet until recently they have either been vilified as 'England's Janissaries' or deliberately forgotten.

Of course, the Loyalists lost and the British withdrawal from the 26 counties of what is now the Republic of Ireland allowed these inconvenient defenders of the old regime to be dismissed as traitors, mercenaries or misguided fools rather than men who 'had their loyalties and stuck to them'.

All successful revolutionaries, whether they are American, French, Russian or even Irish, rearrange the facts to create a 'Liberation Myth' that emphasizes the justness of their cause and vindicates their overthrow of what came before. Thus it was essential that the orthodox Nationalist narrative airbrushed any form of willing Irish participation out of the picture. Even one-time *Taoiseach* and ex-IRA Irregular Seán Lemass conceded 'it was common – and I was also guilty in this respect – to question the motives of those who joined the British forces, but it must in their honour and in fairness to their memory be said that they were motivated by the highest purpose.' Although there are many memorials to the Republicans who fell in the Anglo-Irish War, and despite these significant changes, there is still no memorial in the Republic of Ireland to those who died serving the British Crown during the Troubles, while some exist in Northern Ireland.

Despite surviving for three years after independence the DMP built no memorials to its fallen officers, while the only one for the RIC is a small plaque tucked away in St Paul's Cathedral in London, commemorating its dead from 1836–1922. The only conflict specifically mentioned on it is World War I, which typifies British attempts to brush the entire episode under the carpet. No medal was ever awarded to British veterans of the Troubles and few, if any, British regimental memorials exist to commemorate the dead. Even Republican veterans had to wait until 1941 before they were presented with a campaign medal in recognition of their efforts.

It was the Elizabethan courtier-poet Sir John Harrington (1561–1612) who said 'that treason doth never prosper … For if it prosper, none dare call it treason' and this exemplifies Irish involvement on both sides during the Irish revolution. If the British

Comdt Paddy Daly leads the Dublin Guards through Phoenix Park, Dublin, en route to take over Beggar's Bush Barracks from the British on 30 January 1922. This was the first time that NA soldiers were seen in public. (National Museum of Ireland/Cashman collection)

Arthur Griffiths, left, the founder of Sinn Féin, was a constitutional rather than a revolutionary Republican. He is pictured here with de Valera. (Corbis)

had retained control of Ireland then its Loyalists in the South would have been remembered as they are in the North – as heroes rather than traitors.

The same could be said of the men who rebelled in 1916 and again in 1919. It is easy to forget that the leaders of the Easter Rising were, by their own admission 'a minority within a minority within a minority' on the margins of the Nationalist tradition and their insurrection was condemned throughout Ireland. However, British mismanagement of the Rising's aftermath and the execution of its leaders helped turn them into national heroes and the inspiration of generations of Republicans who have sought to make Ireland 'a nation once again'. Ultimately, their rebellion in 1916 ceased to be treason because its survivors were able to carve out an Irish state in 1922.

Equally, the men who fought the British but then turned on the new *Saorstát* and lost have largely been glossed over in the orthodox narrative of Ireland's struggle. Their memorials are few and controversial. Neligan had commented that 'revolution devours its own children' and when the IRA turned on itself in 1922 both sides in the Civil War viewed the other as having betrayed everything that they had fought for. Thus, from 1923 onwards the two factions that had fought the Civil War dealt with each other, in the words of Oscar Wilde, 'with all the added bitterness of an old friend.' Viewed as traitors and dangerous subversives by the Irish Government the Republicans were marginalized until 1932 when de Valera finally became the state's first *Fianna Fáil Taoiseach*.

Even so, the Civil War had opened so many bitter wounds that it became the great unmentionable event in modern Irish history to the extent that historians like Ryle Dwyer and Helen Litton could comment that they were never taught anything about it in school. In much of Ireland it was simply ignored as something best forgotten, while the very mention of it was enough, until relatively recently, to cause uproar in the Dáil.

In essence the Anglo-Irish War and the Civil War were about the nature of Ireland's relationship with Great Britain. Rightly or wrongly, Ireland legally became an integral part of the UK in 1801 and, ironically, it only took on anything resembling the status of a colony when the *Saorstát* seceded from the Union and became a dominion of the British Commonwealth.

For the bulk of the nineteenth century a broad coalition of Nationalists sought to unpick the Union and in many respects the Treaty unravelled the threads that bound them together and made the Civil War possible, if not inevitable. Supporters of the Treaty tended to be those who favoured devolution rather than independence or Republicans whose pragmatism overruled their idealism and were inclined towards a more democratic, consensus-based approach. On the other hand those who subscribed to a more dogmatic and doctrinaire Republicanism tended to reject the Treaty.

Despite the change of regime, the legacy of the RIC was evident in Ireland's new police force. (National Library of Ireland)

Anglo-Irish relations have been further complicated by the issue of partition. The Government of Ireland Act created a devolved Parliament to govern the six-county province of Northern Ireland, which the *Saorstát* recognized when it ratified the Treaty. However, Nationalists have never really been able to reconcile themselves to the concept of Irishmen who actually wished to remain within the UK. Their only conceivable answer has been to blame British perfidy in wishing to divide and rule Ireland when the reality was that the British government in 1920 had dearly hoped that partition would be a temporary expedient until North and South could reconcile and reunite.

Indeed it has consistently been UK Government policy to support Irish reunification if the majority of the people in Northern Ireland wish it to happen. Sadly, the Civil War merely deepened the divide between Loyalist and Nationalist Ireland and made reunification less rather than more likely.

While it is easier to portray the conflict in Leinster, Munster and Connacht as one between the Irish and the British during 1919–21, the same is not true of the struggle in Ulster, where the majority of its population fiercely defended Ireland's membership of the UK. Here it was without doubt an internecine one between Irishmen who held radically different views of how Ireland should be governed. While Republicans viewed the Treaty as a betrayal of their sacrifices against the British, they also viewed Northern Ireland as unfinished business. It is this that lay at the heart of the Troubles that plagued Northern Ireland since 1969 and seems only now to have come to an end.

Despite being vilified by the Republicans, the RIC left a significant legacy behind it. Both the RUC in Northern Ireland and the *Garda* modelled themselves on the old constabulary. It is true that only the RUC retained the outward trappings of the RIC but the majority of the men who shaped and led the new *Garda* were themselves ex-RIC officers, and Lt Col Sir Walter Edgeworth-Taylor remained Chief Commissioner of the DMP until 1923, while his Assistant Commissioner Denis Barrett stayed until 1925 when the force was absorbed by the *Garda*.

17th August 1921: The Irish parliament, the Dáil, in session with its president Éamon de Valera in the chair. (Photo by Walshe/Topical Press Agency/Getty Images)

Both the DMP and RIC were among the first modern constabularies or 'New Police' to be formed and as such significantly influenced the form and functions of almost every other constabulary created in Britain, Ireland, the Commonwealth and even the USA. Consequently, there has been an upsurge in interest, and pride, in the RIC among the historians of Irish policing on either side of the border as well as in the UK.

Unfortunately for the British, ill-disciplined security forces coupled with its policy of reprisals proved counter-productive in wining 'hearts and minds' in the South. Many senior British officers disapproved of reprisals for just that reason; however, the conflict had begun to unleash forces that were beyond the control of politicians on either side.

The British had no unified command structure in Ireland and, while the military favoured a hardline approach, the Castle viewed rapprochement with the rebels as inevitable, with Lloyd George's policies often undermining the efforts of both. It did not help that many senior politicians dismissed IRA violence as either a massive crime wave, or the beginning of a Bolshevik coup in Britain, or that the Crown's forces were conducting operations against people who were ostensibly 'British' under the full glare of the media, making methods that might have been tolerated in India or Africa unacceptable.

While 'official' British reprisals were directed against property the British did not sanction the assassination of suspected IRA or Sinn Féin activists, and although Loyalist death-squads undoubtedly operated in Ireland they were not condoned by either Whitehall or the Castle. Indeed, under the scrutiny of the Irish, British and world press it would have been impossible for Britain to have openly adopted such a strategy against what were, technically, its own citizens, and members of the security forces who carried out murders were tried and in some cases executed for their crimes. Reprisals, official or otherwise, did nothing to improve the situation and often drove otherwise neutral bystanders into the arms of the rebels. Whereas many could dismiss IRA atrocities as the actions of terrorists and criminals it was a different matter when the assassin or arsonist wore a British uniform.

Equally there is a tendency to forget that assassination was a formal part of the IRA's strategy. The Squad was created and fêted for such jobs and while the Bloody Sunday killings of 1920 are usually discussed in terms of a military operation they were in reality the shooting of a dozen unarmed men who were, for the most part, woken from their slumber to be executed.

The truth is that with regard to the 'military' conduct of the Anglo-Irish War there is little to be proud of on either side and its legacy soured Anglo-Irish relations for decades. Ultimately the IRA campaign of 1919–21 succeeded because Britain was exhausted and overstretched after four years of war in Europe, Asia and Africa, and distracted by commitments in Afghanistan and Iraq. During the Irish Civil War the NA quickly adopted attitudes towards the rebel IRA that were uncannily similar to those of their British adversaries a few months before. This was possibly because so many of the new Army's officers and men had served in the British Army, or equally it may have been because they were faced with the harsh reality of trying to defeat an elusive guerrilla organization.

Defeat in the Civil War did not destroy militant Republicanism, and its remnants smouldered for decades before flaring into life between 1956 and 1962 during the IRA border campaign, and again in 1969. The modern IRA has its roots in these times, posing a threat to both the Irish state and Northern Ireland. Ireland's proximity to Britain, however, made it inevitable that, despite the history of violence, the two countries would have to coexist. The fate of Ulster's Protestants aside, British concerns over Ireland were mainly about defence, which is why the UK retained control of several strategic facilities on the island and limited the size of the Irish Defence Force.

Britain's abandonment of the Treaty Ports in 1938 reiterated its failure to understand Irish domestic politics. Its politicians undoubtedly believed that Éire, as a member of the Commonwealth, would support Britain in any future European war. Unfortunately for Britain, de Valera was *Taoiseach* in 1939 and, despite Churchill's offer of the prospect of Irish reunification if de Valera brought Éire into the war, he made sure that Éire remained firmly neutral during World War II.

Éire's public stance was resented by many in the UK, especially as her survival was as dependent on the North Atlantic convoys as Britain's. De Valera, however, was preoccupied by internal problems, with the IRA exploiting the emergency to steal military supplies, killing three Irish policemen and seven civilians during 1939–41. Despite being neutral, however, Éire provided some covert support to the Allies during the war and the increase of its military to more than 40,000 men helped bring together former adversaries in the defence of Éire.

In the years since 1923 the protagonists on all sides of the Irish revolution have one by one left the stage, but their legacy has shaped Anglo-Irish, North–South and internal Irish relations ever since. Equally their departure has also created the opportunity for old wounds to heal and ghosts put to rest. With hindsight it is fairly obvious that reprisals and coercion had little prospect of convincing the majority of people in Southern Ireland that their future lay within the UK, and equally it is difficult to see how the IRA campaign in Northern Ireland would make Ulster Protestants feel welcome in a unified Ireland.

Since the 1998 Good Friday Agreement there has, at last, been a shift in the pattern of relationships between all parties involved in the politics of 'the Island of Ireland', which recognizes what former Irish Defence Minister Michael Smith TD referred to as its 'complex set of relationships … accepting that each has a right to their heritage and that theirs is a part of ours.' Consequently historians on both sides of the Irish Sea are beginning to revisit the events of 1913–23, examining them as history should be – with objectivity – rather than as a live political issue. In doing so, they are creating the opportunity for both the British and Irish to come to terms with the past and, as neighbours – tied by blood and history – and partners in the EU, move on.

BIBLIOGRAPHY

Primary sources

Hansard, H. C. Deb. (series 5) vol. 82

PRO, Cabinet Office CAB 23/1/2 Extracts of War Cabinet Meetings

PRO, Colonial Office, CO 903/19

PRO Colonial Office, Inspector General and County Inspector's Monthly Confidential Reports, CO 904/102–16

PRO Colonial Office, RIC Weekly Summaries of Actions, CO 904/148–50

PRO Home Office, The 1916 Royal Commission on the Rebellion in Ireland, HO 45/10810/312350

PRO Home Office, 1919–20 Attempted Assassination of the Lord Lieutenant (Lord French), HO 45/10974/484819

PRO Home Office, 1916–18 Civilians Convicted by Field General Courts Martial. Treatment in English Prisons, HO 144/1453/311980

PRO Home Office, 1916–19 Internment of Irish Prisoners in UK, HO 144/1455/313106

PRO Home Office, RIC General Register of Service, HO 184 vols. 31–42, 15/7/1899 – 31/8/1922

PRO Home Office, RIC Officers' Register, HO 184 vols. 47–8, 19/3/1909 – 17/9/1921

PRO Home Office, RIC Auxiliary Division, HO 184 vols. 50–51, 23/7/1920 – 5/12/1921

PRO Parliamentary Papers, 1914, vol. 18

PRO War Office, Registered Files: Ireland, WO 32

PRO War Office, WO 35/67

PRO War Office, WO 35/69, Public Records Office, Kew

PRO War Office, Judge Advocate General's Office: Courts Martial Proceedings. WO 71/344–59 (inclusive) Fields General Courts Martial against Civilians Accused of Armed Rebellion, 1916, WO 71

PRO War Office, Judge Advocate General's Office: Miscellaneous Records. Proclamations and Orders under Martial Law in Ireland 1916, 1917, 1920 and 1921, WO 93/16–29 inclusive WO 93

Coates, T. (ed.), *The Irish Uprising, Papers from the British Parliamentary Archive*, The Stationery Office, London, 2000

M.I.5: The First Ten Years, 1909–1919, Public Records Office, London, 1997

Dáil debates

First Dáil, Vol. F (21/1/1919–10/5/1921)

Second Dáil, Vol. S (16/8/1921–14/9/1921)

Second Dáil, Vol. T (14/12/1921–10/1/1922)

Second Dáil, Vol. S2 (28/2/1922–8/6/1922)

Third Dáil, Vols. 1–4 (9/9/1922–9/8/1923)

Articles

Cottrell, P., *Myth, The Military and Anglo-Irish Policing 1913–1922*, British Army Review, No. 133, 2003

MacDonald, Z., 'Revisiting the Dark Figure', British Journal of Criminology, vol. 41 issue 1, 2001

Secondary sources

Abbott, R., *Police Casualties in Ireland 1919–1923*, Mercier Press, Dublin, 2000

Adair, J., *Puritans: Religion and Politics in Seventeenth Century England and America*, Sutton Publishing, Stroud, 1998

Allen, G., *The Garda Siochána*, Gill & Macmillan, London, 1999

Babington, A., *Military Intervention in Britain: From the Gordon Riots to the Gibraltar Incident*, Routledge, London & New York, 1991

Barry, T., *Guerilla Days in Ireland*, Roberts Rinehart, New York, 1995

Bartlett, T., and Jeffrey, K. (eds.), *A Military History of Ireland*, Cambridge University Press, Cambridge, 1996

Barton, B., *From Behind A Closed Door – Secret Court Martial Records of the 1916 Easter Rising*, Blackstaff Press, Belfast, 2002

Bell, P.M.H., *The Origins of the Second World War in Europe*, 2nd edn, 3rd imp., Longman, London and New York, 1998

Bennett, R., *The Black and Tans*, Spellmount, Staplehurst, 1959; repr. 2000

Bowyer Bell, J., *The Dynamics of Armed Struggle*, Frank Cass Publishers, London, 1998

Bowyer Bell, J., *The Secret Army: The IRA 1916–1979*, Poolbeg Press, Dublin, 1989

Bradbridge, Colonel E. U. (ed.), *59th Division 1915–1918*, Naval & Military Press London

Brady, C., *Guardians of the Peace*, Prendeville Publishing, Dublin, 2000

Breen, D., *My Fight for Freedom*, Anvil Books, London, 1964

Brennan-Whitmore, W. J., *Dublin Burning – The Easter Rising from behind the barricades*, Gill & Macmillan, Dublin, 1996

Brunicardi, D., *The Sea Hound – The Story of an Irish Ship*, Cork: The Collins Press, 2001

Buckley, Capt. D., *The Battle of Tourmakeady, Fact or Fiction: A study of the IRA ambush and its aftermath*, Nonsuch, Dublin, 2008

Caputo, P., *A Rumor of War*, Macmillan, London, 1977

Carr, W., *A History of Germany 1813–1990*, 4th edn., Edward Arnold, London, 1990

Carver, Field Marshal Lord M., *Britain's Army in the 20th Century*, Macmillan, London, 1998

Caulfield, M., *The Easter Rebellion – Dublin 1916*, Roberts Rineheart, Boulder, CO, 1995

Chappell, M., *The British Army in World War 1 (1) The Western Front 1914–16*, Osprey Publishing, Oxford, 2005

Chappell, M., *The British Army in World War 1 (2) The Western Front 1916–18*, Osprey Publishing Oxford, 2005

Clarke, D., *British Artillery 1914–19 Field Army Artillery*, Osprey Publishing, Oxford, 2004

Coffey, T., *Agony at Easter – The 1916 Irish Uprising*, Pelican, Baltimore, 1971

Connolly, S. J. (ed.), *The Oxford Companion to Irish History*, Oxford University Press, Oxford, 1988

Coogan, T. P., *De Valera: Long Fellow, Long Shadow*, Arrow Books, London, 1993

Coogan, T. P., *1916: The Easter Rising*, Orion Books, London, 2005

Coogan, T. P., *IRA*, Fontana Books, London, 1971; repr. 1980, 1984 & 1987

Coogan, T. P., *Michael Collins*, Arrow Books, London, 1990

Coogan, T. P. and Morrison G., *The Irish Civil War*, Weidenfeld & Nicolson, London

Coppard, G., *With a Machinegun to Cambrai*, Papermac, London, 1980

Costick, C., and Collins, L., *The Easter Rising – A Guide to Dublin in 1916*, O'Brien Press, Dublin, 2000

Cottrell, P., *The Anglo-Irish War, The Troubles of 1913–1922*, Osprey Publishing, Oxford, 2005

Cottrell, P., *The Irish Civil War 1922–23*, Osprey Publishing, Oxford, 2008

Curran, J.M., *The Birth of the Irish Free State*, Alabama University Press, Alabama, 1980

Curtis, L., *The Cause of Ireland, from United Irishmen to Partition*, Beyond the Pale Publications, Belfast, 1994

Deasy, L., *Towards Ireland Free*, Mercier Press, Cork, 1973

Doyle, R., *A Star Called Henry*, Vintage Books, London, 2000

Duggan, John P., *A History of the Irish Army*, Gill & Macmillan, Dublin, 1991

Emsley, C., *The English Police: A Political and Social History*, 2nd edn., 5th imp., Longman, London & New York, 1996

Emsley, C., and Weinberger, B. (eds.), *Policing Western Europe: Politics, Professionalism and Public Order, 1850–1940*, Greenwood Press, London, 1991

Falls, C., *Elizabeth's Irish Wars*, Constable & Robinson, London, 1996

Fanning, R., *Independent Ireland*, Dublin, 1983

Ferguson, N., *The Pity of War*, Penguin Books, London, 1999

Forester, M., *Michael Collins – The Lost Leader*, Sidgwick and Jackson, London, 1971

Foucault, M., *Discipline and Punishment: The Birth of Prison*, Penguin Books, London, 1991

Griffith, K., and O'Grady, T., *Curious Journey – An Oral History of Ireland's Unfinished Revolution*, Mercier Press, Cork, 1998

Litton, H., *The Irish Civil War, An Illustrated History*, Wolfhound Press, Dublin, 2006

Hart, P., *The IRA and its Enemies, Violence and Community in Cork 1916–1923*, Oxford University Press, Oxford, 1999

Hart, P., *The IRA at War 1916–23*, Oxford University Press, Oxford, 2003

Harvey, D., and White, G., *The Barracks – A History of Victoria/Collins Barracks*, Mercier Press, Cork, 1997

Hayes-McCoy, G. A., *A History of Irish Flags From Earliest Times*, Academy Press, 1979

Hogan, J. J., *Badges, Medals and Insignia of the Irish Defence Forces*, Dublin, 1987

Haythornthwaite, P. J., *The World War One Source Book*, Arms and Armour Press, London, 1994

Hazel, Major. D., *Attrition*, DETS(A), Upavon, 1999

Herlihy, J., *The Dublin Metropolitan Police: A Short History and Genealogical Guide*, Four Courts Press, Dublin, 2001

Herlihy, J., *The Royal Irish Constabulary: A Complete Alphabetical List of Officers and Men, 1816–1922*, Four Courts Press, Dublin, 1999

Herlihy, J., *The Royal Irish Constabulary: A Short History and Genealogical Guide*, Four Courts Press, Dublin, 1997

Hezlet, Sir A., *The B Specials, A History of the Ulster Special Constabulary*, Tom Stacey, London, 1972

Holmes, R., *The Western Front*, BBC Worldwide, London, 1999

Hopkinson, M., *Green against Green: The Irish Civil War*, Gill & Macmillan, Dublin, 1988, repr. 2004

Hough, R., *Winston and Clementine, The Triumph of the Churchills*, Bantam Books, London, 1990

Kautt, W., and Showalter, D., *The Anglo-Irish War*, Praeger Publishing, London & New York, 1999

Kee, R., *The Green Flag, A History of Irish Nationalism*, Weidenfield & Nicolson, London, 1972

Kee, R., *Ireland: A History*, Wiedenfield & Nicholson, London, 1980

Kenny, K., *Ireland and the British Empire*, Oxford University Press, Oxford, 2005

Knox, O., *Rebels and Informers, Stirrings of Irish Independence*, John Murray, London, 1997

Laffin, J., *Jackboot: The Story of the German Soldier*, Cassell & Company, London, 1989

Lumsden, R., *A Collector's Guide to The Allgemeine-SS*, Osprey Military, London, 1993

MacArdle, D., *The Irish Republic*, Victor Gollancz, London, 1937

MacCarron, D., *The Irish Defence Forces since 1922*, Osprey Publishing, Oxford, 2004

Martin, F. X. (ed.), *The Howth Gun Running*, Browne and Nolan, Dublin, 1964

Martin, F. X. (ed.), *The Irish Volunteer 1913–1915*, James Duffy & Co., Dublin, 1963

Maguire, M., Morgan, R., and Reiner, R. (eds.), *The Oxford Handbook of Criminology*, 2nd edn., Oxford University Press, Oxford, 1997

McLaughlin, E., and Muncie, J. (eds.), *Controlling Crime*, Sage Publications & OU, London, 1996 repr. 1998

McNally, M., *Easter Rising 1916: Birth of the Irish Republic*, Osprey Publishing, Oxford, 2007

McNiffe, L., *A History of the Garda Siochána*, Wolfhound Press, Dublin, 1997

Morrison, G., *The Irish Civil War – An Illustrated History*, Gill & Macmillan, Dublin, 1981

Neeson, E., *The Civil War in Ireland*, Mercier Press, Cork, 1968

Neillands, R., *The Great War Generals on the Western Front 1914–1918*, Robinson, London, 1998

Neligan, D., *The Spy in the Castle*, MacGibbon & Kee, London (repr. Prendeville Publishing, Dublin), 1968, repr. 1999

O'Connor, U., *The Troubles: The Struggle for Irish Freedom 1912–1922*, Mandarin Paperbacks, London, 1975

O'Donoghue, Florence, *No Other Law*, Anvil Books, Dublin, 1954

O'Farrell, P., *Who's Who in the Irish War of Independence and Civil War 1916–23*, (Dublin, 1997

O'Halpin, E., *Defending Ireland, The Irish State and its Enemies*, Oxford University Press, Oxford, 1999

O'Mahony, S, *Frongoch: University of Revolution*, FDR Teoranta, Killiney, Dublin, 1987

O'Malley, E., *On Another Man's Wound*, Rich and Cowan, Dublin, 1936

O'Malley, E., *The Singing Flame*, Anvil Books, Dublin, 1978

O'Sullivan, D. J., *Irish Constabularies 1822–1922*, Mount Eagle Publications, Dublin, 1999

O'Toole, E., *Decorations and Medals of the Republic of Ireland*, Medallic Publishing, USA, 1990

Pakenham, T., *The Year of Liberty, The Great Irish Rebellion of 1798*, 2nd edn., Abacus, London, 1997

Phillips, K., *The Cousins' Wars: Religion, Politics and the Triumph of Anglo-America*, New York, 1999

Reilly, T., *Cromwell: An Honourable Enemy*, Brandon, Dingle, 1999

Reiner, R., *The Politics of the Police*, Harvester-Wheatsheaf, Hemel Hempstead, 1985

Reith, C., *The Blind Eye of History*, Faber and Faber, London, 1952

Ryan, D., *Sean Treacy and the Third Tipperary Brigade IRA*, Alliance Press, London, Tralee), 1945

Ryan, M., *The Day Michael Collins was Shot*, Poolbeg Press, Dublin, 1998

Ryan, M., *The Real Chief: The Story of Liam Lynch*, Mercier Press, Cork, 2005

Ryan, M., *The Tom Barry Story*, Cork, 1982

Ryan, M., *Tom Barry, Column Commander and IRA Freedom Fighter*, Mercier Press, Cork, 2003

Ryder, C., *The RUC 1922–2000, A Force under Fire*, Arrow Books, London, 1989; repr. 1992, 1997 & 2000

Sheehan, W., *British Voices from the Irish War of Independence 1918–1921*, The Collins Press, Cork, 2005

Sloan, G.R., *The Geopolitics of Anglo-Irish Relations in the Twentieth Century*, Leicester University Press, London, 1997

Smith, M. L. R., *Fighting for Ireland? The Military Strategy of the Irish Republican Movement*, Routledge, London and New York, 1995

Stephens, J., *The Insurrection in Dublin*, introduction by John A. Murphy, Colin Smythe, Gerrards Cross, 1916 repr. 1978, 1992 & 2000

Sturgis, M., *The Last Days of Dublin Castle*, ed. Michael Hopkinson and Tim Pat Coogan, Irish Academic Press, Dublin, 1999

Taylor, D., *The New Police in Nineteenth-Century England: Crime, Conflict and Control*, Manchester University Press, Manchester & New York, 1997

Taylor, P., *Loyalists*, Bloomsbury, London, 1999

Taylor, P., *Provos: The IRA and Sinn Féin*, Bloomsbury, London, 1997

Thompson, E. P., *The Making of the English Working Class*, Penguin Books, London, 1991

Thompson, F.M.L. (ed.), *Cambridge Social History*, vol. 3, Cambridge University Press, Cambridge, 1990

Townshend, C., *The British Campaign in Ireland, 1919–1921*, Oxford University Press, Oxford, 1998

Townshend, C., *Ireland*, Edward Arnold, London, 1999

Townshend, C., *Political Violence in Ireland*, Oxford University Press, Oxford, 1984

Valiulis, M. G., *Portrait of a Revolutionary*, Irish Academic Press, Dublin, 1992

Walsh, P. V., 'The Irish Civil War 1922–1923: A Military Study of the Conventional Phase 28 June – 11 August 1922' (paper delivered New York), 1998

White, G., and O'Shea, B., *Irish Volunteer Soldier 1913–23*, Osprey Publishing, Oxford, 2003

Younger, C., *Ireland's Civil War*, Fontana, London, 1970

Unpublished papers

Richard Abbot's papers on the RIC Auxiliary Division.

Periodicals

An Cosantoir, The Journal of the Irish Defence Forces, 1941–2002

Papers

The O'Donoghue Collection, National Museum of Ireland, Dublin.

Interview

Taped interview with General Tom Barry, 1979

Collections

Captain Tom O'Neill's Collection of Irish Defence Force Memorabilia, stathan@indigo.ie

INDEX

References to illustrations are shown in **bold**.